Machine Transcription:
A Comprehensive Approach for Today's Office Professional

Complete Course

Fourth Edition

Carol A. Mitchell
John A. Logan College
Carterville, Illinois

Glencoe McGraw-Hill

New York, New York Columbus, Ohio Woodland Hills, California Peoria, Illinois

Library of Congress Cataloging-in-Publicaiton Data

Mitchell, Carol A. (Carol Ann),
Machine Transcription : a comprehensive approach for today's office professional : complete course : student text / Carol a. Mitchell.—4th ed.
p. cm
Includes bibliographical references and index.
ISBN -0-07-822831-X (pbk.)
1. Dictation (Office practice) 2. Transcription. 3. Office practice I. Title

HF5547.5 .M583 2003
651.7'4—dc21 2001033798

Glencoe/McGraw-Hill

A Division of The ***McGraw-Hill*** *Companies*

Machine Transcription: A Comprehensive Approach for Today's Office Professional, Complete Course, Fourth Edition

Printed in the United States of America.

Send all inquiries to:
Glencoe/McGraw-Hill
21600 Oxnard Street, Suite 500
Woodland Hills, CA 91367

ISBN 0-07-822831-X (Student Edition)

5 6 7 8 9 045 10 09 08

Dedication

To Sam Mitchell, my anchor;
to Angela, my greatest joy;
and to Loyd and Alice Jacobs,
who provided the education
that made this possible.

Acknowledgements

I appreciate all the time and effort of the classroom teachers who have adopted my textbook and have taken the time to make suggestions. A special thanks goes to those who have edited and those who have marketed all the editions of my work.

Most of all, thank you to my family for your support.

Contents

To The Student

The lessons and assignments in this textbook will prepare you to meet the challenges of working in the expanding field of machine transcription. When you have completed the course, you will be able to:

1. Demonstrate the correct procedures for placing a recording in transcribing machine and for removing it.
2. Manipulate the machine controls properly.
3. Demonstrate ear-finger-foot coordination in transcribing material from the transcription equipment.
4. Keep the word processor in constant motion while transcribing material from the transcription equipment.
5. Transcribe a mailable copy on the first draft from the transcription equipment.
6. Correctly use words taken from the Word Study portion of each section when transcribing dictated material.
7. Supply the proper punctuation in dictated copy.
8. Transcribe at or above the minimum acceptable transcription speed.
9. Spell correctly the words listed in the Spelling Review in each section.
10. Match words taken from the Word Study portion of each section with their proper definitions.
11. Edit letters properly using proofreaders' marks.
12. Effectively use the spelling checker feature of your word processing program, a dictionary, and other reference sources to assist in producing mailable or usable transcripts.

COURSE ORGANIZATION

Machine Transcription will build on abilities you may already have in the areas of language development and listening and will help you apply them to transcription. Each lesson will reinforce the objectives so that by the time the course is over, you will feel confident about using your new skills. The following is an explanation of how the text and tape materials are organized to help you reach these objectives.

The Textbook

Part 1 introduces you to career opportunities, equipment, procedures, and techniques for machine transcription. Part 2 contains 21 sections that provide the punctuation, spelling, grammar, and guidelines you must know in order to correctly transcribe the section's dictation. Each section of Part 2 is organized as follows:

OBJECTIVES. The Objectives describe the goals that have been established for the section.

PUNCTUATION REVIEW. The Punctuation Review presents punctuation rules and example sentences illustrating those rules. You will not be asked to apply any punctuation rule until it has been introduced in the Punctuation Review. Once a punctuation rule has been introduced, however, you will be expected to apply that rule when transcribing all of the following transcription tapes.

WORD STUDY. The Word Study portions introduce words that sound alike or similar when dictated but are spelled differently and have different meanings. Definitions and parts of speech are given for each word, followed by example sentences showing how the word is used.

SPELLING REVIEW. The Spelling Review contains words that will be dictated on the transcription tape for that section. By studying these words before you transcribe the dictation, you should be able to improve your transcription speed and efficiency. In addition to the words introduced in the Word Study, the review includes other words that will be used in dictated documents. If you are unfamiliar with any of the words, consult a dictionary. Following this practice will prepare you for the Exercises.

TRANSCRIPTION GUIDELINES. Under this heading are guidelines for formatting, answers to questions of style, and examples that will help you during transcription.

ASSIGNMENTS. This part lists the work you will do to complete the section. It first lists the text exercises to be completed before you transcribe. Next, it lists the tests you should complete for the section. These tests are either given to you by your instructor or located on the dictation recordings. Any special instructions for the section's dictation are also noted.

EXERCISES. The text contains three types of exercises that prepare you for transcription:

PUNCTUATION EXERCISES. The Punctuation Exercises give you practice in applying punctuation rules in textbook exercises before you are asked to insert the proper punctuation in dictated sentences.

WORD STUDY EXERCISES. These exercises provide practice in choosing the correct word from groups of troublesome words according to the meaning of a sentence. Complete these exercises before you transcribe the dictation for that section.

PROOFREADING EXERCISES. Because a machine transcriptionist must be able to produce accurate documents, you must be a proficient proofreader. The proofreading exercises in each section will sharpen your skill at recognizing and correcting errors in punctuation, spelling, formatting, keying, and word usage. A list of proofreaders' marks appears in the Reference Handbook at the back of the textbook. Use these marks to correct the Proofreading Exercises in each section. In addition, proofreading guidelines are given in the Part 1, Section 3, Transcribing Techniques.

The Dictation Recordings

PRE-TRANSCRIPTION TRAINING. This dictation will ease you into the actual transcription process. Complete it before you transcribe the dictation for Part 2, Section 1. It contains some spelling words and punctuation exercises from Part 2, Section 1; three practice paragraphs; and a very short letter.

TRANSCRIPTION. Each section of Part 2 has a corresponding transcription recording. The documents you will transcribe stress the punctuation rules presented in the Punctuation Review and the words presented in the Word Study portions of each section. They may also cover punctuation and word usage presented in earlier sections. The last item on each section's dictation is the list of spelling words for the next section. Transcribe these to help yourself prepare for the upcoming transcription items.

Part 1

Orientation To Machine Transcription

SECTION 1
You—A Machine Transcriptionist

SECTION 2
Machine Transcription—On the Job

SECTION 3
Transcribing Techniques

SECTION 4
Effective Listening

SECTION 5
Dictation

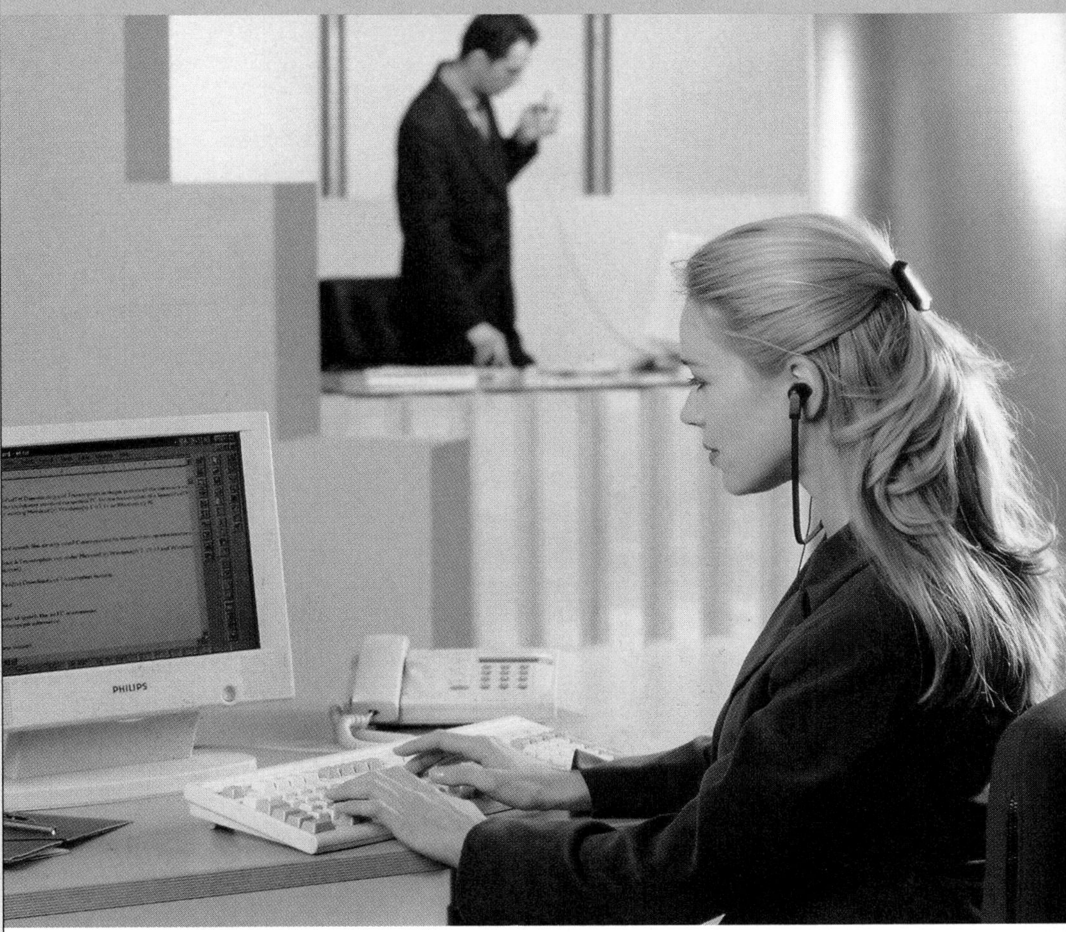

Welcome to *Machine Transcription*! Today's skilled professional transcriptionists—those who can produce quality work using a variety of equipment—secure rewarding employment in many different settings. Just a few examples include working in media and entertainment, in the hotel industry, for legal firms, in medical settings, in travel and tourism, and in home-based transcriptionist businesses.

This program has been written specifically to provide you with both the technical and the language skills you will need to succeed. Study the program carefully to develop these skills and to move forward toward achieving your career goals. What type of employment do you intend to pursue?

Section 1

You—A Machine Transcriptionist

INTRODUCTION

Introduction

The machine transcriptionist has greater employment opportunities than ever before. More and more executives are realizing the efficiency of using machine dictation. Employers can make use of what would otherwise be nonproductive time by using the small handheld units to dictate. Productive dictation is possible almost anywhere—in a waiting room at the airport, in a hotel room, at home, in a car, or on a plane. Depending on the type of dictating and transcribing equipment used by a company, traveling executives can call in the dictation or mail in a completed tape that can be played on a transcription unit.

No matter how flexible and efficient the dictation methods and equipment are, the words will not reach their destinations without capable transcriptionists to produce written copies. The greater value placed on machine dictation naturally has led to an increased demand for good transcriptionists—not just those who key exact copies of what they hear, but trained transcription specialists who can produce documents that are accurate in every way, sometimes in spite of inaccuracies in the dictation.

Executives are learning that transcriptionists have superior skills in listening, proofreading, and language arts (word usage, spelling, and punctuation) as a result of their specialized training. Transcriptionists are trained to make decisions, accept responsibility for their work, and turn to appropriate reference sources when questions arise. They can proofread the dictator's communication for accuracy and clarity. You will be capable of such tasks after completing this machine transcription course.

In your job you may someday be asked to train others in proper dictation techniques. You may help choose new office equipment, or you may serve on a committee to develop an office procedures manual. The learning starts with this course, but it doesn't end here.

1.1 BE PROFESSIONAL

Your professionalism plays an important part in your position and in your chances for promotion. Just what is *professionalism?*

If you asked ten people this question, you would probably receive ten somewhat different answers. What is appropriate in one environment may be perceived differently in another. For example, proper office conduct might be quite different in Japan or France than it is New York, Los Angeles, or Carbondale. For our purposes, *professionalism* means "a collection of appropriate skills, attitudes, behaviors, and images." Improving your professionalism is affected by both how others see you and how you perceive yourself. *Your professionalism begins with your image of yourself.*

Beginning now and continuing throughout your office career, read professional journals to keep up to date on new equipment developments in the industry. You may have an opportunity in your job to help select or recommend new equipment from time to time. In order to be effective, you must be aware of what is available in the field. Technology changes *rapidly.* You will likely have to retrain several times in your working career. For example, let's say that 20 or 25 years ago you were a successfully employed mimeograph operator. (You may not even

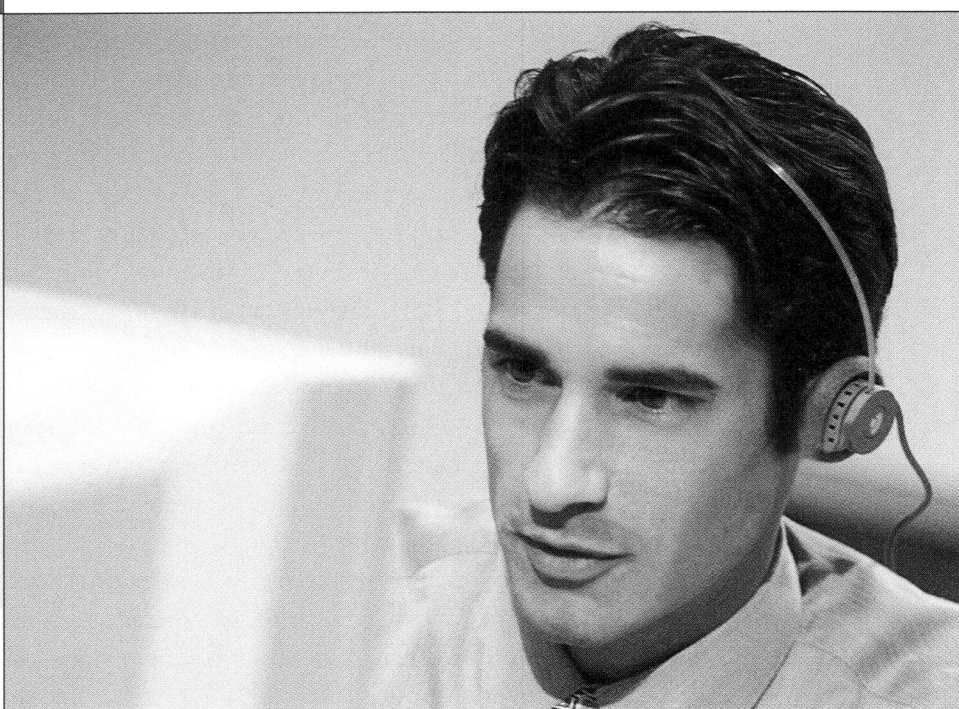

Figure 1.1
Imagine that you are an entry-level transcriptionist who aspires to positions of more responsibility.
What can you do to make sure that you will be considered for promotions and that you will be ready for the challenges?

know what a mimeograph machine is! It makes duplicate copies by using an ink-filled drum.) You were the best. You could turn out beautiful copies and never get a drop of ink on you. Where would you be today if you had not retrained? *Unemployed!* You must be ready and willing to change as technology does or be left behind. The job you have today may not even exist in a few years due to advances in technology, competition from foreign markets, or budget cuts. Keep your skills up to date. Be flexible, and be willing to look at new ways to approach your job. For example, learn to use the Internet to research topics and locate facts you need to complete your work.

Don't assume that your formal education is over once you have received your degree. Update your knowledge by attending workshops that give information about new and more efficient work procedures. Take refresher courses occasionally to maintain or improve your level of skill. Some skills may be used infrequently in your current position. However, it is important to maintain your overall skill level so that these skills, which may be important for future advancement, will not be lost. Refresher courses will also help strengthen any skills that are weak.

Membership in professional organizations can also help improve your skills and update your knowledge of new equipment and more efficient work methods. Consider an active membership in one or more professional organizations such as International Association of Administrative Professionals (IAAP), which was formerly known as Professional Secretaries International (PSI); National Association of Legal Secretaries (NALS); National Association of Educational Office Personnel (NAEOP); American Association of Medical Assistants (AAMA); American Association for Medical Transcriptionists (AAMT); Office Automation Society International (OASI); Association of Business Support Services International, Inc.

(ABSSI), which was formerly known as National Association of Secretarial Services (NASS); Administrative Management Society (AMS), Association of Information Systems Professionals (AISP); Office Systems Research Association (OSRA); Association of Records Managers and Administrators, Inc. (ARMA); Association of Information Technology Professionals (AITP); and Data Processing Management Association (DPMA). Choose organizations that will assist you in both the position you now have and the one you aspire to have.

You must maintain a professional attitude to achieve your highest potential. This includes exhibiting a pleasant personality, helping fellow employees, sounding cheerful on the telephone, accepting work assignments without complaint, and seeing that the job at hand is always done well.

Your professional image is determined by what you say, how you say it, and how you look when you are saying it. Be in control. Self-control helps you radiate competence. If you lose self-control, the image you project is "I can't handle my job." Keep in mind that your work history will include everything you do on the job, every task you perform, every memo you write, and every meeting you attend. Always put forth your best effort to assure that you have a work history that you can proudly present when applying for a promotion. Your value to the firm begins with your opinion of yourself. Believe in yourself; you will be a better employee and will be more likely to get that promotion you want.

1.2 SET GOALS FOR YOURSELF

Set goals for yourself and a timetable for achieving them. If I were to ask you to drive to Petrolia, Illinois, you would have to look at a map to plan the trip. *(Good luck in finding it.)* If you want to achieve anything in life, you must have a plan—goals. Be realistic when you set long-term and short-term goals. Decide what it will take to achieve those goals. Work toward your goals by putting your plan into action. Periodically review your goals and plans to determine whether you need to make changes. Maybe the job you have is the one you want forever. If that is the case, work to make yourself the absolute best you can possibly be in that job. If you aspire to a higher level, examine what it takes to achieve that goal. Then work systematically to reach it.

Did you notice that all these points are in terms of action? I did not say, *"Sit back, relax, and wait for something wonderful to fall in your lap."* Be in control. You have ultimate control over how you respond to a situation. Act in a positive, confident manner; but ACT. Believe in yourself. Remember that the image others have of you starts with your image of yourself.

There is an old Chinese proverb—

If you would be happy for one hour, take a nap.

If you would be happy for a day, go fishing.

If you would be happy for a month, take a long vacation.

If you would be happy for a year, inherit a fortune.

If you would be happy for life, love your work.

Section 2

Machine Transcription—On the Job

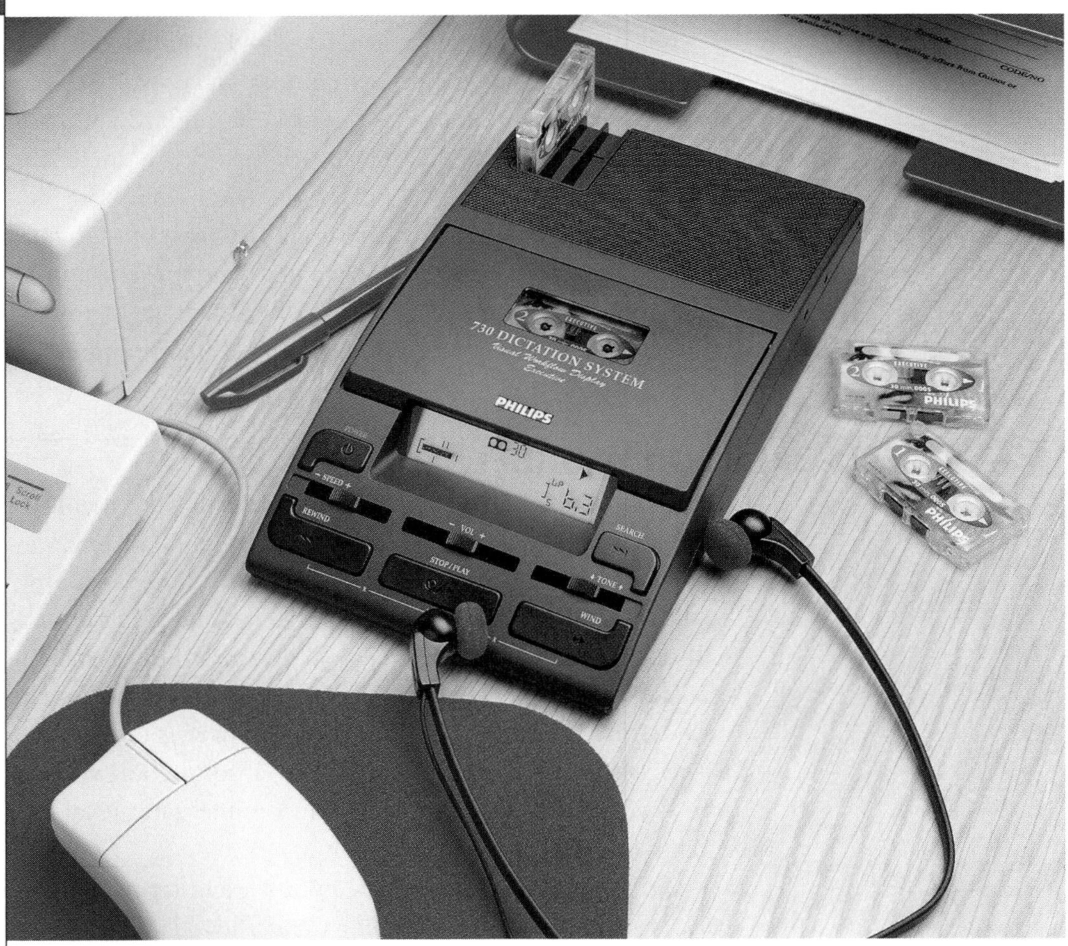

INTRODUCTION

2.1 Recording the Message

2.2 Voice-Recognition Software

2.3 Remote Transcription

2.4 Transcribing the Message—Word Processing

2.5 Sharing Files—Local Area Networks

2.6 Record-Keeping

Introduction

Although your employer may use other methods to transmit correspondence to you (dictation at the word processor, shorthand, or handwritten copy), machine dictation is generally considered to be the most efficient. This assessment is based on the best use of both the dictator's and transcriptionist's time.

Your instructor will introduce you to the features of the particular dictation and transcription equipment available in this class. To understand thoroughly how transcription occurs, it is helpful to learn first about the dictation process. This chapter explores the basic equipment used for dictation and how this equipment is arranged in the office.

2.1 RECORDING THE MESSAGE

The parts of a basic dictation unit include a microphone, a recorder, and some type of medium (such as a tape or a CD ROM) on which the message is recorded.

Analog dictation units use magnetic media. The cost of operation is reduced because magnetic tapes can be reused an unlimited number of times by recording over previously dictated material. It is easy to review dictation and make corrections. The dictator may record for long, uninterrupted periods, and sound quality is good.

The magnetic tape may be housed in either a discrete system or a continuous-loop system.

Discrete Systems

A discrete system is called external because the medium is removable and can be handled by the dictator and the transcriber. There are two basic types of discrete systems—portable units and desktop units. Most machines use cassettes in one of four sizes.

Figure 2.1
Cassette tapes for use in discrete dictation/transcription units come in four sizes.

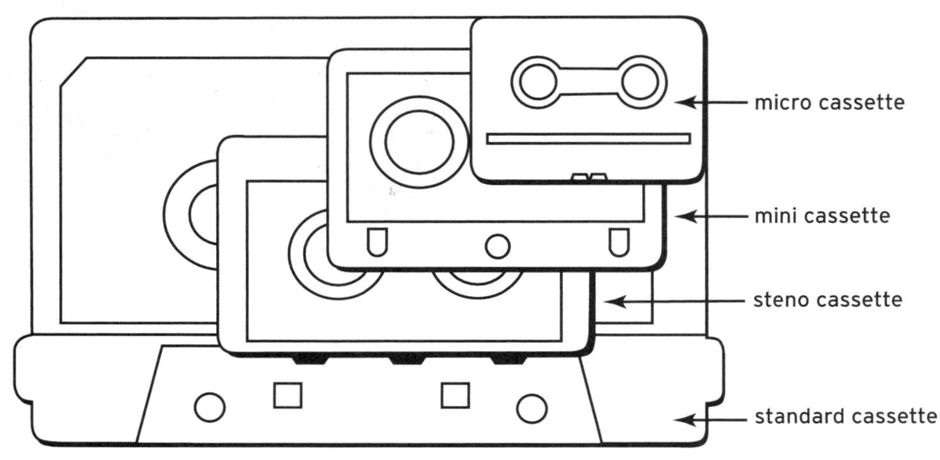

NOTE:
When the equipment in the office is changed or updated, it is important to check the size of the tapes used on the old equipment for compatibility with the new units. Some equipment suppliers offer adapters for other tape sizes.

ADVANTAGES AND DISADVANTAGES. Discrete media have several advantages. Tapes are economical, convenient, and readily available from electronics and office supply stores. They can be distributed among several transcriptionists when a project is needed quickly or is long. Since tapes can be used with portable units, the dictator is not limited to using them in the office. Tapes can be mailed to the transcriptionist if the dictator is away from the office or if the keyboarder works at a different location. Tapes may be erased or filed for future reference.

Discrete media also have some disadvantages. When a tape is full, the dictator must replace it in the machine with another one. This may be done manually; or in an automatic system, the dictator must wait until the new cassette falls into place. The transcriptionist must wait until the dictator finishes a tape before starting to transcribe. When being transferred from the dictator to the transcriptionist, the tape can be lost or misplaced.

PORTABLE UNITS. Portable units are battery powered and use magnetic tapes. The standard functions found on most portable units include record, play, rewind, fast forward, volume, and an electronic cue for marking instructions to the transcriptionist and signaling the end of a document. Some units weigh less than a half pound and are only 4 or 5 inches long. The portable units are especially useful to executives and others who travel, work in the field rather than in an office, have long commutes to the office, or do some of their work at home.

Figure 2.2
Portable dictation units such as this Voice Processor are used to record transcription at any location. (Dictaphone)

DESKTOP UNITS. Desktop units are larger and remain in the office. Many units use magnetic tapes. Record, rewind, fast forward, play, and volume controls are standard functions of most machines. Virtually all machines are equipped with some type of electronic cue or manual system for marking instructions and signaling the end of a document. Most machines have an audible signal that warns the dictator that the tape is almost full. Tone and speed controls are common features but are not available on all machines. Some machines are equipped with automatic scanners or automatic search features designed to locate special instructions. Other special features, such as a conference hookup and telephone call recording capability, are available on some equipment. Some desktop models may also function as transcription units when the microphone is replaced by a headset and a foot pedal.

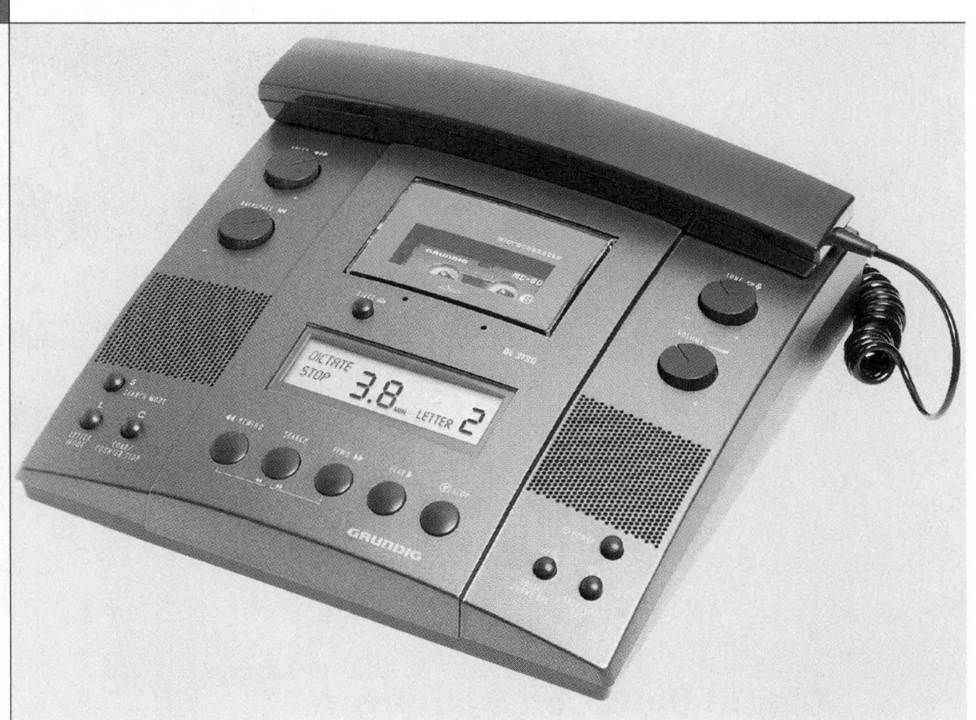

Figure 2.3
Desktop dictation equipment. (Grundig)

Continuous-Loop Systems

Continuous-loop systems are internal systems—that is, the medium is never handled. The tape is kept permanently inside individual tanks. The system gets its name from the fact that the ends of the tape inside the tank are joined to form a "continuous loop" that can hold 4 to 6 hours of dictation. When the tape is full, the dictator receives a message (usually an audible signal) that such is the case. After the transcriptionist transcribes the dictation, further dictation can be recorded over the old dictation.

Internal storage, or tank, systems have several advantages. Since the tape is not handled, there is no danger of its being lost or misplaced. Within seconds after the employer begins dictating, the transcriptionist can start to transcribe.

This feature allows transcriptionists to pace their work more efficiently, thus speeding delivery of the finished product. The dictating and transcribing units are always ready for use; the tape does not have to be loaded first.

Continuous-loop systems have some disadvantages, however. Only one transcriptionist can transcribe from the loop at one time; therefore, the work cannot be distributed among several transcriptionists. The dictated tape cannot be filed for future reference. Since the tank is stationary and the transcription unit is wired directly to the tank, the transcriptionist cannot move to another location.

Figure 2.4
The Lanier VoiceWriter 300 uses either mini or micro cassettes. (Lanier)

Digital Dictation Systems

Most manufacturers now market digital dictation systems. These are computer-based systems. The dictation is stored in digital rather than analog form on floppy disks or CD-ROMs. The quality of the dictation is better than the dictation on magnetic tape. However, these systems cost more than the desktop and portable units. Digital computer-based systems require additional wiring and installation, in contrast to desktop units that can be unplugged and moved easily. Digital portable recorders are popular for use with these dictation systems.

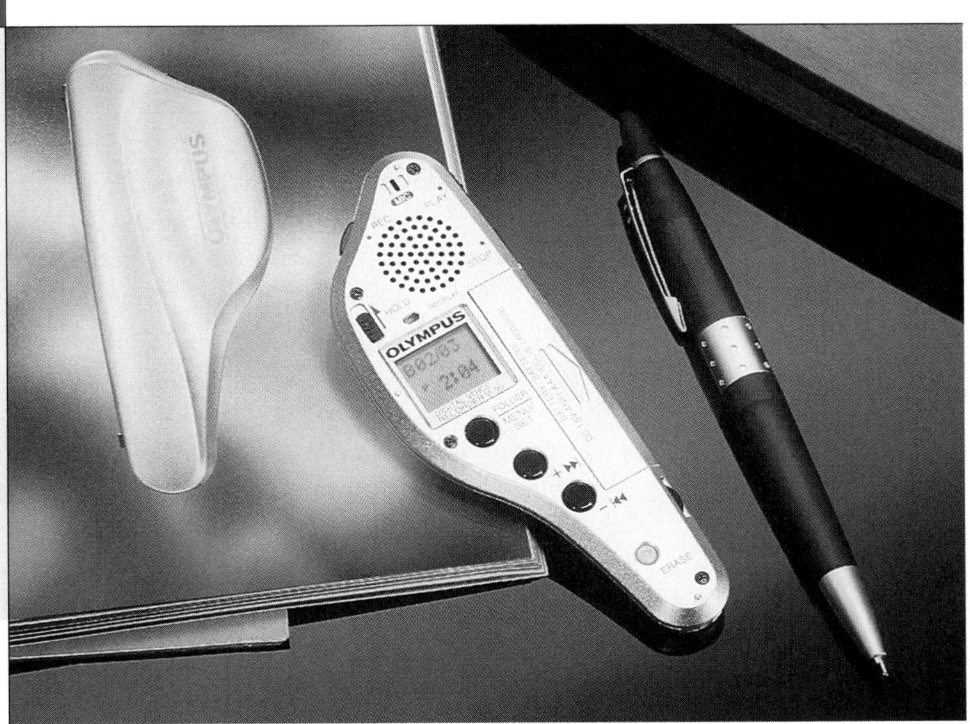

Figure 2.5
Digital remote recording unit. (Olympus)

Central Recording Systems

Central recording systems may contain a discrete system, a continuous-loop system, or a digital computer-based system. Central recording systems are separately wired or use existing telephone lines. In a separately wired system, each dictating unit is wired directly to a remote recorder or a computer located away from the microphone. Systems that use existing telephone lines are designed for many originators with all lines connected to one or more remote recorders or a computer. Every telephone may be an input device when the user dials a special number and a code for access to the recording device. These systems can be programmed so that the dictating operations are controlled by telephone buttons. This allows originators to call from outside phones as well as from internal company phones to record dictation. This feature increases the flexibility and efficiency of the system. Some units allow the dictator to dictate by telephone from a remote location and also to direct the dictation to a specific employee.

Advantages vary with the type of system chosen. If your firm chooses a multicassette (discrete) dictation system, there is a great deal of flexibility. The tapes may be dedicated to specific uses. For example, the system may be programmed to record high-priority dictation on one cassette, foreign-language dictation on another, notes to the file on another, and routine correspondence on still another. Each dictator may record dictation on a separate cassette. The dictator merely dials in the designated code to access the appropriate cassette. An audible signal alerts the dictator that the end of the tape is near. The dictation may be distributed to the transcriptionists according to workloads, ability, and priority.

In a multicassette dictation system, cassettes are stacked in the central recorder. As each cassette is filled, it is ejected so that a new one may slip into the record slot.

Flexibility is also a feature of the continuous-loop system since several tanks may be available. By merely pressing a code number on the telephone or a button on the dictation unit, the employer can direct incoming dictation to the tank with the least amount of dictation, to the tank designated to handle certain types of dictation, or to a specific transcriptionist. Tanks designated to handle specific types of dictation or dictation from only a certain individual or department are called dedicated tanks. Digital displays remind the transcriptionist how much dictation remains to be transcribed.

On a digital computer-based system, the dictator is able to insert dictation without dictating over previous dictation. This is accomplished in much the same way that you insert material on a word processor. The previous dictation is preserved merely by being moved over to allow room for the inserted material. With digital computer systems, the transcriptionist does not have to rewind the tape when the transcription is complete.

The multicassette, continuous-loop tank, and computer-based systems can be programmed to handle priority dictation. Cassette systems can eject a priority cassette as soon as the dictator hangs up. With continuous-loop tank and computer systems, a supervisor may be cued when priority material is received and can assign it for immediate transcription. On some systems, the dictator can press a button to indicate priority work, and a corresponding button on the transcription unit allows the transcriptionist to locate it quickly. On digital computer-based systems, priority dictation is automatically moved to become the first item for transcription.

2.2 VOICE-RECOGNITION SOFTWARE

Some firms use voice-recognition software. When the speaker dictates into a microphone, the transcript appears on the computer screen immediately. The various software packages achieve this transcript with varying degrees of accuracy. The first step is for the dictator to train the computer to understand his or her speech and pronunciation. The more time spent training the computer, the greater the accuracy of the transcript.

Using voice-recognition software, you can also edit text and correct mistakes verbally. You can verbally enter commands such as bold, underline, and all caps. The degree of accuracy of the software will determine its worth to you in your work. If you are an extremely slow typist, it may be faster for you to use voice-recognition software. If you are a fast typist, you may find that using this software is actually slower than keying the text yourself by the time you correct the transcription errors made by the software. As the technology improves, the value and prevalence in the workplace of voice-recognition software will increase. Your goal should be to efficiently produce quality documents regardless of how you accomplish the task.

When a firm uses voice-recognition technology, transcriptionists use proofreading skills extensively. They *must* proofread for content, not just scan for

Figure 2.6
The Dictaphone Boomerang system converts the speaker's voice to a transcript on a computer screen. (Dictaphone)

misspelled words. Transcriptionists need to be familiar with the vocabulary that is customary and appropriate for the type of transcripts that are produced. They proofread the transcripts carefully to be sure that the proper words have been transcribed and that the punctuation is appropriate. It is important to be particularly watchful for homonyms such as *their, there,* and *they're* or *principal* and *principle*. The more familiar the transcriber is with the dictator's customary vocabulary, the easier it is to proofread and correct the transcripts.

Types of Errors Experienced Using Voice-Recognition Software

When PC Magazine ("Say That Again????" PC Magazine Online, October 20, 1998, <http://search.zdnet.com/pcmag/features/speech98/intro.html> 8/4/99.) tested four voice-recognition software packages, errors occurred, including the following.

What the testers said	What the programs heard
"cold training and mop-up"	college training in Moscow
"travel to California"	troubled California
"draw a cube"	draw on Cuba
"Genevieve Haldeman"	Genevieve, haul them in
"for immediate release"	for a meeting at reliefs

"Personally, I want to let you know how much I enjoyed your book."	Personally, I want to let you know how much I enjoyed your brother.
"By December 31, you'll receive a $50,000 bonus"	By December 21, you'll receive $8 by defective gas and bonus.
"to our finest restaurant"	postwar France restaurant
"less-than-fashionable summer attire"	Last and vegetable are attacked.

2.3 REMOTE TRANSCRIPTION

Some hospitals and some doctors in private practice are outsourcing the transcription of their dictation rather than purchasing transcription equipment and employing transcriptionists to work at their facilities. The dictation is transmitted through secure Internet connections to one of several companies that hire transcriptionists who work in their homes. Some doctors directly hire individual transcriptionists as independent contractors who then work at home. These remote transcription procedures open up many new employment possibilities for skilled transcriptionists. These jobs allow much greater flexibility of work hours than is possible in many on-site transcription facilities. For example, under this arrangement, a parent caring for young children at home and unable to work at an on-site transcription facility may be able to work at home.

2.4 TRANSCRIBING THE MESSAGE—WORD PROCESSING

In many companies, dictation is transcribed by assistants or machine transcriptionists within each department. Firms that use this approach often require the assistant to perform other duties in addition to word processing. The assistant may work for only one executive or for several executives. This decentralized approach (see Figure 2.7) is often preferred when the executives' work is very confidential or must be completed within tight deadlines.

In other companies, machine transcriptionists work in a centralized or partially centralized word processing department (see Figures 2.8 and 2.9). The centralized department may receive dictation from all other departments within the building or from employees who call from remote locations to record their dictation. A supervisor assigns the dictation to transcription specialists according to the priority of the documents and the transcriptionists' workloads. A single transcriptionist may transcribe the dictation of many different originators or may be assigned to handle work in certain subject areas.

Figure 2.7
A decentralized word processing arrangement.

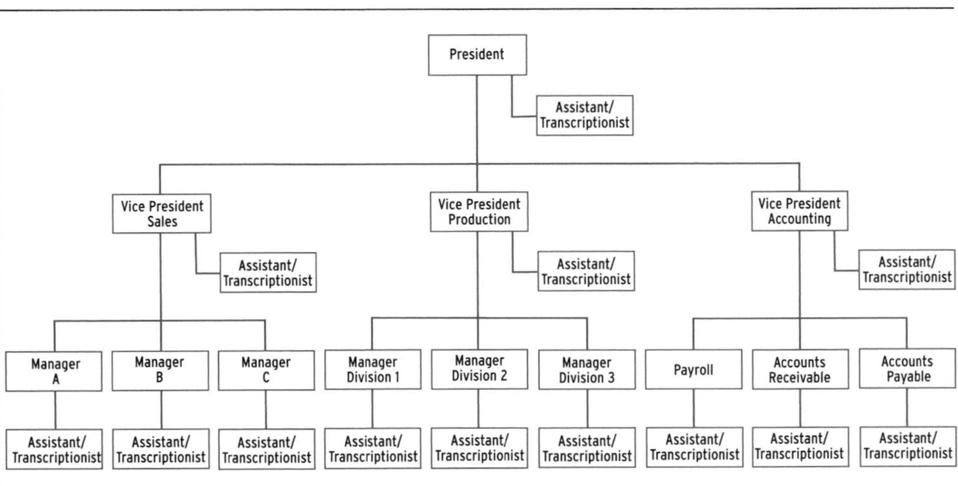

Figure 2.8
A centralized word processing arrangement.

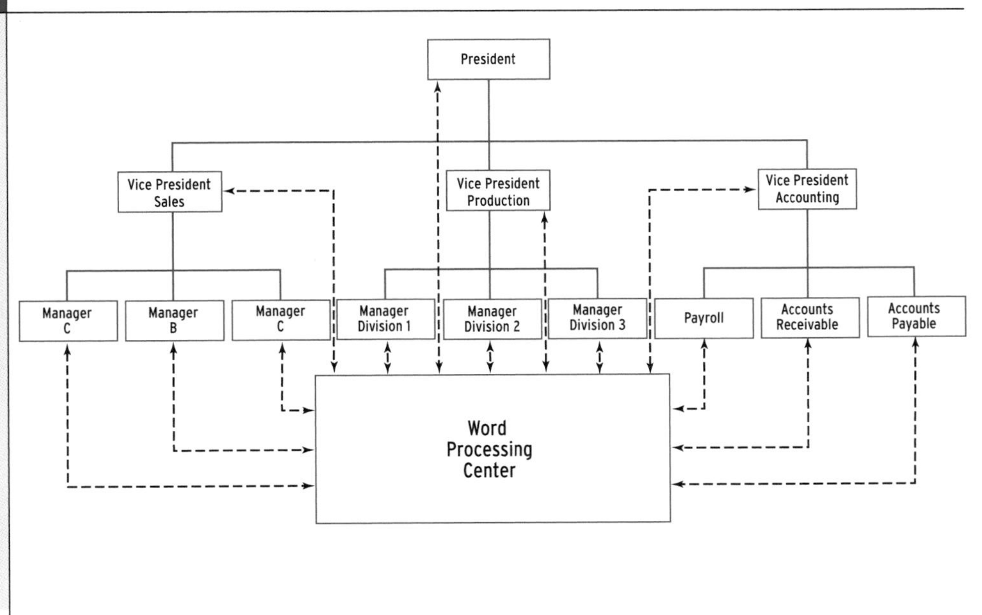

Figure 2.9
A partially centralized word processing arrangement.

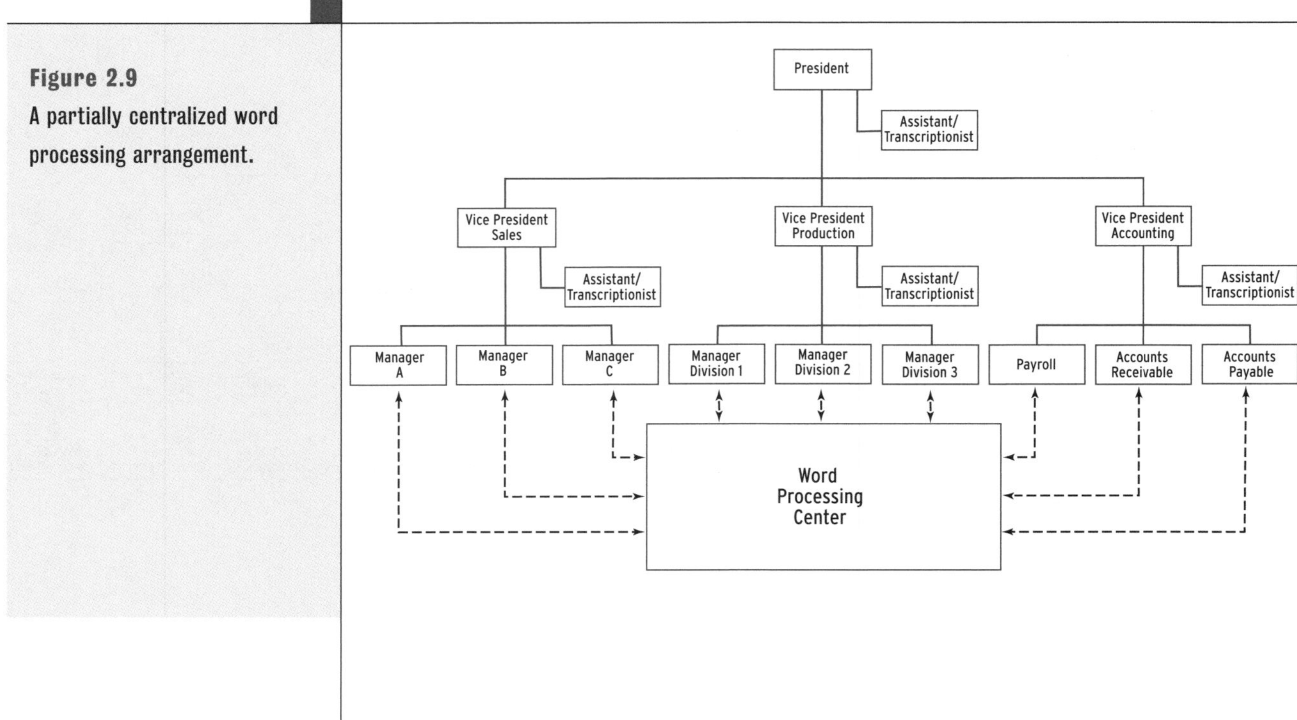

2.5 SHARING FILES—LOCAL AREA NETWORKS

Local area networks allow employees to share data and to communicate easily through the workstations at their desks. Employees have shared access to hardware, application software, and databases. The hardware that controls the network is referred to as the *server*. The server can be located in a remote location in the building; that is, in a closet, in the basement, and so forth. The server for the dictation equipment works in the same way as a server for a word processing system. The dictating stations and transcribing stations are part of the network. Hospitals use local area networks extensively. Doctors dictate reports at dictating stations located in examining rooms. This dictation goes to the server and is then distributed to the transcription stations automatically or through a supervisor who assigns work.

Figure 2.10
Handheld dictation units are often used by health care providers to document patients' care. (Phillips)

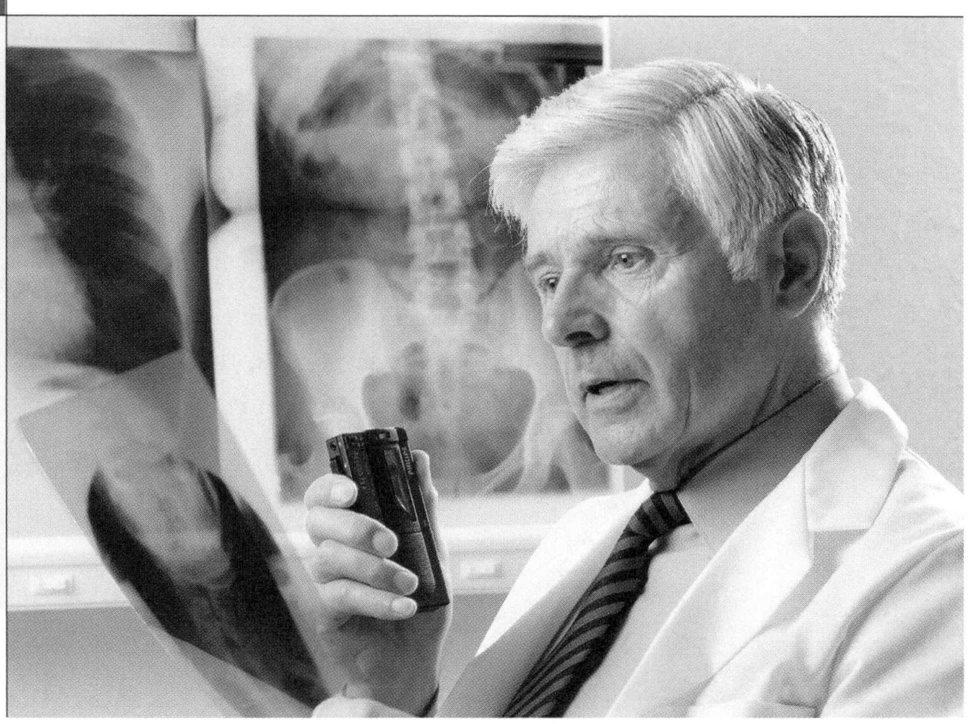

Figure 2.11
Many transcriptionists work in a hospital setting. (Phillips)

2.6 RECORD-KEEPING

Transcriptionists often keep more records of their work in a centralized environment than in a decentralized office. A transcription log is kept by the transcriptionist as a record of the work and contains details about its completion and distribution. A dictation evaluation form may be sent to the dictator by the transcriptionist with suggestions for improving the efficiency of the dictation and the transcription process.

In a centralized system, supervisors may use management consoles with display screens and printers to generate work-flow reports concerning:

1. Amount of incoming dictation.
2. Individual transcription workloads and output.
3. Amount of dictation from individual authors.
4. Dates of dictation.
5. Dates of transcription.
6. Turnaround time.
7. Number of priority jobs.
8. Productivity reports for the day, week, month, and year.
9. Amount of dictation from specific workstations.

TRANSCRIPTION LOG

Transcriptionist ______________________________

Date ______________________________

Dictator ______________________________

Time started ______________________________ Time ended ______________________________

Total time in minutes ______________________________

Account to be charged ______________________________

Distribution of transcribed items:

1. ______________________________
2. ______________________________
3. ______________________________
4. ______________________________
5. ______________________________
6. ______________________________
7. ______________________________
8. ______________________________
9. ______________________________
10. ______________________________
11. ______________________________
12. ______________________________
13. ______________________________
14. ______________________________
15. ______________________________

DICTATION EVALUATION FORM

Name of Dictator ____ Date __________________________

PLEASE

____________ Dictate at a slower rate.

____________ Dictate in a louder voice.

____________ Dictate more distinctly.

____________ Spell proper names.

____________ Spell unusual words.

____________ Give complete instructions.

____________ Specify kind of stationery or form required.

____________ Use proper correction procedure.

____________ Specify number of copies.

____________ Indicate unusual punctuation or capitalization.

____________ Specify distribution of transcribed material.

____________ Give woman's preferred title.

____________ Indicate end of letter or item.

Other ____

____

____

____

____

____

____

____

Name of Transcriber ____

Section 3

Transcribing Techniques

Introduction

You have studied the basic parts of a transcription unit and how to operate it. However, there is much more to the process than pushing a button and keying what you hear. In addition to these mechanical functions, the transcriptionist must constantly be attentive to spelling, word meaning, grammar, punctuation, sentence structure, placement of copy, the dictator's pronunciation, and special instructions given by the dictator. This chapter discusses some very important processes that occur before, during, and after listening to dictated material.

3.1 BEFORE YOU BEGIN TRANSCRIBING

There are a few things to be accomplished before you listen to the first word of dictation. These include building a reference library, both general and specialized; setting up the dictation equipment; listening to dictated instructions; and calculating letter placement or other format from the clues you are given about the length of each document.

Build Your Reference Library

Be sure to equip your work area with the reference books and supplies needed to make your transcription fast, efficient, and accurate.

GENERAL REFERENCE LIBRARY. Everyone should have a good desk dictionary. Every office should have an unabridged dictionary. You also should obtain telephone directories for all of the areas you call frequently and an area code directory. A good reference or office procedures handbook can provide a great deal of assistance, as can an English grammar handbook. A ZIP Code directory is essential for efficient mail preparation.

NOTE:
If the ZIP Code is not provided, use the Internet to find it. Using your search engine, search for the key word ***ZIP Code*** and make a note of the Internet address.

You should have the equipment manual for your word processor readily available. Your firm may have an office handbook or manual of letter styles to be used and procedures to be followed. Be sure you have a copy for easy reference. This office handbook may also contain helpful information about the personnel with whom you work, including flowcharts that can direct you to the proper personnel in case of questions or problems in particular departments or areas. A thesaurus is sometimes helpful in transcription. A city directory is useful for locating proper names, addresses, and telephone numbers. Remember that your local library staff can help you locate information that is not available in any of your reference books.

The Internet is an excellent tool for reference. For example, if you log on to the Internet and go to http://www.refdesk.com/, you will find links to dictionaries, encyclopedias, almanacs, U.S. Postal Service, news, maps, and many more reference sites.

SPECIALIZED REFERENCE LIBRARY. Acquire any reference books applicable to your particular career field. For example, if you work for a law firm, you will need a certified list of domestic and foreign corporations, a *Martindale Hubbell Law*

Directory, an insurance directory, tax tables, *Black's Law Dictionary*, and a medical dictionary. Some of these reference books should be available in the firm; therefore, you will not have to purchase them yourself. If you work in a medical office or hospital, you will need a *Physician's Desk Reference Manual*, medical dictionaries from more than one source, and supply house catalogs. Most employers are happy to purchase any reference books that you feel are necessary.

Set Up Your Machine

If you have a desktop transcriber, you will have a headset, a foot pedal, and a transcribing unit that holds the tape or disk and has the controls. If you are using a continuous-loop system, you will have a headset, a foot pedal, and a control unit. A control unit is somewhat smaller than a transcribing unit since it does not hold the media.

Your instructor will demonstrate where the controls are located on the specific transcribing units you will be using in your classroom. The following illustration shows the location of the power switch and the controls for tone, volume, speed, counter, search, play, stop, rewind, and fast forward on one unit. It also illustrates the location of the area designed to receive a tape. Plug the headset into the receptacle labeled "headset." Plug the machine into an electric outlet. Be sure the foot control is plugged into the transcription unit. Open the media compartment, and insert the cassette. Close the media compartment, and turn on the machine. On most machines an indicator light will remind you that the machine is turned on. If your machine is designed for use with indication slips or index strips, find the one that corresponds with the tape you are going to transcribe, and

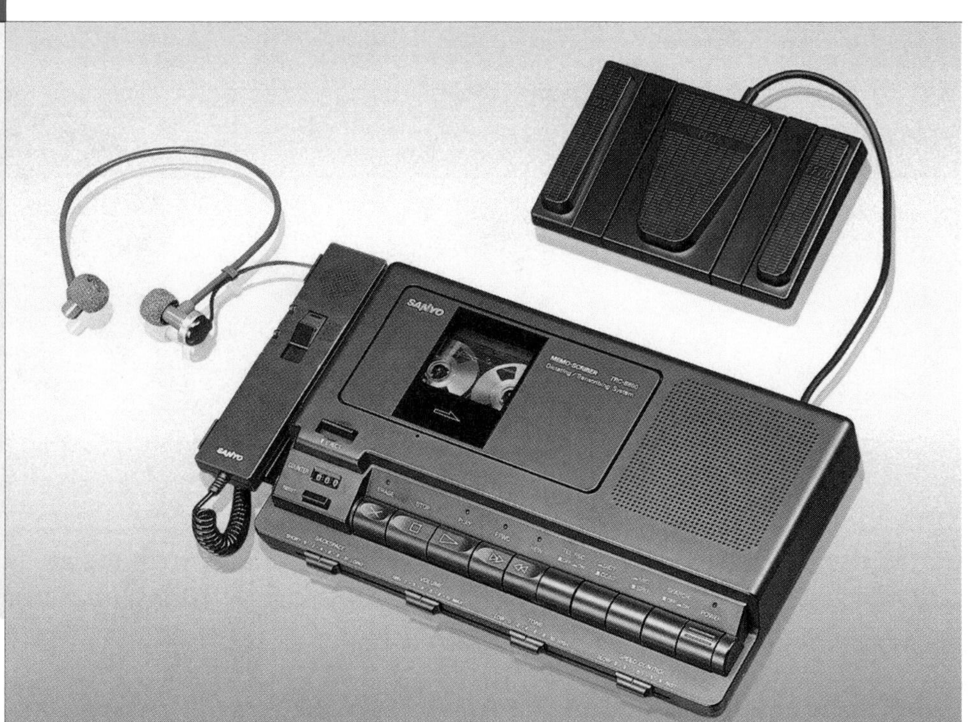

Figure 3.1 Memo-Scriber TRC-8800 Dictating/Transcribing System control unit showing tape location, counter, and controls for erase, stop, play, fast forward, rewind, search, power, backspace, volume, tone, and speed control. The headset and foot pedal are also shown. (Sanyo)

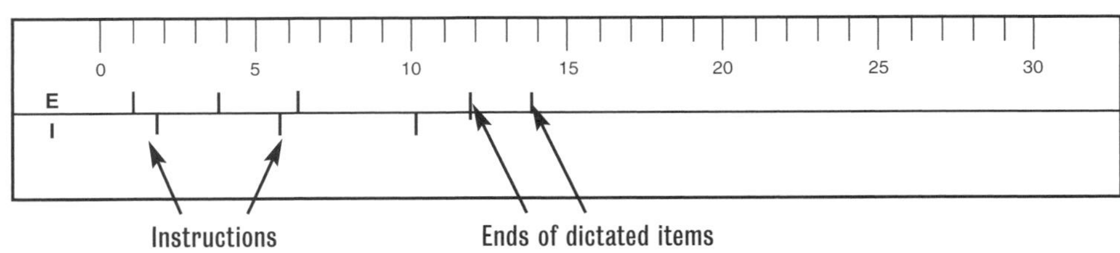

Figure 3.2
The marks on an index strip help the transcriptionist understand an assignment.

place it on the transcribing machine. The marks at the top of the indication slip show the approximate number of minutes of dictation for each document. Corrections and instructions are indicated by marks at the bottom of the indication slip. Adjust the volume, speed, and tone controls for your own listening comfort.

Listen to Instructions

Before you begin to transcribe, always listen to any corrections or instructions. The instructions may contain information about the order in which you should key the items dictated. You and your employer would be very unhappy if you had not listened to the instructions before you began to transcribe and then found the next day that one of the last items dictated should have been transcribed first and mailed immediately. Press the fast forward key to advance the tape to corrections or instructions as shown on the indication slip or on the lighted display.

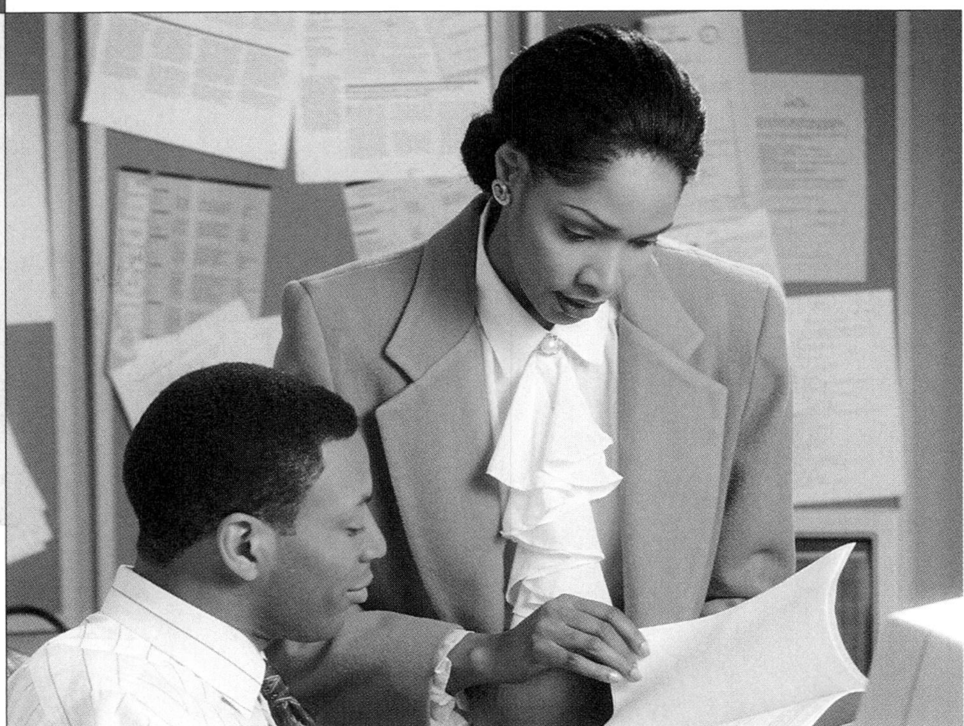

Figure 3.3
Listen carefully to instructions about assigned work.
What can you do to improve your listening skills?

If your machine has no indication slip or lighted display, your employer should list the counter numbers at which the corrections or instructions begin. If you are working on a transcribing machine that has electronic cuing, the corrections and instructions can be found through the scanning or search mechanism. If you are working from a centralized dictation system, check any priority notations before you begin transcribing.

Calculate Vertical Letter Placement

As a transcriptionist, you will have to translate the amount of time shown on the indication slip, counter, or lighted display into length of typed copy. Once you have estimated the length of the item to be transcribed, choose the appropriate margins for the document. Some firms prefer that you use the default margins of the word processing program. Others want you to vary the margins to adjust the width of the document based on the letter's length. If you are keying a letter, the letter placement chart shown in Table 3.1 may help you. Another option is to use the word processor's vertical center command if the item should be centered on the page. There is another copy of this chart and other transcription guidelines summarized in the Reference Handbook at the back of the textbook. You may find it most efficient to keep a copy of the letter placement guidelines beside your keyboard.

Table 3.1

LETTER PLACEMENT CHART - WORD PROCESSORS

Length of Letter	Number of Minutes	Margin Settings Courier New 10-point	Margin Settings Courier New 12-point	Top Margin Inches	Top Margin Line
Short	1 or less	2"	2"	3.32	20
Medium	1 ½	1.75"	1.7"	2.96	18
	2	1.75"	1.5"	2.61	16
	2 ½	1.5"	1.2"	2.25	14
Long	2 ½-3	1.25"	1.2"	2.07	13
Two-Page	3 or more	1"	1"	2.07	13

The letter must begin at least a double space below the letterhead. If the letter contains extra lines such as attention line, subject line, company name in the closing lines, and mailing notations, adjust the position of the date line upward. Press Enter four times after keying the date. If you choose a different font, the placement may need to be adjusted.

3.2 HOW TO BEGIN TRANSCRIBING

To start transcribing, depress the foot pedal to listen to a phrase or sentence. Then key what you have heard. Listen to as much as you can remember at one time. Try to avoid rewinding and listening to the same material twice. Rewinding is time consuming and inefficient. At first, you will probably listen to only a short phrase before you release the foot pedal and begin keying. With practice, you will be able to listen to longer sections of dictation before you release the foot pedal. At first, you may find yourself pausing to listen to additional dictation before you resume keying. Strive to eliminate the pauses. Just before you finish keying a phrase or sentence, depress the foot pedal again and listen to the next phrase or sentence. Your goal is to key without pauses.

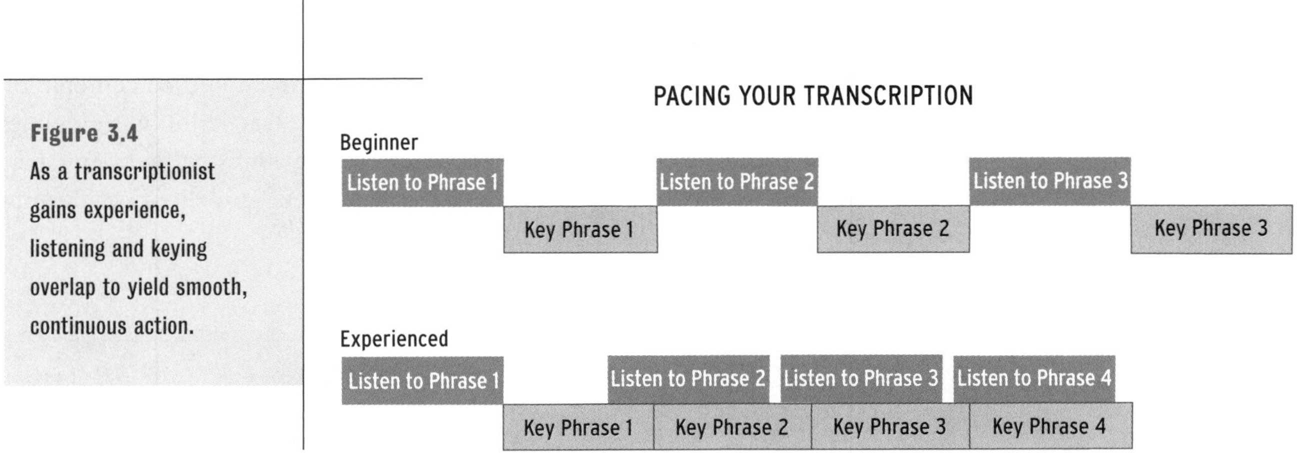

Figure 3.4 As a transcriptionist gains experience, listening and keying overlap to yield smooth, continuous action.

Automatic Recall Feature

Although many transcribing machines have an automatic recall feature that repeats the last one to ten words that you heard just before releasing the foot pedal, this practice is inefficient and should be avoided. Most of the time you will not need to repeat the dictation you just heard. You may even find that you will accidentally rekey the repeated words if your machine is set for automatic recall. The better procedure is to set the automatic recall feature of your transcribing unit to zero. For the rare times that you must listen to the dictation a second time, use the backspace feature on the foot pedal. You will develop a fast transcription speed more easily by using this procedure than by using the automatic recall feature of the transcribing equipment.

Concentrate and THINK!

As you transcribe, think about what you are keying. The dictation should not go directly from your ears to your fingers without passing through your brain. If you are not thinking about the content of what you are transcribing, you may confuse words such as *advice* and *advise*; *affect* and *effect*; *know* and *no*; *to*, *too*, and *two*; *assistance* and *assistants*; *brake* and *break*; and *compliment* and *complement*. If you are concentrating on the content of what you are transcribing, you will be able to detect inconsistencies in the dictated material. Suppose, for example, at the beginning of a letter, the dictator mentions June 26 as the date; however, at the end of the letter, the date is repeated incorrectly as June 25. If you are concentrating on the content of the dictation, you will detect this inconsistency and check to see which date is correct. Always check figures, dates, names, and addresses.

Ask Yourself: Does It Make Sense?

If a sentence does not make sense to you, it probably will not make sense to the reader. If you cannot understand a word or phrase, adjust the tone control slightly. Sometimes this will enable you to understand the dictation. Increasing the volume is not always the answer. If you increase the volume too much, you may actually distort the voice, making understanding the word more difficult. Think about the point the dictator is trying to make. Perhaps that will help you decipher the dictation. As you become familiar with the dictator's speech patterns and word usage, deciphering mumbled words and phrases will become easier.

Apply the Rules

The transcriptionist must make sure there are no errors in the presentation of the transcribed material. Errors may be grouped in three categories: grammar, punctuation, and spelling.

GRAMMAR. The dictator will rely on you to correct grammatical errors. The dictator is concentrating on the idea he or she is trying to convey and may dictate a sentence that is grammatically incorrect—using, for example, a singular verb with a plural subject. This does not mean that the dictator does not know the proper word or words to use; it may merely mean that the dictator was concentrating on content rather than form. It is up to you to supply the correct form. Be certain that you are correct before you make changes.

PUNCTUATION. The dictator also will rely on you to supply the correct punctuation. Listen for pauses in the dictation as clues to punctuating transcribed sentences. There are also other kinds of clues. For example, if the sentence starts with a subordinate conjunction (*if*, *when*, *as*, *since*, *although*, and so forth), you know that the sentence begins with a dependent clause and that you will need to separate that clause from the independent clause with a comma.

SPELLING. If you are unsure of the correct spelling of a word, use a dictionary; don't guess. Briefly check the definition to be sure the spelling that you have found matches the intended meaning. For example, suppose you can't remember whether *calendar*, a table that shows the months and days of the year, is spelled with an *ar* or an *er*. If you find *calender* in a dictionary and do not check the definition, you will type the wrong word.

Each time you use a dictionary to look up the correct spelling of a word, put that word on a list. When you have a little extra time, learn the spelling of the words on this list so that you will not have to look them up repeatedly.

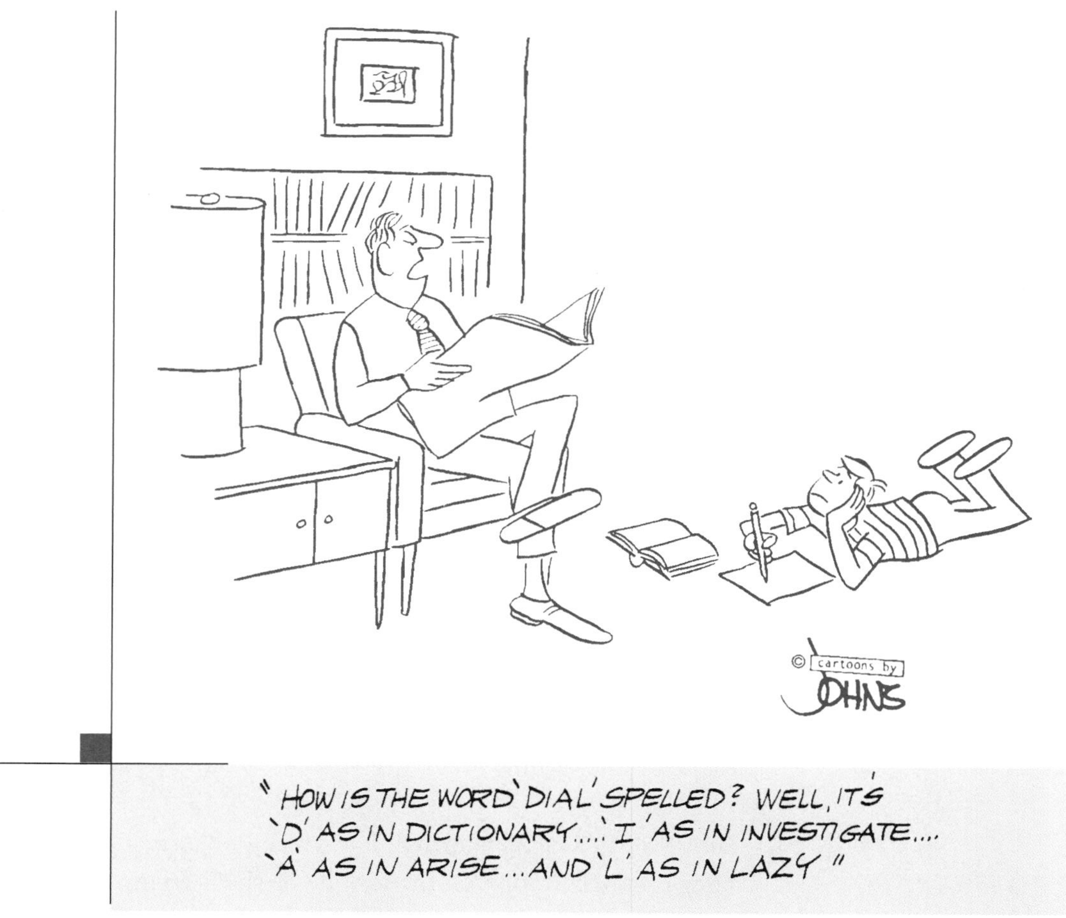

" HOW IS THE WORD 'DIAL' SPELLED? WELL, IT'S 'D' AS IN DICTIONARY.... 'I' AS IN INVESTIGATE.... 'A' AS IN ARISE... AND 'L' AS IN LAZY "

Don't Forget Enclosures

If the letter mentions an enclosure, be certain to type the enclosure notation and put the enclosure with the transcribed letter. The dictator may or may not dictate the enclosure notation. It is up to you to remember to include the notation and the enclosure.

3.3 PROOFREAD CAREFULLY

Proofread each item before you print it. Check the grammar, punctuation, spelling, and format. Proofread more slowly than your normal reading rate. ***THINK*** about what you are proofreading. Don't overlook errors such as *you* for *your* or *will* for *well*. Never mail a letter that says, "Please send you check." The spelling checker will not find this error because "you" is a dictionary word, and the spell-check feature finds only words that are not in its dictionary. If you do not ***THINK*** about the sense of what you are proofreading, you may miss this type of error since it is not obvious. These errors will be found only when you are thinking about the content as well as the grammar, punctuation, spelling, and format. Even the spell-check function of your equipment cannot distinguish between words that sound alike but are spelled differently and have different meanings.

If you are proofreading statistical information, land descriptions, legal contracts, wills, or technical reports, you should seek the assistance of another employee. If you transcribed from a rough draft, read the original and have the proofreading partner check your copy. It is easier to recognize someone else's errors than to find your own. You should double-check all punctuation and unusual spellings, paragraph divisions, and format. If you have transcribed the information from a tape, rewind the tape so you can listen to the material again as you proofread your copy.

If you are proofreading a long document, take a break occasionally, and perform some other task.

In some circumstances, it may be necessary to proofread the document more than once. Proofread for format first; then proofread for content, spelling, and grammar. After you have corrected the errors, proofread a final time. You will find a list of proofreaders' marks in the Reference Handbook at the back of the textbook.

3.4 PRODUCE MAILABLE TRANSCRIPTS

You should always strive for a mailable or usable transcript the first time you key each dictated letter or item. Your employer cannot afford to allow you to produce rough drafts routinely. The following checklist will help you determine the mailability of your transcripts.

MAILABILITY CHECKLIST

Your transcript is mailable or usable if it contains:

1. No spelling errors.
2. No punctuation errors.
3. No grammatical errors.
4. No typographical errors (*if* for *it*, *in* for *on*, and so forth.)
5. A proper format.
6. The proper vertical and horizontal placement on the page.
7. The appropriate number of copies.
8. An enclosure notation, when appropriate. (Make notes of any information about enclosures that are not mentioned in the body of the letter so that you will not forget to include the notation in the letter.)
9. No smudges.

Use this checklist as a guideline for all your transcription exercises. You may want to keep a copy of this list in a convenient location for quick reference.

3.5 ASSEMBLE YOUR TRANSCRIPTS

As a machine transcriptionist or office assistant, present your transcripts to your employer in a folder. Arrange the items in the folder so that the most important items are signed or viewed first. If you transcribe an item that has been designated as a priority or rush, immediately submit it to your employer for signing and processing. The rest of the transcribed items should be presented for signing and processing according to the mail schedule and your employer's schedule. Attach any enclosures to the original letter or item. Use a paper clip to attach each unfolded letter under the flap of its envelope; the flap may be at the top or left side of the stationery.

If your employer wishes to check the address on the envelope, place the letter under the flap of the envelope with the address side up. If your employer does not wish to check the address, place the letter under the flap of the envelope with the address side down. Any photocopies or printouts of outgoing letters should be stapled on top of the pieces of mail to which you are responding and placed under the original transcripts in the folder. These photocopies or printouts will be filed after your employer has signed the correspondence or approved other items. If any photocopies or printouts are to be mailed, the envelopes should be prepared and the copies presented in the folder in the same manner as the original letter. These copies should be placed in the folder under the original letter and envelope. By submitting your transcripts in a folder, you keep them clean and protect them from loss and from unauthorized viewing.

Figure 3.5
Transcripts are presented to an employer for signature and mailing.
What is the proper order for assembling transcripts for presentation?

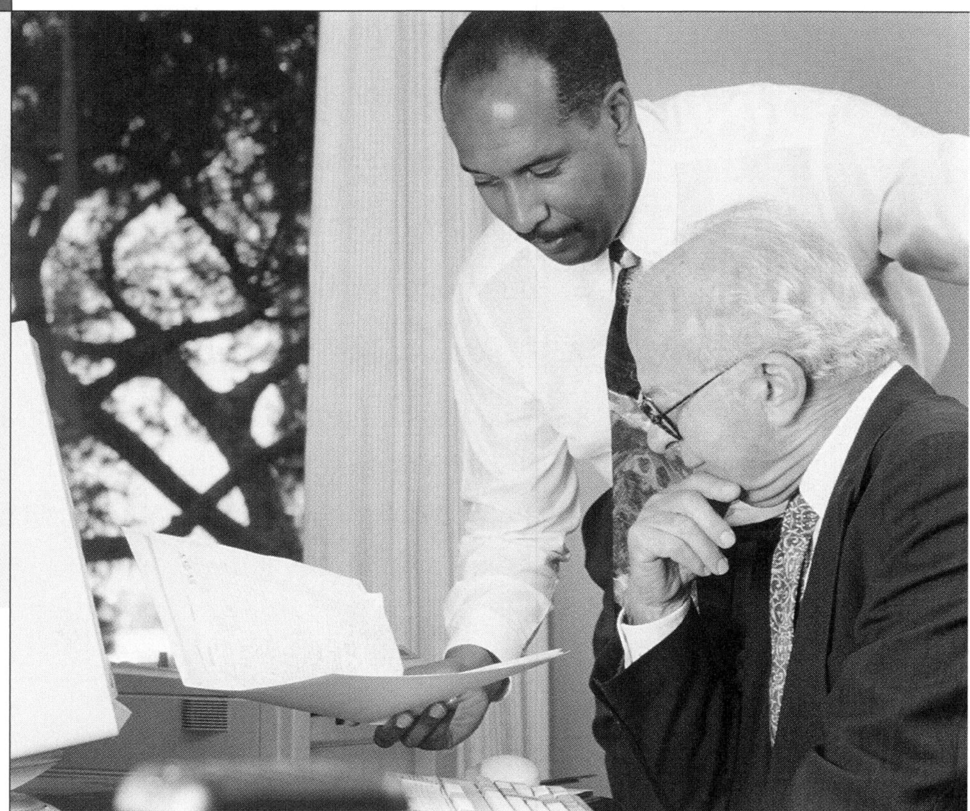

3.6 BE PROUD OF YOUR WORK

The high cost of doing business demands that you be efficient as well as highly skilled. This course can do much toward building your efficiency and skill. The ingredient that you add is pride in a job well done.

The foundation of skill development is confidence in your ability to perform. Even though at the beginning of this course you may not be able to produce a mailable copy the first time, your skill at machine transcription will improve steadily as you proceed through these lessons. Your ultimate goal should be to produce a mailable transcript the first time. By always giving your best effort, your confidence will grow along with your skill.

3.7 TIME MANAGEMENT

Use the following Time Management Schedule to plan your time efficiently. First, for a week, make a chart similar to the Time Management Schedule, and keep track of what you actually do with your time. Then use your Time Management Schedule to plan how to use your time more efficiently. You will be surprised at how much more *free* time you have when you plan your time carefully. Try it; it works.

Following the Time Management Schedule is a Student Progress Record that will help you keep track of your work as you complete assignments during the course.

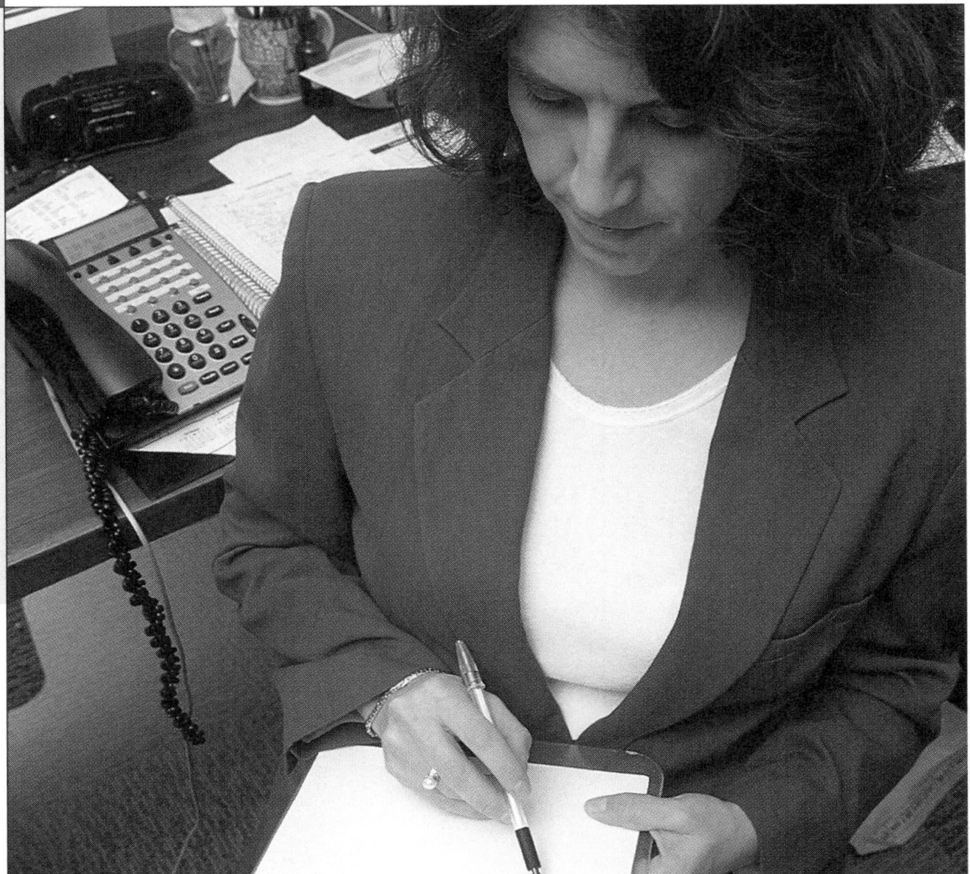

Figure 3.6
Effective time management improves productivity.
What do you think is the best way to keep track of your work?

TIME MANAGEMENT SCHEDULE

	Sunday	Monday	Tuesday	Wednesday	Thursday	Friday	Saturday
5 a.m.							
6 a.m.							
7 a.m.							
8 a.m.							
9 a.m.							
10 a.m.							
11 a.m.							
12 Noon							
1 p.m.							
2 p.m.							
3 p.m.							
4 p.m.							
5 p.m.							
6 p.m.							
7 p.m.							
8 p.m.							
9 p.m.							
10 p.m.							
11 p.m.							

STUDENT PROGRESS RECORD

Part 1 Assignments	Started	Completed	Grade
Reference Exercises			
Listening Exercises			
Dictation Exercises			
Pre-Transcription Dictation			
Proofreading Exercise			

Part 2 Assignments			
SECTION 1			
Punctuation Exercises: Part 1			
Punctuation Exercises: Part 2			
Word Study Exercises: Part 1			
Word Study Exercises: Part 2			
Proofreading Exercise 1-A			
Proofreading Exercise 1-B			
Proofreading Exercise 1-C			
Spelling Test 1			
Section 1 Dictation: 1.1			
1.2			
1.3			
1.4			
SECTION 2			
Punctuation Exercises: Part 1			
Punctuation Exercises: Part 2			
Word Study Exercises: Part 1			
Word Study Exercises: Part 2			
Proofreading Exercise 2-A			
Proofreading Exercise 2-B			
Proofreading Exercise 2-C			
Spelling Test 2			
Section 2 Dictation: 2.1			
2.2			
2.3			
2.4			
Word Study Test 1			
SECTION 3			
Punctuation Exercises: Part 1			
Punctuation Exercises: Part 2			
Word Study Exercises: Part 1			
Word Study Exercises: Part 2			
Proofreading Exercise 3-A			
Proofreading Exercise 3-B			
Proofreading Exercise 3-C			
Spelling Test 3			
Section 3 Dictation: 3.1			
3.2			
3.3			
3.4			
3.5			

STUDENT PROGRESS RECORD continued

Part 2 Assignments	Started	Completed	Grade
SECTION 4			
Word Study Exercises			
Proofreading Exercise 4-A			
Proofreading Exercise 4-B			
Proofreading Exercise 4-C			
Spelling Test 4			
Section 4 Dictation: 4.1			
4.2			
4.3			
4.4			
4.5			
SECTION 5			
Punctuation Exercises: Part 1			
Punctuation Exercises: Part 2			
Word Study Exercises: Part 1			
Word Study Exercises: Part 2			
Proofreading Exercise			
Word Division Exercises			
Spelling Test 5			
Section 5 Dictation: 5.1			
5.2			
5.3			
5.4			
5.5			
Word Study Test 2			
Practice Transcription Test			
(Optional)			
SECTION 6			
Word Study Exercises			
Proofreading Exercise 6-A			
Proofreading Exercise 6-B			
Proofreading Exercise 6-C			
Spelling Test 6			
Section 6 Dictation: 6.1			
6.2			
6.3			
6.4			
6.5			
SECTION 7			
Punctuation Exercises: Part 1			
Punctuation Exercises: Part 2			
Word Study Exercises: Part 1			
Word Study Exercises: Part 2			
Proofreading Exercise 7-A			
Proofreading Exercise 7-B			
Proofreading Exercise 7-C			
Spelling Test 7			
Section 7 Dictation: 7.1			
7.2			
7.3			
7.4			
7.5			

STUDENT PROGRESS RECORD continued

Part 2 Assignments	Started	Completed	Grade
SECTION 8			
Word Study Exercises: Part 1			
Word Study Exercises: Part 2			
Proofreading Exercise 8-A			
Proofreading Exercise 8-B			
Proofreading Exercise 8-C			
Spelling Test 8			
Section 8 Dictation: 8.1			
8.2			
8.3			
8.4			
8.5			
Word Study Test 3			
Transcription Test 1			
SECTION 9			
Punctuation Exercises: Part 1			
Punctuation Exercises: Part 2			
Word Study Exercises: Part 1			
Word Study Exercises: Part 2			
Proofreading Exercise 9-A			
Proofreading Exercise 9-B			
Proofreading Exercise 9-C			
Spelling Test 9			
Section 9 Dictation: 9.1			
9.2			
9.3			
9.4			
9.5			
SECTION 10			
Word Study Exercises: Part 1			
Word Study Exercises: Part 2			
Proofreading Exercise 10-A			
Proofreading Exercise 10-B			
Proofreading Exercise 10-C			
Spelling Test 10			
Section 10 Dictation: 10.1			
10.2			
10.3			
10.4			
10.5			

STUDENT PROGRESS RECORD continued

Part 2 Assignments	Started	Completed	Grade
SECTION 11			
Punctuation Exercises: Part 1			
Punctuation Exercises: Part 2			
Word Study Exercises: Part 1			
Word Study Exercises: Part 2			
Proofreading Exercise 11-A			
Proofreading Exercise 11-B			
Proofreading Exercise 11-C			
Spelling Test 11			
Section 11 Dictation: 11.1			
11.2			
11.3			
11.4			
11.5			
Word Study Test 4			
Transcription Test 2			
SECTION 12			
Word Study Exercises: Part 1			
Word Study Exercises: Part 2			
Proofreading Exercise 12-A			
Proofreading Exercise 12-B			
Proofreading Exercise 12-C			
Spelling Test 12			
Section 12 Dictation: 12.1			
12.2			
12.3			
12.4			
12.5			
12.6			
Transcription Test 3			
SECTION 13			
Punctuation Exercises			
Word Study Exercises: Part 1			
Word Study Exercises: Part 2			
Proofreading Exercise 13-A			
Proofreading Exercise 13-B			
Proofreading Exercise 13-C			
Spelling Test 13			
Section 13 Dictation: 13.1			
13.2			
13.3			
13.4			
13.5			
Transcription Test 4			

STUDENT PROGRESS RECORD continued

Part 2 Assignments	Started	Completed	Grade
SECTION 14			
Punctuation Exercises			
Word Study Exercises: Part 1			
Word Study Exercises: Part 2			
Proofreading Exercise 14-A			
Proofreading Exercise 14-B			
Proofreading Exercise 14-C			
Spelling Test 14			
Section 14 Dictation: 14.1			
14.2			
14.3			
14.4			
14.5			
14.6			
14.7			
Word Study Test 5			
SECTION 15			
Proofreading Exercise 15-A			
Proofreading Exercise 15-B			
Proofreading Exercise 15-C			
Proofreading Exercise 15-D			
Spelling Test 15			
Section 15 Dictation: 15.1			
15.2			
15.3			
15.4			
15.5			
15.6			
Transcription Test 5			
SECTION 16			
Proofreading Exercise 16-A			
Proofreading Exercise 16-B			
Proofreading Exercise 16-C			
Spelling Test 16			
Section 16 Dictation: 16.1			
16.2			
16.3			
16.4			
16.5			
16.6			
Transcription Test 6			
SECTION 17			
Proofreading Exercise 17-A			
Proofreading Exercise 17-B			
Proofreading Exercise 17-C			
Proofreading Exercise 17-D			
Spelling Test 17			
Section 17 Dictation: 17.1			
17.2			
17.3			
17.4			
17.5			
Transcription Test 7			

STUDENT PROGRESS RECORD continued

Part 2 Assignments	Started	Completed	Grade
SECTION 18			
Proofreading Exercise 18-A			
Proofreading Exercise 18-B			
Proofreading Exercise 18-C			
Proofreading Exercise 18-D			
Spelling Test 18			
Section 18 Dictation: 18.1			
18.2			
18.3			
18.4			
18.5			
18.6			
SECTION 19			
Proofreading Exercise 19-A			
Proofreading Exercise 19-B			
Proofreading Exercise 19-C			
Proofreading Exercise 19-D			
Spelling Test 19			
Section 19 Dictation: 19.1			
19.2			
19.3			
19.4			
Transcription Test 8			
SECTION 20			
Proofreading Exercise 20-A			
Proofreading Exercise 20-B			
Proofreading Exercise 20-C			
Proofreading Exercise 20-D			
Spelling Test 20			
Section 20 Dictation: 20.1			
20.2			
20.3			
20.4			
Final Spelling Test			
Final Word Study Test			
Final Transcription Test			
SECTION 21			
Optional Bonus Section 21 Dictation: 21.1			
21.2			
21.3			
21.4			

Name/Class ____________________

ASSIGNMENT: SECTION 3

Complete the Reference Exercises below. Tear the completed exercises out of the textbook, and give them to your instructor before you proceed.

Reference Exercises

Locating ZIP Codes

DIRECTIONS: ***Using a current ZIP Code directory or the Internet, locate the proper ZIP Codes for the following addresses, and list them in the answer blanks provided:***

1. 567 Cooper Street, Aspen, Colorado ____________

2. P.O. Box 108, Sarasota, Florida ____________

3. 414 Fifth Avenue, New York, New York ____________

4. 625 North Michigan Avenue, Chicago, Illinois ____________

5. 918 Main Street, Eagle Creek, Oregon ____________

Using References

DIRECTIONS: ***Using appropriate reference books, answer the following questions in the answer blanks provided:***

1. When you add the suffix ing to the word *control*, do you double the *l*?

____

2. Which spelling is preferred—*usable* or *useable*?

____

3. What is the appropriate salutation and complimentary closing to use when you write a letter to a United States senator?

____

4. How should you address the envelope for the above letter?

____

5. What is the telephone number of the local library?

____

EXERCISE Name/Class ____________________

6. Which is the correct spelling—*preferrably* or *preferably*?

____

7. If a person's title is followed by an appositive, do you capitalize the title? For example:
   John called the vice president, Joe Brown.
   OR
   John called the Vice President, Joe Brown.

____

8. Indicate the proper capitalization in the following sentence:
   the sales in our north central region have increased 5 percent.

____

9. Locate the name and address of a local caterer who could cater a dinner for 25 people.

____

10. Circle the correct conjugation of the verb *light*.
    light - lighted - lighted
    OR
    light - lit - lit

11. What is the phone number of the sheriff's office?

____

12. List the name, address, and telephone number of a local pest control service.

____

13. Is the place of business of a barber spelled as one word or two words (barbershop or barber shop)?

____

14. Choose the proper way to express the fractions in the following sentences:
    We have (3/4, three-fourths) of our work done.
    Our office is (4 1/2, four and one-half) miles from the airport.

____

15. Locate and list the addresses and telephone numbers for two office supply businesses.

____

____

____

____

____

____

Section 4

Effective Listening

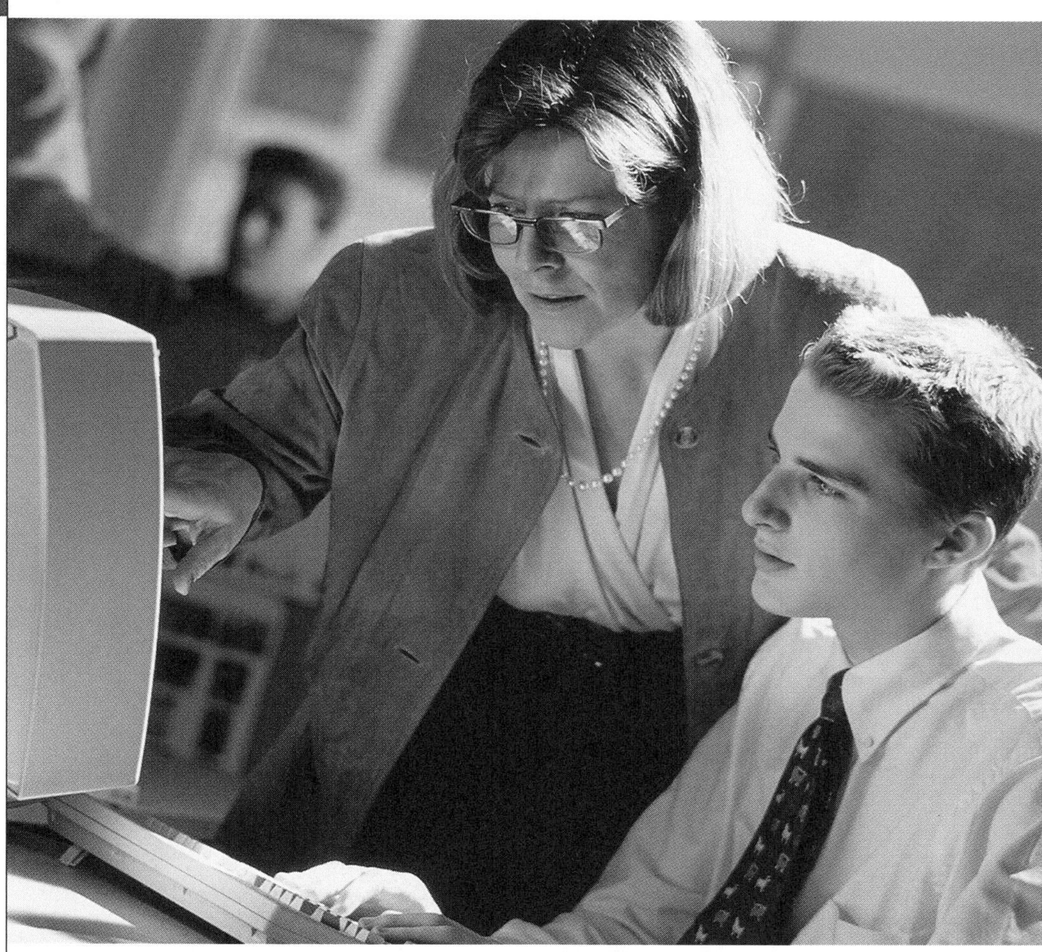

WHY YOU SHOULD LISTEN

Why You Should Listen

Effective listening and efficient transcribing are inseparable and are essential to your job performance. Effective listening is an important part of all office duties whether they involve transcribing, taking instructions, answering the telephone, attending business meetings, acting as receptionist, or answering questions from clients or customers. You will be able to improve your listening ability and, therefore, your job performance by practicing the guidelines presented in this chapter.

Effective listening is active, not strictly passive, behavior. Passive listening is really just hearing. The kind of listening talked about in this course is the kind needed to understand the message thoroughly. Such effective listening is the result of hearing plus the increased mental energy in order to comprehend what is being said.

You spend a great deal of your time listening to others. Ralph G. Nichols, a renowned listening expert, reports that we spend 45 to 70 percent of our time listening, depending on our occupations (Ralph G. Nichols and Leonard A. Stevens, *Are You Listening?* McGraw-Hill Book Company, New York, 1957, pp. 6–8). Think of all the time you spend listening: you listen to your instructors in class; you listen to instructions from your employer; you listen to music; you listen to television and radio; and you listen to your friends and family.

In *Are You Listening?* Ralph G. Nichols and Leonard A. Stevens wrote:

> We think much faster than we talk. The average rate of speech for most Americans is around 125 words per minute... It is common to find people who read and understand 1,200 words per minute, and even much more... It has been found that people can comprehend speech at more than 300 words per minute without significant loss from what can be comprehended and retained at much slower speeds... It might seem logical to slow down our thinking when we listen to coincide with the 125-word-per-minute speech rate. But slowing down thought processes is a difficult thing to do—almost painful. Therefore, when we listen, we continue thinking at high speed while the spoken words arrive at low speed. In the act of listening the differential between thinking and speaking rates means that our brains work with hundreds of words in addition to those we hear, assembling thoughts other than those spoken to us. To put it another way, we can listen and still have spare time for thinking. (pp. 78–79)

4.1 FACTORS THAT INFLUENCE LISTENING

Your ability to listen is influenced in many ways. The following factors apply to listening generally. Some apply more directly to transcription than others. The important thing to remember is that it is part of a transcriptionist's job and a sign of professionalism to overcome factors that inhibit listening and, therefore, interfere with producing the best work. For example, whatever your prejudices or your attitude toward the speaker, the job requires that you listen and transcribe efficiently.

1. **Past experiences.** Experiences influence how well you can relate to the speaker. Do you have any common experiences, or are you from completely different backgrounds?
2. **Intelligence, vocabulary, and education.** Your ability to listen effectively to the speaker is influenced by the intelligence, vocabulary, and education of both you and the speaker. If there is a great disparity between your level of achievement and that of the speaker, effective listening may be more difficult.
3. **Prejudices.** All your prejudices affect your attitudes as you listen to a speaker. For example, if you are listening to a political speech, your listening ability may be greatly influenced by whether you are a Democrat or a Republican. There are certain words that are emotionally charged as far as you are concerned. Nichols calls these words "emotional filters" (Nichols and Stevens, pp. 89–103). When the speaker uses any of these words, your listening ability may be affected. The following are examples of words that could be emotionally charged for some people: communist, red, scab worker, union, Democrat, Republican, and Internal Revenue Service. There are, of course, words that evoke positive emotional reactions in most people: mother, father, home, and so forth.

Figure 4.1
These people are listening to a business presentation.
How do your past experiences and attitudes affect what you hear when you listen?

4. **Attitude toward speaker.** If you dislike the speaker, it is much more difficult to listen carefully than if the speaker is someone you like. If you consider the speaker an equal or superior, you will be a better listener than if you consider the speaker to be inferior to you. You will find it easier to listen carefully to someone you respect rather than to someone for whom you have little regard. If you have already decided that the speaker has nothing interesting to say, you will find it difficult to pay attention.
5. **Language skills.** The speaker's language skills also affect your ability to listen. If the speaker fails to enunciate carefully, you may have difficulty concentrating on what is being said. Can you easily understand the speaker's words, or does the speaker have an unfamiliar accent? If the speaker uses incorrect grammar, you may tend to discount the value of his or her ideas. Don't always equate the value of the content with the quality of the delivery.
6. **Attitudes of others.** When listening to a public speaker, the attitudes of the people with you tend to influence your attitude. You may find it more difficult to listen objectively to what the speaker is saying if your friends have already voiced negative opinions about it.
7. **Health.** If you are sick, tired, or hungry, it is more difficult to pay attention to the speaker's words. It may be difficult to overlook the sounds of your growling stomach; it's even more difficult to process information while you are dozing.
8. **Comfort.** If the room is too hot or too cold, if your chair is uncomfortable, if you have to strain to hear the speaker, or if you cannot see the speaker, you will have difficulty concentrating on the material being presented.
9. **Distractions.** People talking, people shifting in their seats, faulty air-conditioning or heating units, traffic, construction work, telephones ringing, or a television or radio playing may hinder listening.
10. **Daydreaming.** Since you can listen much faster than the speaker can speak, you have "extra" time that is not used for listening. You may find yourself daydreaming.
11. **Demands on your time.** If you are worried about deadlines and commitments, it may be difficult to block out those concerns and concentrate on a speaker's words. Preoccupation with your schedule can be one of the most difficult obstacles to effective listening.
12. **Desire.** If you have a sincere desire to be a good listener and to improve your listening ability, you will find it easier to concentrate.
13. **Poor listening habits.** Selective listening, false listening, interrupting, and impatient listening are examples of poor listening habits that we should try to overcome ("Active Listening," *Public Management*, Vol. 79, No. 12, December 1997, pp. 25–28). If you listen only to portions of what the speaker is saying (selective listening), you may perceive a very different message than the one the speaker intends to convey. Pretending to listen while you are actually concentrating on something else (false listening) may cause you to miss important instructions. Don't concentrate on your response while the other person is speaking (impatient listening). This makes it difficult to truly listen to the speaker's message. Your focus is on your response and not on what the other person is saying to you.

4.2 WAYS TO IMPROVE YOUR LISTENING

There are several things you can do to become a better listener. Make a real effort to practice these suggestions so that you will become more informed, more effective, and, therefore, a better employee.

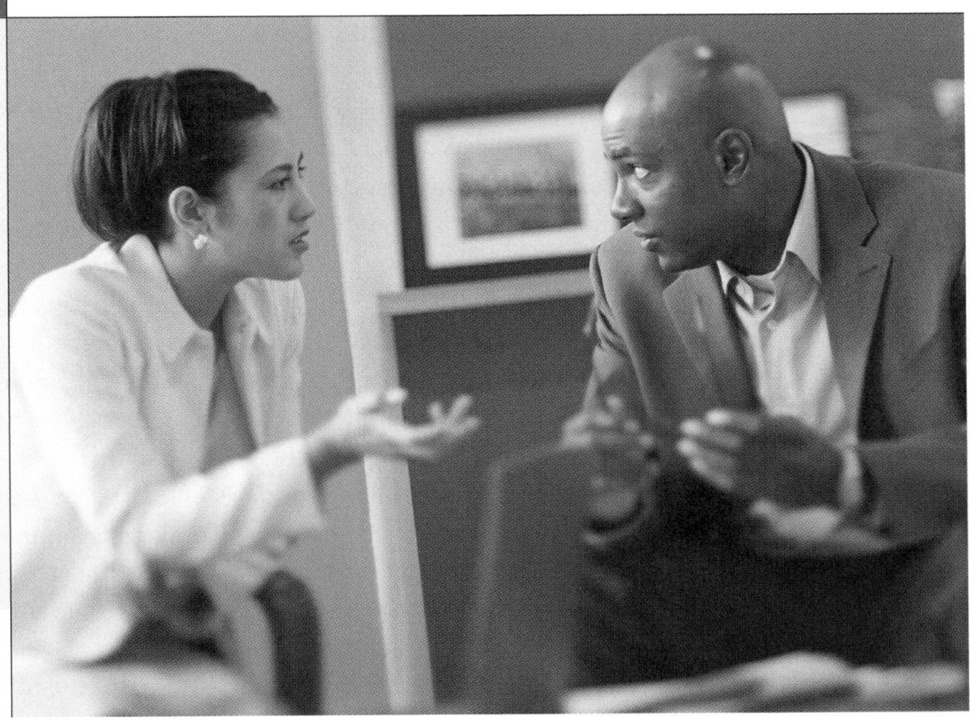

Figure 4.2
Active listening is demonstrated by actions and facial expression.
Is this person exhibiting good listening skills? Why, or why not?

As with the factors that influence listening, some of the following points apply more directly to listening during transcription than others. Nevertheless, your efforts to improve your general listening ability will undoubtedly result in improved listening skills on the job, no matter what the circumstances.

1. **Talk less.** If you are among those people who feel they must be talking most of the time, remember this: You cannot listen and talk at the same time. If you are having a discussion, give the other person a fair chance to contribute. Don't rush the speaker by your actions or by your facial expressions. While the other person is talking, think about what he or she is saying and not just about what you are going to say next.
2. **Don't interrupt.** The only acceptable time to interrupt is when you want to clarify what is being said. You may say, "Pardon me, but when did you say this happened?" Otherwise, interrupting the speaker is inconsiderate and shows that you have little regard for the other person's point of view. Let the other person finish his or her sentence.
3. **Practice good health habits.** This is always valuable advice, particularly where listening is concerned. Try to eat properly and get enough rest. During long periods of transcription, fatigue is a special problem. Take short breaks away from the keyboard. Focus your attention away from the work. Stretch and relax.

4. **Consider the speaker's subject.** "Do your homework" in situations where it is possible. That is, spend some time thinking about the speaker's subject area ahead of time. Consider the points you would make if you were speaking, and then see how your points compare with those actually made by the speaker.
5. **Choose to listen.** Consciously decide to be attentive to a speaker. Even if you are not very interested in the topic, you can use the opportunity to practice good listening procedures. This requires self-discipline. You may be able to learn something from the speaker's manner of presentation (at the very least, what *not* to do as a public speaker). When you choose to work in transcription, you make a general commitment to spend a lot of time listening; however, you may still need to motivate yourself on a day-to-day basis.
6. **Reduce surrounding noises.** Do anything that you can to reduce the noise level around you. For example, close doors or windows and turn off the television or radio. Do your best to block out noises over which you have no control, such as others' shifting in their seats or talking.
7. **Choose your seat carefully.** In a lecture situation, choose a seat that gives you a clear view of the speaker and is away from obvious competing noises.
8. **Recognize prejudices.** Try to recognize the prejudices that you have as well as those exhibited by the speaker, and choose not to let them prevent you from listening to the speaker's point of view. Listen with an open mind, and try to consider the speaker's opinions, even if you disagree. Don't let emotionally charged words be roadblocks to listening.
9. **Consider the speaker's perspective.** Try to understand what the speaker is saying from his or her point of view. You may not agree with the speaker, but you will have a better understanding of the message being conveyed (Paul C. Blodgett, "Six Ways to Be a Better Listener [Training 101: The Art of Listening]," *Training & Development,* Vol. 51, No. 7, July 1997, pp. 11–12).
10. **Concentrate on the content of the message.** If you feel, for example, that the speaker is dressed inappropriately for the occasion, listening may become more difficult. Perhaps, the speaker has a cold with some distracting symptoms. Try not to be so influenced by physical factors that you miss out on an important message.
11. **Maintain eye contact.** In one-to-one or small-group situations, eye contact is vital to maintain the flow of communication. Even in a large-group situation, an obviously attentive audience (as evidenced by all eyes focused on the speaker) will encourage the speaker to make a more effective and, therefore, more interesting presentation. Eye contact is the most basic form of the next point—feedback.
12. **Provide the speaker with feedback.** If appropriate, make comments or ask questions. Your opportunity to respond will be determined by the situation. In a lecture setting, you may not have an opportunity to speak. In that case, any feedback you give the speaker must be through facial expression or head movements. On the other hand, if you are talking with one individual, you may want to make a comment or restate something the other person has said in order to encourage more discussion on a point. Asking questions to clarify what has been said shows that you were listening to the speaker.

Figure 4.3
Taking notes is required in many situations.
How can you remain focused on the speaker as you take notes?

13. **Mentally summarize.** During the "extra" time you have while you are listening to a prepared speech or lecture, mentally summarize what the speaker has said.
14. **Take notes.** When appropriate, take brief notes. However, don't become so involved in the note-taking process that you lose track of what the speaker is saying.

Since you spend so much of your time listening to others, work to make that time as productive as possible. By improving your listening skills, you will learn more. Your self-confidence will increase as your knowledge increases. Though effective listening is hard work, you will reap benefits in terms of improved personal relationships and job performance.

4.3 LISTENING AND TRANSCRIPTION

Your attention to all the above suggestions will help you to become a better listener. However, machine transcription presents special listening problems. For example, the dictator may have a tendency to slur certain combinations of letters. Words may not be pronounced distinctly. As you become familiar with the dictating style and vocabulary of the dictator, transcription will become easier and more fluent. The dictator may use a word that has variations in spelling and meaning, such as *cite*, *sight*, and *site*. Your language skills and vocabulary will help you choose the correct word. Don't guess; if you are unsure, use a dictionary. The dictator may dictate numbers and refer to that data incorrectly later in the message; it is your job to catch such errors. As you can see, listening is more than just hearing. It requires concentration.

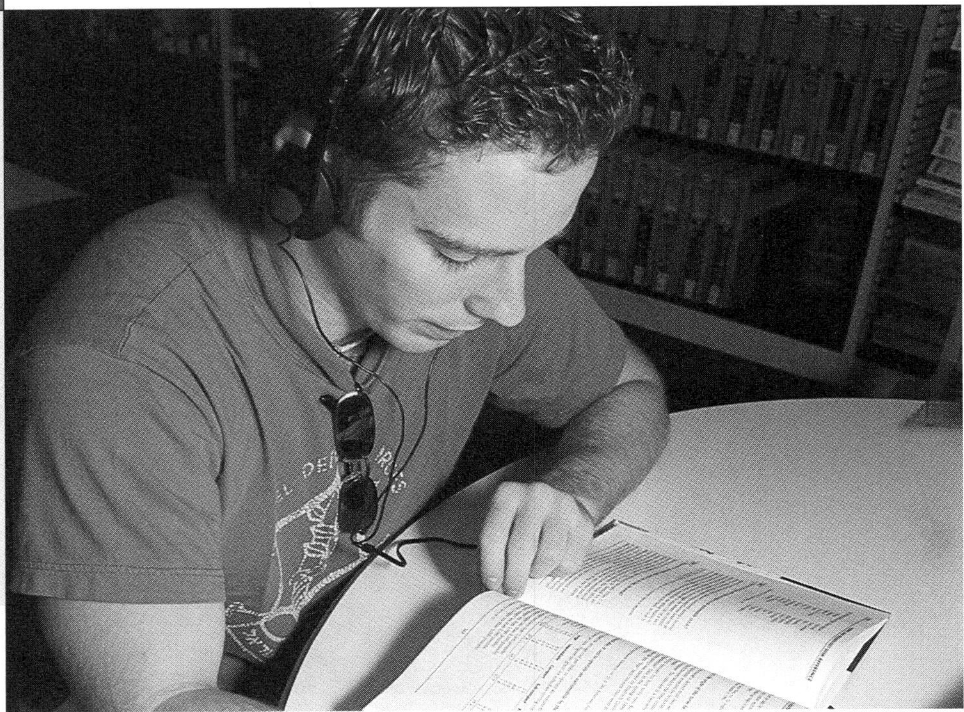

Figure 4.4
Listening effectively while transcribing may require research to choose the correct word.
Listening is more than just hearing!

Throughout this course you will study sets of words that sound alike or similar but have different meanings and are spelled differently. On the transcription recordings, you will practice choosing the correct word in context. The following listening exercises will sharpen your general powers of concentration and recall.

ASSIGNMENT: SECTION 4

EXERCISE

Obtain the Listening Exercises recording from your instructor. Complete the six Listening Exercises using the following answer sheets. Some of the exercises require you to recall dictated lists of numbers or words. Others ask you to answer questions after listening to paragraphs. Concentrate and listen closely.

Go To...
Listening Exercises

Name/Class ______________________

Listening Exercises

Answer Sheets

EXERCISE 1: Which Word Is Different?

1. ______________________
2. ______________________
3. ______________________
4. ______________________
5. ______________________
6. ______________________
7. ______________________
8. ______________________
9. ______________________
10. ______________________

EXERCISE 2: How Many Items Can You Remember?

1. ______________________
____
____
____
____

2. ______________________
____
____
____
____

3. ______________________
____
____
____
____

Name/Class ______________________________

4. ______________________________

____

____

____

____

____

Exercise 3: Can You Recall the Numbers?

1. ______________________________
2. ______________________________
3. ______________________________
4. ______________________________
5. ______________________________
6. ______________________________
7. ______________________________
8. ______________________________
9. ______________________________
10. ______________________________

Exercise 4: Can You Recall the Sentences?

1. ______________________________

____

____

____

2. ______________________________

____

____

____

3. ______________________________

____

____

____

Name/Class ______________________________

4. ______________________________

5. ______________________________

6. ______________________________

7. ______________________________

8. ______________________________

9. ______________________________

10. ______________________________

EXERCISE

Name/Class

Exercise 5: Can You Recall the Paragraphs?

1.

2.

3.

4.

5.

Exercise 6: Can You Answer the Questions About What You Have Heard?

1.

2.

3.

4.

5.

Section 5

Dictation

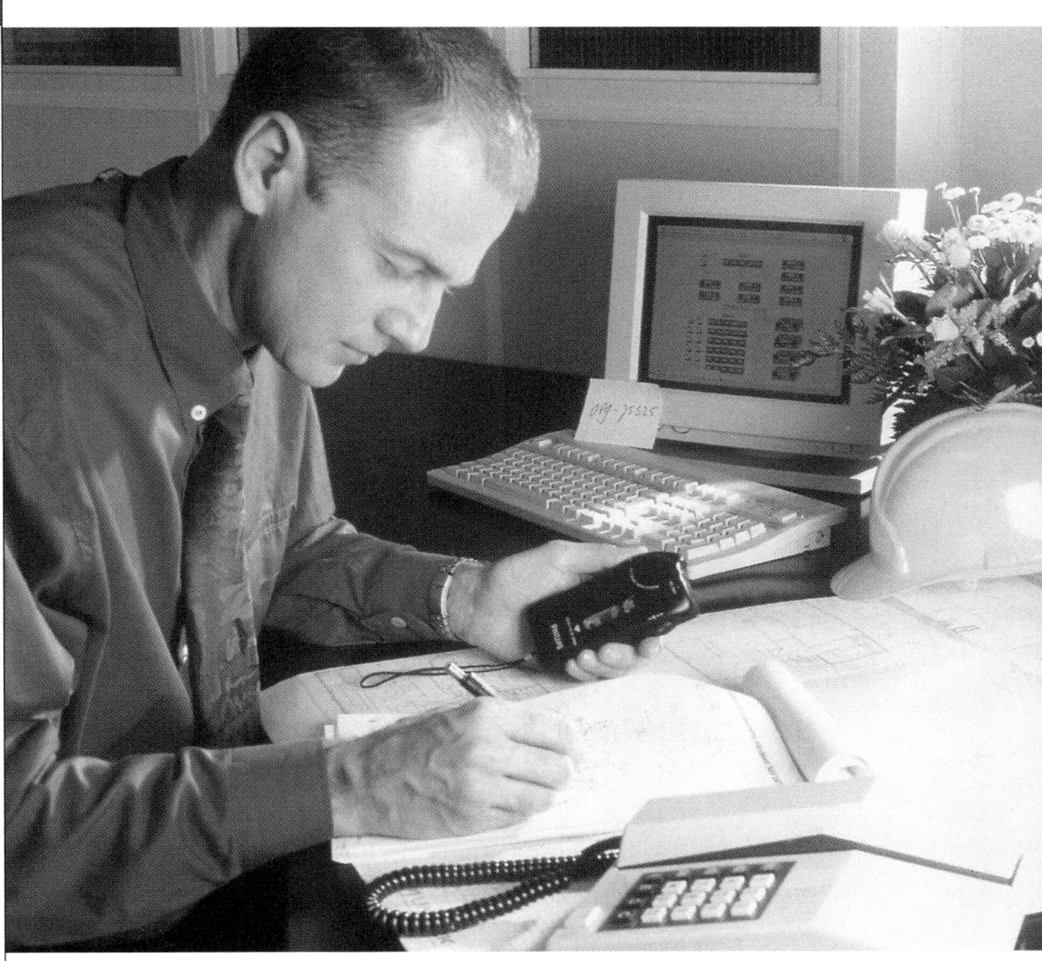

Introduction

As you demonstrate your competence and value to an employer, you will be given greater responsibilities. For example, your employer might rely on you to write some of the correspondence. You may have the opportunity to dictate letters for others to transcribe. If you have not already done so, you should take a course in business letter writing to prepare yourself for this opportunity.

5.1 GUIDELINES FOR DICTATION

Following are some of the things you should know before dictating:

Become Familiar with Dictation Equipment

Read the operator's manual and become familiar with the operation of the machine. If the operator's manual is not available, ask the manufacturer's representative for a copy.

Organize Information

Organize your thoughts before you begin to dictate. Write notes on the letter that you are answering or write a short outline on another sheet of paper. If you need other materials to help you prepare your answer, gather them before you begin to dictate. Arrange the items that you are going to dictate so that the most urgent item will be transcribed first.

Be Natural

Visualize your reader; write your letter as if you were having a conversation. Cover all of the points on your outline, but be concise. Time is money for both you and your reader.

Be Considerate of the Transcriptionist

If you are good at dictating correspondence, the transcriptionist will be able to produce mailable letters easily and efficiently. Here is a list of things you can do to help the transcriptionist:

1. If the transcriptionist works for more than one person, be sure to identify yourself properly.
2. Before you dictate each item, tell the transcriptionist how many copies you want and how you want them distributed.
3. Before you dictate each item, dictate any special mailing instructions, such as priority mail, Express Mail, certified mail, registered mail, Federal Express, delivery confirmation, and so forth.

4. Before you dictate an item, identify any special stationery requirements.
5. Before you dictate an item, tell the transcriptionist what type of item it will be: a letter, an interoffice memorandum, a report, and so forth.
6. If you are dictating using analog equipment, mark the end of each item and any corrections you make on an index strip or indication slip. If the transcriptionist works for more than one person, write your name on the index strip. If the transcribing machine has no indication strip but does have a counter, make a note of the number on the counter at the end of each item and at the beginning of all corrections. Be sure to give these notes to the transcriptionist so he or she can judge the length of the dictated items and transcribe efficiently. If the transcribing machine has a lighted display or automatic scanner, be sure to press the appropriate button on the microphone to mark the tape so that the ends of the items and the corrections will be indicated on the tape. If you are dictating on a centralized dictation system, you may press a code number on the telephone to indicate the end of an item or a correction.
7. Enunciate your words carefully. Don't mumble, chew on a pencil, chew gum, smoke, or drop the ends of your words. Don't try to dictate while you are eating. If the transcriptionist has to come to you for verification of what you said, additional time and money have been wasted.
8. Dictate at an even rate. Don't try to impress the transcriptionist with how fast you can dictate.
9. If you pause to organize your thoughts during dictation, be sure to release the dictation button to avoid blank or "dead" space. Transcription rates will suffer if the transcriptionist must listen to blank space while transcribing.
10. Spell names, technical terms, or foreign words. *When in doubt, spell it out!* Don't spell so rapidly that the transcriptionist has to go back and listen twice to what you said.
11. Indicate the end of each paragraph and sentence by saying, "paragraph" or "period." This helps avoid confusion and speeds transcription.
12. As you dictate, turn each answered letter face down in a stack along with any accompanying materials. When you give the transcriptionist the finished dictation, include the stack of answered mail for reference and filing.
13. If you dictate information that is to be keyed on a printed form, do so in a logical order; that is, dictate the fill-ins from top to bottom or from left to right. Keep the form in front of you as you dictate.
14. After you finish your dictation, say, "End of dictation." When a tape or CD is reused, old material may be transcribed again by mistake if the end-of-dictation instruction is not given.

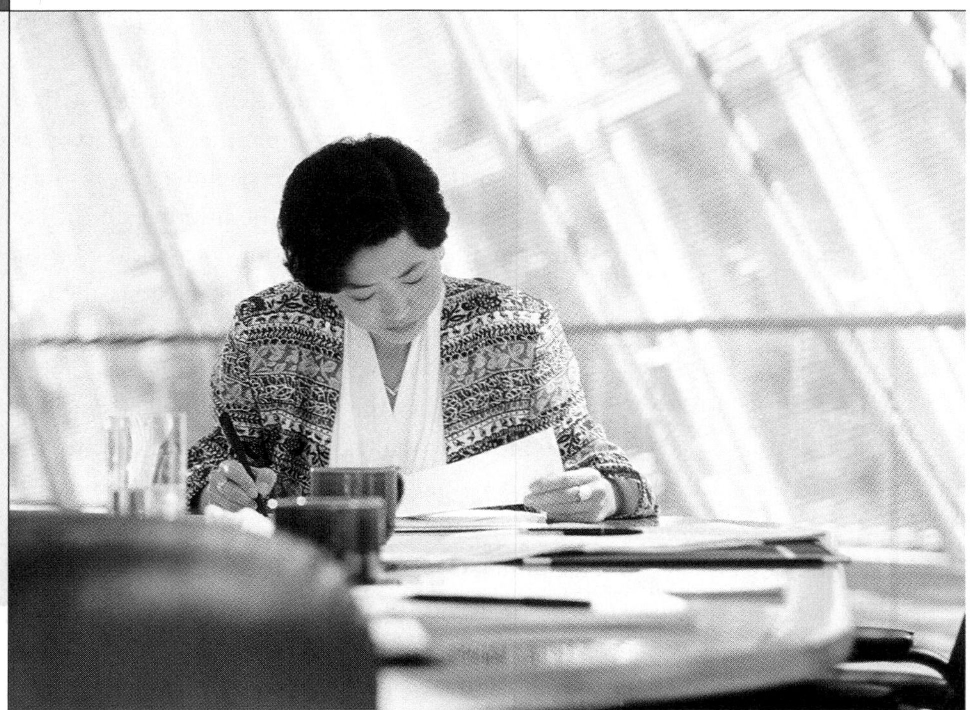

Figure 5.1
The good dictator organizes thoughts and materials before beginning dictation.
What other guidelines should be followed before starting to dictate?

After you have dictated a small amount, listen to your dictation. Ask yourself whether you would find it easy to transcribe. Be honest with yourself. Be efficient when you dictate, and make your dictation as easy to transcribe as possible.

5.2 SAMPLE DICTATION

The following sample dictation script will help you prepare to dictate the letters assigned. The words in boldfaced print are directions to the transcriber.

This will be a letter on company stationery with a file copy only. This letter goes to Mr. Loyd **(L-o-y-d)** Jacobs **(J-a-c-o-b-s),** 209 East Oak Street, Lawrenceville **(L-a-w-r-e-n-c-e-v-i-l-l-e),** Illinois 62439 Dear Mr. Jacobs Thank you for your assistance in obtaining the antique miniature lamp that I have been searching for to complete my collection. **(Period)** Enclosed is my check for $1500 to cover the cost of the lamp. **(Period Paragraph)** I understand that you will be participating in the antique show in Dallas during the first week in May. **(Period)** Since I will be attending that show, I would prefer to pick up the lamp at that time rather than risk shipping it. **(Period Paragraph)** Thank you for your assistance. **(Period)** I will look forward to visiting with you in your booth at the show. **(Period)** Sincerely yours **(Type the company name in the closing lines.**) OLD WORLD ANTIQUES Elizabeth A. Childers **(C- h-i-l-d-e-r-s) Operator, please make a photocopy of this letter for me to take to the Dallas antique show the first week in June. Thank you. This is the end of this letter.**

Take a moment to analyze this letter from the transcriptionist's point of view. These are the points you should particularly note in this sample dictation:

1. *Loyd* is an unusual spelling; therefore, it should be spelled for the transcriber. If the dictator forgets to spell a name, always check the spelling before you submit the letter for signature.
2. Would you have spelled *assistance* correctly?
3. By dictating **(Period)** or **(Period Paragraph)**, you avoid confusion and aid the transcriptionist with the structure of the document.
4. Would you have typed the dollar amount correctly?
5. Would you have inserted the comma after *Since I will be attending that show?* Remember to look for clues to proper punctuation—sentences beginning with subordinate conjunctions, the intonation of the dictator, and so forth.
6. Did you notice that the month in the direction to the operator at the end of the letter is different from the month listed in the letter? As the transcriptionist, you must determine which is correct.
7. Would you have made the photocopy for your employer to take to the antique show?
8. Would you have made a note on the calendar to send the photocopy with your employer when she goes to Dallas?
9. Would you have typed the enclosure notation?
10. Would you have enclosed the check with the letter?

As you can see, there is more to machine transcription than just keying. As you proceed through this course, the practice you receive will help make many of these necessary skills automatic.

Figure 5.2
Transcriptionists develop skills in listening, proofreading, and language arts.
Focus on gaining these skills as you progress through this course.

ASSIGNMENT: SECTION 5

DIRECTIONS: ***Dictate letters for three of the following exercises:***

1. Your employer, Mrs. Alice Jacobs, has a business selling antiques. She is out of town on business for two weeks. You receive a letter from Mr. James Rudolfo, 2975 East Main Street, Carbondale, IL 62901, requesting a meeting with Mrs. Jacobs during the first week of June to discuss purchasing her antique miniature lamp collection. She will be out of town during the first week of June, but she will be available the rest of the month. Answer his letter and set up an appointment.
2. You are the purchasing manager for Elliott Enterprises. Write a letter to Sutton Business Furniture, 7984 East Division Street, New York, NY 10002, ordering one Model 1175 conference table and six Model 1175-273 chairs. The price of the table is $625. The chairs cost $179 each. The chairs are to be covered with a royal blue fabric, Color 198. You should also inquire about the delivery date of the furniture.
3. You are the purchasing manager for Elliott Enterprises. The Model 1175 conference table and six Model 1175-273 chairs that you ordered from Sutton Business Furniture, 7984 East Division Street, New York, NY 10002, arrived today. The conference table has a broken leg. One of the chairs was also damaged. Write a letter requesting replacement of the damaged items and instructions for disposition of the damaged items.
4. You have been asked to speak at the regional meeting of the Association of Office Managers on April 10. Write a letter to Ms. Sandra Blakemore, Association of Office Managers, 2182 East Oakland Avenue, Bloomingdale, OH 43910, accepting the invitation to speak. Your topic will be "Improving Office Efficiency."
5. You are employed by Rogers, Inc., a mail-order company. You receive an order for a heating pad from Catalog 7945. This item is no longer available. Offer to substitute a similar heating pad from Catalog 7999. The customer is Mr. J. R. Fisher, 4715 East Oak Street, Aspen, CO 81611.

Part 2

Transcription Lessons

Pre-Transcription Training

Part 2 begins with Pre-Transcription Training that will help you begin to learn how to transcribe. By completing this recording first, you will be able to practice transcribing before you transcribe material that will be graded. If you have not read "Transcribing Techniques" in your textbook, do that now. Then complete this recording. The Pre-Transcription Training recording contains:

Pre-Transcription Training

- Spelling words and punctuation exercises from Section 1
- Three practice paragraphs
- A very short letter

Listen to the intonation of the dictator's voice to help you decide where to insert the punctuation marks. The Reference Handbook in Part 3 at the back of the textbook describes letter styles.

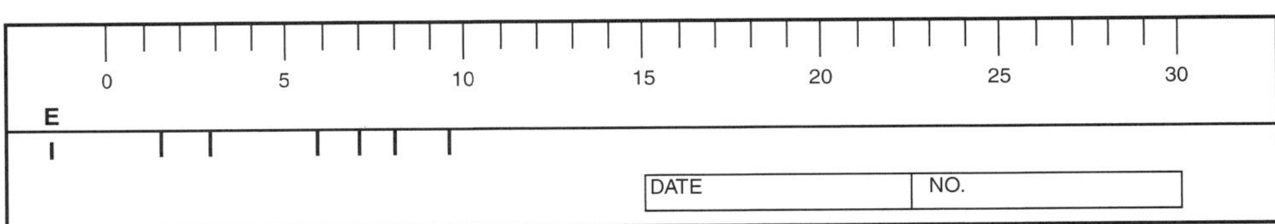

Pre-Transcription Portion

Name/Class____

When completed, tear this exercise out of the textbook and give it to your instructor.

Pre-Transcription Proofreading Exercise

DIRECTIONS: *Use proofreaders' marks to correct the memorandum below. A list of proofreaders' marks is in the Reference Handbook at the back of the textbook. There are no punctuation errors, and the wording is not to be changed except for the errors.*

MEMO TO: Action Committee
FROM: Sara Land, Chair
DATE: November 9, 20__
SUBJECT: Planning Meeting

We have several times that most be discussed at the meeting in Thursday. Pleas by thinking about the following agenda and by prepared too offer sum suggestions for a plan if action:

1. Sales in the Northeast Region gave declined by 12 percent in the last moth.

2. We are planning to trail test are knew soap product during June. We must design the area in which we well conduct this trail test.

3. We most fine a solution too the space problem we have in the main office.

4. Discuss the applications if the for remaining candidates fur the sales position that we have available in the Central Region.

Are meeting will be held on the Andrew conference Room it 1:30 p.m.

acm

Did you find 26 errors? None of the errors in this exercise would have been found by the spelling checker of your equipment because they are all words found in the dictionary. The spelling checker is a great time-saving feature that you should use for every document; however, you must proofread for content as well as spell check your documents.

Section 1

1.1 OBJECTIVES

In Section 1, you will work toward the following objectives:

- Correctly insert commas in sentences containing a series of elements.
- Correctly format symbols, company name in the closing lines, numbers, enclosure notations, expressions of time, and copy notations when transcribing the dictation for this section.
- Correctly complete Punctuation Exercises, Word Study Exercises, and Proofreading Exercises in preparation for transcription.
- Complete Spelling Test 1 with at least 80 percent accuracy.
- Select the appropriate words and the correct spelling according to the context of the dictation when transcribing this section's documents.

1.2 PUNCTUATION REVIEW

Use a comma to separate three or more items in a series. Place a comma before a conjunction. Do not use a comma to separate a series of only two items.

Examples: Bob ordered ballpoint pens, paper clips, computer disks, and file folders from Fisher Office Supply Company.

Chicago and Atlanta are on the itinerary for Mrs. Jacobs.

1.3 WORD STUDY

The words listed here are frequently confused in transcription because they sound alike when dictated but have different meanings. Study the words carefully so that you will be able to select the appropriate word according to the context of the dictation.

assistance (noun) help or aid

I need your *assistance* in lifting this box.

assistants (noun) helpers; workers

Mr. White requested three *assistants* to help him in the new division.

desert (verb) to abandon; to leave; to forsake

We will *desert* our plan to build a new factory.

desert (noun) an arid region

Death Valley is a *desert*.

dessert the final course of a meal, such as pie, cake, or pudding

We ate peach pie for *dessert*.

personal (adjective) relating to or affecting a person

Do not make *personal* calls from the office.

personnel (noun) employees

One-half of our *personnel* work on Saturdays.

their (possessive pronoun) belonging to or done by them

This is *their* car. This is *their* work.

there (adverb) at or in that place; used to introduce a clause

I assure you that I will be *there*.

There is plenty of time to finish the report.

they're contraction for *they are*

They're scheduled to arrive at 7 p.m.

to (preposition) in the direction of; toward; used to introduce a verb in the infinitive; regarding or concerning

John was on his way *to* work.

She did not want *to* be late for the meeting.

He was attentive *to* the telephone while everyone was at lunch.

too (adverb) more than enough; also

Jane ate *too* much for lunch.

He wanted to help *too*.

two (adjective) one plus one

Mrs. Davis dictated *two* letters before the meeting.

1.4 SPELLING REVIEW

The dictation for this section contains the words listed here. Study them carefully to help you transcribe more rapidly. If you hear other words in the dictation that you do not know how to spell, make a list of those words and learn their correct spellings. This practice will help you improve your transcription speed.

accommodations
advantageous
agenda
application
appreciate
arrangements
assistance
assistants
available
buffet
commercial
convention
creating
customers
cyberspace
descriptions
equipment
equipped
estimate
facilities
hyperlinks
immediately
include
limousine
opportunities
performance
personal
personnel
podium
requirements
security
session
sincerely
successful
suitable
tremendous
variety

1.5 TRANSCRIPTION GUIDELINES

NOTE:
For a more in-depth list of number rules, consult an office reference manual such as ***The Gregg Reference Manual*** by William A. Sabin.

NUMBERS. As a general rule, the numbers *one* through *ten* are written as words, and numbers *11* and above are written as digits. There are some exceptions to this general rule.

If a number appears as the first word in a sentence, it must be written in word form.

Example: Fifty-three members were present for the meeting.

Line, page, paragraph, size, and verse numbers are always typed in digits. The words *line, page, paragraph, size,* and *verse* are not capitalized unless they appear as the first word in a sentence. Other words appearing with numbers are capitalized.

Examples: Our new copier is Model 4956X.

We will be on Flight 482.

This refers to Invoice 2371.

We received Model 684.

I will need the dress in a size 4.

We will meet in Room 2.

They broke Rule 896.

Please read paragraph 2, line 29 on page 3.

Page 2 shows the music for the next song.

We will sing verse 4.

SYMBOLS. Use symbols (#, ¢, %, @) in technical writing, in tables, and on business forms only. Spell out or abbreviate these designations in business letters. All percentages are expressed in digits.

Examples: Please send 25 No. 39 shirts.

Please send 50 cents for handling.

We expect to increase profits 2 percent over last year.

TIME. Use digits to express time with *a.m.* or *p.m.* Omit the colon and the zeros when keying even times. However, in lists containing several hour and minute expressions, add two zeros to exact times to maintain a uniform appearance. Use either words (for formality) or digits (for emphasis) to express time with *o'clock*.

Examples:	6:35 p.m.	8 a.m.	ten o'clock
WRONG:	five p.m.	9:00 a.m.	11:00 o'clock

COMPANY NAME. If the company name appears in the closing lines of a letter, double-space after the complimentary closing and key the company name in all-capital letters. Use a comma to separate *Inc.* or *Ltd.* from the rest of the company name if the company uses a comma. Then return (or press Enter) four times before keying the signature line.

> **NOTE:**
> When you are using company stationery, the company name is not necessary; however, some firms prefer to use the company name in the signature block. When you start working in a new position, check the preference of your employer.

Example:

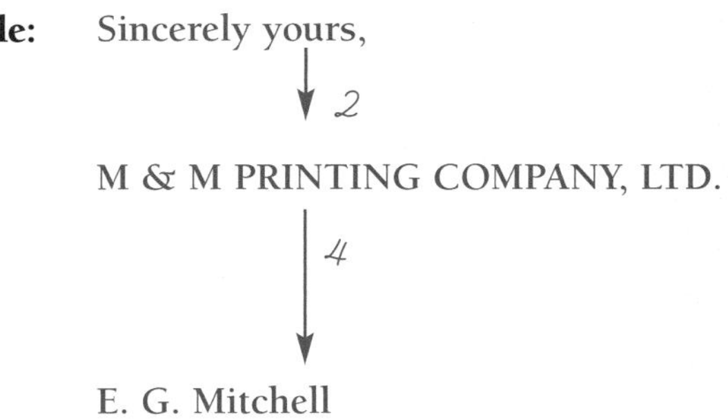

Sincerely yours,
2
M & M PRINTING COMPANY, LTD.
4
E. G. Mitchell

ENCLOSURE NOTATION. The enclosure notation is keyed at the left margin on the line below the reference initials. If you have more than one enclosure, you may want to list the enclosures.

Examples: Enclosure

Enclosures 3

Enclosures:
1. Contract
2. Check
3. Credit application

The notation *Attachment* is more appropriate on a memorandum if you are not using an envelope.

If you are sending additional material under separate cover (that is, separately), you should key a separate cover notation in the same location as you would enter the enclosure notation. If you are sending enclosures with the letter and items under separate cover, list the separate cover notation under the enclosure notation.

Examples: Separate cover 2   Enclosures 2
Separate cover 2

Under separate cover:
1. Contract
2. Book

COPY NOTATION. A copy c notation is used when you want to send a copy of the letter to someone in addition to the addressee. The order of the notations at the end of a letter is as follows:

1. Reference initials
2. Enclosure notation
3. Delivery notation
4. Copy notation
5. Postscript
6. Blind copy notation
7. Blind postscript

Examples: c Mr. L. V. Jacobs   c: Ms. Angela Mitchell

E-MAIL ADDRESSES. When you type an e-mail address, never change the capitalization, punctuation, spacing, or symbols contained in the address. The first part of the address is the name the person has chosen for his or her *mailbox*. This is followed immediately by the @ symbol. The @ symbol is followed by the *domain* (the system used to deliver the e-mail message). If an e-mail address falls at the end of a line, you may divide the address before the @ symbol or before a dot in the address. However, it is best to avoid dividing e-mail addresses.

ASSIGNMENTS

Complete the Punctuation, Word Study, and Proofreading Exercises that are located on pages 67–72 at the end of this section. The purpose of these exercises is to assist you with the transcription assignment. Tear the completed exercises out of the textbook, and give them to your instructor before you take Spelling Test 1 and before you transcribe the dictation for this section.

Page 67

SPELLING TEST 1

Ask your instructor for Spelling Test 1. Complete this test before you transcribe the dictation for Section 1.

SECTION 1 DICTATION

Recording for Section 1

Transcribe all of the letters for Section 1 in block style with open punctuation. If no date is dictated for a letter, use the current date. Refer to the Reference Handbook for sample letter styles. Be sure to check your transcript for usability. You should always strive for a mailable or usable transcript the first time you transcribe each dictated letter or item. The following checklist will help you determine the mailability of your transcripts for this course.

NOTE:
If you have not transcribed the Pre-Transcription Training Recording, do so now before you transcribe the dictation for Section 1. This is also a good time to review the Spacing Guide in the Reference Handbook.

MAILABILITY CHECKLIST

Your transcript is mailable or usable if it contains:

1. No spelling errors.
2. No punctuation errors.
3. No grammatical errors.
4. No keying errors (*if* for *it, in* for *on,* and so forth).
5. A proper format.
6. The proper vertical and horizontal placement on the page.
7. The appropriate number of copies.
8. When appropriate, an enclosure notation. (Make notes of any information about enclosures that are not mentioned in the body of the letter so that you will not forget to include the notation in the letter.)
9. No smudges.

Assembling Your Transcripts

When you submit your classroom transcription assignments, staple the items in the upper left corner, and arrange them in the same order as they occur on the recording. Label each assignment in the upper right corner with your name and the section number.

NOTE:
Letterhead templates are located on the CD ROM accompanying this text-workbook.

Use the following letterheads when you transcribe:

1. Randolph Enterprises, Inc.
2. High Road
3. Madison Hardware Corporation
4. No letterhead provided—agenda

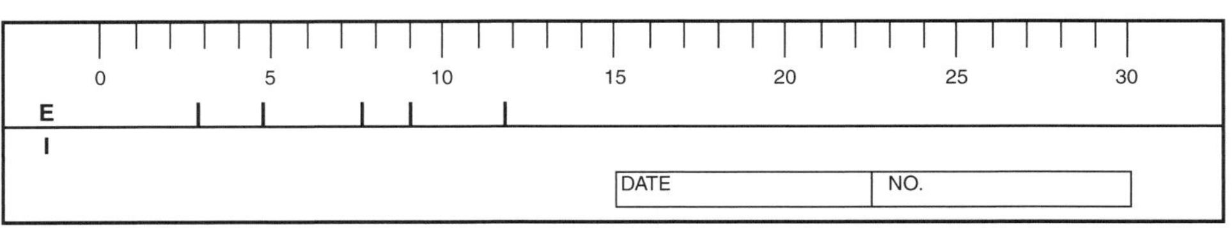

Name/Class ____________________

Section 1 Exercises

When completed, tear these exercises out of the textbook and give them to your instructor.

Punctuation Exercises—Commas in a Series

DIRECTIONS: ***Insert commas where needed in the following sentences.***

PART 1

1. This afternoon we must choose the color for the walls in the new conference room decide which conference table we are going to order and agree on the style of the chairs.
2. Please schedule meetings with the Advertising Department the Marketing Department and the Personnel Department for Wednesday Thursday and Friday, respectively.
3. Mr. James will be in St. Louis on Monday in Chicago on Tuesday in New York City on Wednesday and in Atlanta on Thursday.
4. Sam answered the telephone dictated several letters revised the complaint and interviewed three new clients.
5. We must complete the moving plans for the office staff make arrangements for temporary employees to help with the relocation assignments and notify all our clients of the move before November 9.
6. Our management consultant can show you how to increase efficiency improve sales and improve morale.
7. Please make reservations for the eight o'clock flight for a rental car and for a room at the Continental Hotel.
8. John Hall Janice Harris and James Moore attended the meeting in Chicago.
9. The real estate broker had listings for apartments houses farms and small businesses.
10. Transcribing answering the telephone and ordering supplies are my duties.
11. Juan bought paper clips legal pads and a stapler at O'Daniel's Office Supply.
12. The bookkeeper wrote checks for the electric bill the telephone bill and the rent.
13. We purchased new desks chairs filing cabinets and book shelves.
14. Packing moving and unpacking are exhausting.

Name/Class ____________________

15. Please pick up the contracts mail the package and deliver the proposal for the new advertising campaign.

PART 2

1. Our itinerary includes stops in Chicago St. Louis New York and Baltimore.
2. Enclosed are a check a contract and a purchase order.
3. The parade will proceed down State Street Washington Avenue Wabash Avenue and Elm Street.
4. Suits slacks sweaters shirts and coats are on sale at Grants Clothing Store until next Friday.
5. You will find the information you are looking for on pages 48 53 107 and 296.
6. The seminar will be held in Chicago on September 10 in St. Louis on December 5 in Atlanta on January 20 and in New York on March 3.
7. Our tour will take us to England France Germany and Italy.
8. Our test market for the new product includes the states of California Nevada New Mexico Arizona and Oregon.
9. Please mail Check 5370 to Mr. Robert Thompson a copy of the lease agreement to Mr. James Green and the certified letter to Mr. Samuel Robinson.
10. He broke his arm his leg and his thumb in the accident.
11. Mi Lin informed me that we will need a dog four cats and three goldfish when we take the photographs for the new ad.
12. Angela ordered paper clips pens staples and file folders.
13. George Aaron Ishmel Peppi and Johann were chosen to work on the new research project.
14. We stopped at our office at the bank at the real estate office and at the airport.
15. Jack Mason Cary Wilson and Tim Grant are the three new assistants.

Word Study Exercises

DIRECTIONS: ***Highlight or circle the correct word choice in each of the following sentences.***

PART 1

1. The (personal, personnel) manager introduced the (to, too, two) new (assistance, assistants) and explained (their, there, they're) duties.
2. (Their, There, They're) going (to, too, two) meet for a working lunch at (their, there, they're) favorite restaurant.

Name/Class____________________

3. (Their, There, They're) planning (to, too, two) attend the seminar for (personal, personnel) managers.

4. (Their, There, They're) is a possibility that the (personal, personnel) manager will ask you (to, too, two) attend the seminar (to, too, two).

5. What is your (personal, personnel) transportation preference if you are asked (to, too, two) attend the seminar along with the (to, too, two) new (assistance, assistants) from the (personal, personnel) office?

6. All (personal, personnel) are expected (to, too, two) provide (assistance, assistants) during the upcoming move (to, too, two) our new facilities.

7. Any (personal, personnel) items in or on the desks will be the responsibility of the individual (personal, personnel) during the move (to, too, two) our new facility.

8. Since the door prize at the first general session is a laptop computer, be sure (to, too, two) register as soon as you get (their, there, they're).

9. One of the (to, too, two) new (assistance, assistants) provided CPR (assistance, assistants) after the worker received a severe electric shock.

10. (Their, There, They're) going (to, too, two) need additional (personal, personnel) insurance coverage.

11. The drilling operations were halted because of the impending (desert, dessert) sandstorm.

12. The manager of the restaurant sent the new (desert, dessert) menu (to, too, two) the printer.

13. The committee decided to (desert, dessert) the original plan (to, too, two) hire (to, too, two) new (personal, personnel) for the marketing division.

14. We are planning (to, too, two) include a light (desert, dessert) with the luncheon menu for the conference.

15. The doctor suggested that the patient retire (to, too, two) a (desert, dessert) environment for health reasons.

PART 2

1. Ann Coleman has requested my (assistance, assistants) in completing the arrangements for the seminar.

2. The (Personal, Personnel) Department is hiring (to, too, two) (assistance, assistants) for the new vice president.

3. Each employee is allowed (to, too, two) (personal, personnel) leave days per year.

4. Most of our (personal, personnel) are members of the credit union.

5. Three employees from our department are going (to, too, two) the seminar.

6. We have (to, too, two) many requests for vacations during the weeks of December 15 and 22.

7. The names of the (to, too, two) new members are John Mason and Sylvia Grand.

8. John and Mary were the (to, too, two) (assistance, assistants) chosen (to, too, two) go (to, too, two) the national conference. Sam decided (to, too, two) attend (to, too, two).

9. Our (personal, personnel) are not permitted (to, too, two) receive (personal, personnel) telephone calls during working hours.

10. Alice will need your (assistance, assistants) when she sets up the display.

11. Gina is (their, there, they're) child.

12. John will be (their, there, they're) at 8 a.m.

13. (Their, There, They're) going (to, too, two) Disney World for (their, there, they're) vacation.

14. (Their, There, They're) planning (to, too, two) meet you (their, there, they're).

15. He assured John that he would be (their, there, they're) on time.

Proofreading Exercise 1-A

DIRECTIONS: ***Use proofreaders' marks to correct the following memorandum. A list of proofreaders' marks is in the Reference Handbook at the back of the textbook.***

MEMO TO: All Department Managers

FROM: Jane Morgan, Vice President

DATE: March 14, 20__

SUBJECT: Sales Meeting, Wednesday, March 20

Their will be a meeting of all department managers in the conference room on the third floor on Wednesday, March 20, form 8:30 a.m. to 11:30 a.m. Please arrange for you assistance too take over your duties during that period of time on March 21. It is essential that you by free to attend this important meeting.

acm

EXERCISE Name/Class ______________________________

Proofreading Exercise 1-B

DIRECTIONS: ***Use proofreaders' marks to correct the letter below. A list of proofreaders' marks is in the Reference Handbook at the back of the textbook.***

January 19, 20__

Ms. Rita Harvard
1440 North Elm Street
Collinsville, IL 62234

Dear Miss Harvard:

SUBJECT: Order 497-3502

Thank you for your order. We have shipped the following items:

No. 2349	Towel Sets	2 @ $25.95	$51.90
No. 4780	Place Mats	4 @ $3.25	13.00
No. 1561	Napkin Rings	4 @ $2.29	9.36
		Total	$74.26

The sheets have been back ordered and should be shiped on Feburary 10. We apreciate you business and look forward to serving you again.

Sincerely

Martin Guido

acm

Name/Class____

Proofreading Exercise 1-C

DIRECTIONS: ***Use proofreaders' marks to correct the memorandum below. A list of proofreaders' marks is in the Reference Handbook at the back of the textbook.***

MEMO TO: Ralph Atkins

FROM: Jack Fuller, Producer

DATE: October 30, 20__

SUBJECT: Celebration

Please organise a celebration for all the cast and production personal after the last day of filming. The author of *Desert Sun*, the book that was the basis for the movie, will receive a personal invitation from me.

The menu should include appetisers, at least four entrees, and several desert choices. Be sure to include a vegatarian entree.

Prepare a letter to the investors announcing that the completed film was within three percent of the estimated budget. We have every expectation that the movie will be very successfull at the box office.

Your assistants in completing these tasks will be apreciated.

xxx

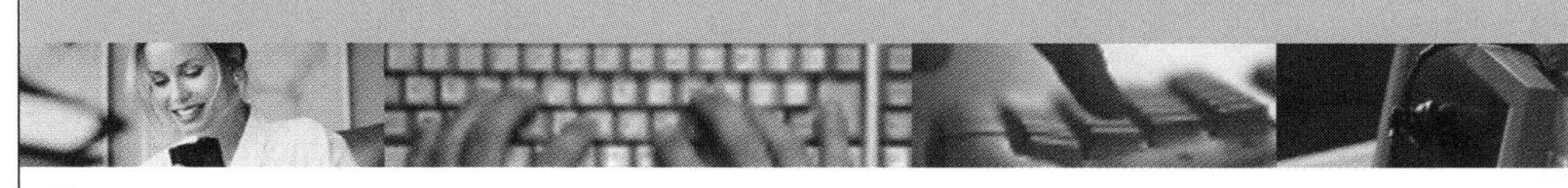

Section 2

2.1 OBJECTIVES

In Section 2, you will work toward the following objectives:

- Correctly insert commas where appropriate in sentences containing independent words or expressions and direct address, and when the word *and* is omitted.
- Correctly insert hyphens in compound expressions.
- Correctly format two-page letters; postscripts; Jr., Sr., II; and ages when transcribing the dictation for this section.
- Correctly complete Punctuation Exercises, Word Study Exercises, and Proofreading Exercises in preparation for transcription.
- Complete Spelling Test 2 with at least 80 percent accuracy.
- Select the appropriate words and the correct spelling according to the context of the dictation when transcribing this section's documents.
- Complete Word Study Test 1 on the word study vocabulary in Sections 1 and 2 with at least 80 percent accuracy.

2.2 PUNCTUATION REVIEW

Independent words or expressions are not necessary to the meaning of a sentence; therefore, they are set off by commas. The following are some examples: *besides, consequently, furthermore, however, I hope, I think, in addition, in my opinion, indeed, nevertheless, of course, on the contrary, therefore,* and *unfortunately.*

Examples: We all knew, however, that he would succeed.

In my opinion, we should reject the proposal.

If you are unsure whether the words or expressions are independent, read the sentence without them. If the meaning is unchanged, the words are independent. Use commas to set off names and titles used in direct address.

Example: Chris, please sharpen these pencils.

When two or more consecutive adjectives modify the same noun, they should be separated by commas. To help you decide whether a comma is necessary, try inserting *and* between the adjectives or try reversing the adjectives. If the meaning is not changed, you need to insert a comma between the two adjectives. However, do not use a comma between the adjectives if the first adjective modifies the combined idea of the second adjective plus the noun. Do not use a comma between adjectives connected by *and, or,* or *nor.*

Examples: She was an intelligent, conscientious student.

The accounting department prepared the annual financial statement.

In the first example, *and* could be inserted between the two adjectives without changing the meaning, and the adjectives could be reversed. Therefore, a comma is necessary. In the second example, *annual* modifies the combined idea of the adjective *financial* and the noun *statement*. Therefore, no comma is needed.

Compound expressions such as *past due* and *follow up* sometimes require hyphens. If a noun follows the expression, use a hyphen.

Examples: The results of the follow-up survey surprised the research team.

Please make a payment on your past-due account.

If the compound expression is not followed by a noun, do not use a hyphen.

Examples: To check on the efficiency of the new procedure, we must follow up with employees in June.

Your account is seriously past due.

Do not use a hyphen if the first word of the compound expression is an adverb ending in *ly*.

Example: He was a poorly trained employee.

2.3 WORD STUDY

The words listed here are frequently confused in transcription because they sound alike when dictated but have different meanings. Study the words carefully so that you will be able to select the appropriate word according to the context of the dictation.

> **NOTE:**
> Do not underestimate the value of the Word Study Exercises. While you may be familiar with the words when you see them written, working with them from dictation is quite different.

allowed (verb) permitted

Three representatives of our division were *allowed* to attend the conference.

aloud (adverb) in an audible voice

Please state your objections *aloud.*

cite (verb) to quote

Please *cite* your favorite poem.

sight (noun) something seen; the act of seeing

The sunset was a beautiful *sight.*

The *sight* of the tornado terrified them.

sight (verb) to observe

The soldier used binoculars to *sight* the enemy planes.

site (noun) location

This is the *site* for the new building.

envelop (verb) to surround

NOTE:
Be careful not to confuse the possessive pronoun *its* with the contraction *it's*. Try to substitute the words *it is* in the sentence. If the substitution makes sense, use the apostrophe and key "it's." If the substitution does not make sense, key "its" to indicate possession. You can make similar substitutions for other possessive pronouns and contractions to determine whether you need an apostrophe.

The convention hotel is designed to *envelop* a center courtyard.

envelope (noun) a folded paper container for a letter

The assistant addressed the *envelope* before inserting the letter.

farther (adverb) to a greater distance

Mr. Whitmer has come *farther* than anyone else.

further (adverb) to a greater degree or to a greater extent

We will discuss the plans *further* at the next meeting.

it's contraction for it is

It's time for the meeting to begin.

its (possessive pronoun) belonging to or done by it

The budget committee made *its* position clear in the report.

presence (noun) the fact or condition of being present

His *presence* could be felt in the room.

presents (noun) gifts

She received three *presents* on her birthday.

presents (verb) gives

Listen carefully as he *presents* his report.

2.4 SPELLING REVIEW

The dictation for this section contains the words listed here. Study them carefully to help you transcribe more rapidly. If you hear other words in the dictation that you do not know how to spell, make a list of those words and learn their correct spellings. This practice will help you improve your transcription speed.

adjacent	division	presence
analyze	efficient	presents
atmosphere	envelop	recommendation
brochure	envelope	reference
cabana	exercise	replacement
certificate	expansion	reservations
concise	farther	restaurant
condominiums	further	schedule
confirmation	garage	shopping
convenient	hopefully	soothing
cordially	invigorating	surveys
courteous	laboratory	truly
coverage	photography	unfortunately
delicious	premiums	various

2.5 TRANSCRIPTION GUIDELINES

TWO-PAGE LETTERS. The heading on the second page of a two-page letter may be keyed in block style or in horizontal style. The margins should be the same on all pages of the letter. The first line of the heading is keyed on line 7 from the top of the page. Double-space or triple-space before you key the rest of the letter. Do not leave fewer than two lines of a paragraph at the bottom of the first page. Do not carry fewer than two lines of a paragraph to the second page.

The second page should be typed or printed on plain paper that matches the letterhead stationery.

BLOCK STYLE

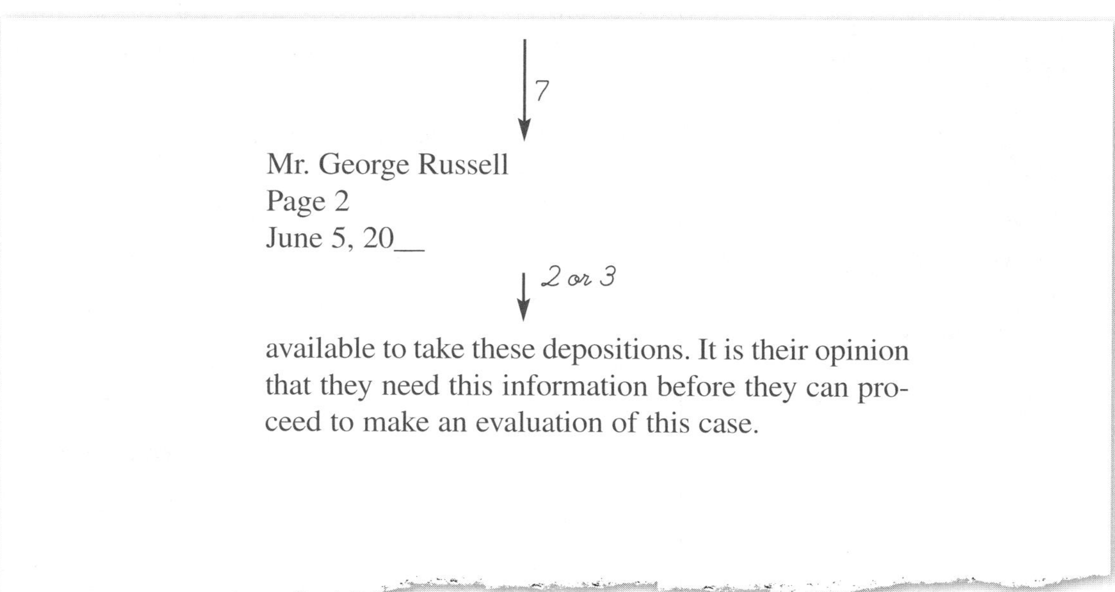

HORIZONTAL STYLE

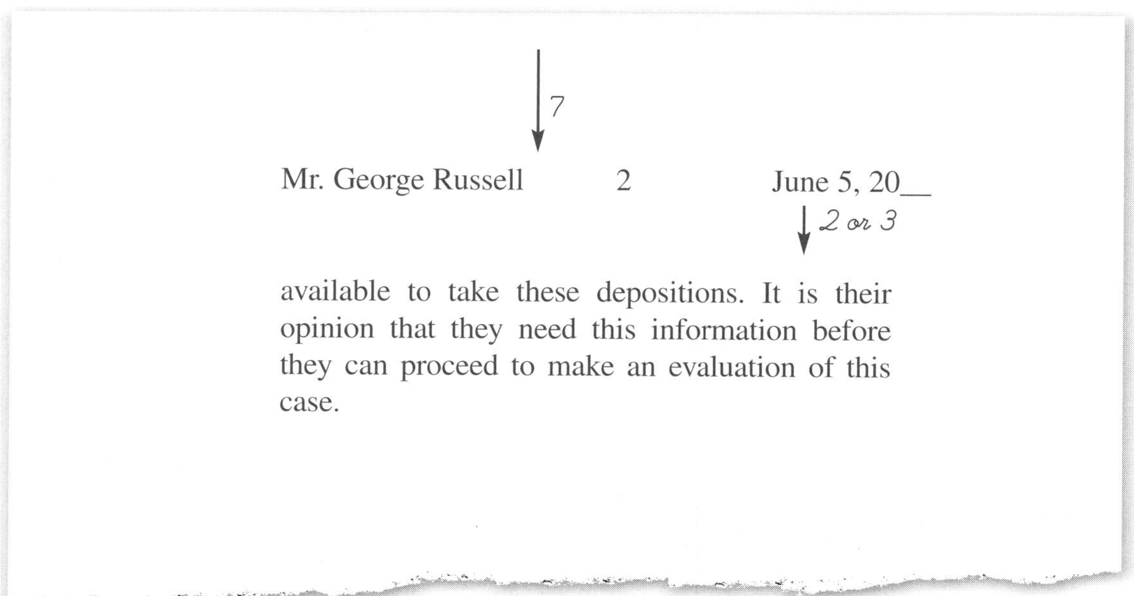

AGES. Ages are generally expressed as words. Use digits for expressing age when the age immediately follows the person's name or when the age is used in a technical sense. Use digits when expressing age in years, months, and days.

Examples: Karen, 60, has chosen early retirement.

Your insurance policy will be paid up at the age of 65.

When we bought the house, William was 5 years 11 months and 3 days old. (Do not separate the years and months with commas.)

Angela is nineteen years old.

The applicant is in her twenties.

E-MAIL. Keep in mind that e-mail messages are not private. Do not send an e-mail message that you would not want everyone in your firm to read. Always use a subject line. When composing the subject line, think of what you would write on a file folder label to help you keep it brief. Restrict each e-mail message to one subject. If you have more than one subject to write about, send more than one e-mail message. Never change the spacing, punctuation, symbols, or capitalization of an e-mail address.

In the e-mail dialog box, type the recipient's name and e–mail address after *To* or *Mail To* and type the subject line after *Subject* or *Re*. The date, your name, and your e-mail address will be inserted automatically.

You may omit the salutation or insert the recipient's name at the beginning of the message. The complimentary closing is generally omitted. You may close simply with your name. These items are a matter of personal preference.

POSTSCRIPT. A postscript is keyed a double space below the copy notation or previous notation. If the paragraphs in the letter are indented, you should also indent the first line of the postscript. If the paragraphs are in block style, begin the postscript at the left margin. You may omit the PS abbreviation.

JR., SR., II, AND SO FORTH. Use a comma between a person's name and *Jr., Sr.,* or *II* if the person uses a comma in his signature. Use a comma after *Jr., Sr.,* or *II* if a comma precedes the designation in the sentence.

ASSIGNMENTS

Complete the Punctuation, Word Study, and Proofreading Exercises that are located on pages 79–84 at the end of this section. The purpose of these exercises is to assist you with the transcription assignment. Tear the completed exercises out of the textbook, and give them to your instructor before you take Spelling Test 2 and before you transcribe the dictation for this section.

Page 79

SPELLING TEST 2

Ask your instructor for Spelling Test 2. Complete this test before you transcribe the dictation for Section 2.

SECTION 2 DICTATION

Go To...
Recording for Section 2

Transcribe all of the letters in modified-block style with open punctuation and blocked paragraphs. Refer to the Reference Handbook for sample letter styles. Be sure to check your transcripts for mailability using the checklist in Section 1.

Use the following letterheads when you transcribe:

1. Andersen Insurance Corporation
2. Beckmann Brothers, Inc.
3. No letterhead provided—e–mail
4. Carefree Village

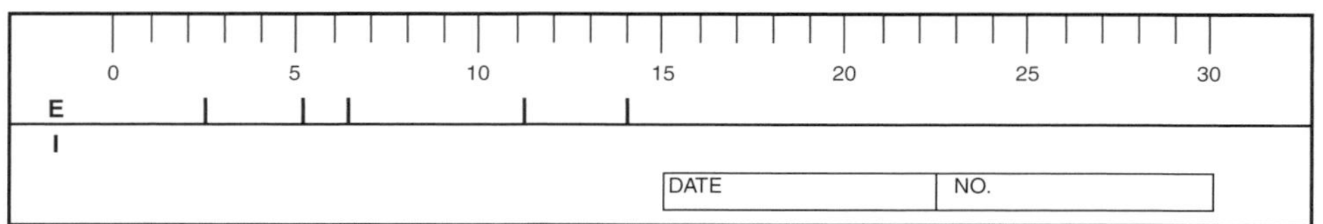

WORD STUDY TEST 1

Ask your instructor for Word Study Test 1. This test covers the word study information contained in Sections 1 and 2. The Word Study Review Summary in the Appendix will help you prepare for this test. Complete this test after you transcribe the dictation for Section 2. The following is a list of words you should study before you take the test:

NOTE:
Review the Word Study portions of Sections 1 and 2 before you take this test. It is much easier to understand a word in context than to match a word with its definition.

allowed
aloud
assistance
assistants
cite
desert
dessert
envelop
envelope
farther
further
it's
its
personal
personnel
presence
presents
sight
site
their
there
they're
to
too
two

Name/Class ____________________

Section 2 Exercises

When completed, tear these exercises out of the textbook and give them to your instructor.

Punctuation Exercises—Independent Words or Expressions, *And* Omitted, Direct Address, and Hyphens in Compound Expressions

DIRECTIONS: ***Insert the proper punctuation where needed in the following sentences.***

PART 1

1. Did you notice Mr. Cockrum that you will receive an additional 15 units free under our new promotion with an order of this size?
2. In other words be tactful when refusing a request.
3. Consequently we have enclosed a check to cover the difference.
4. Thank you Mrs. Martin for your help.
5. Yes sir I would be glad to deliver the papers for you.
6. The efficient capable transcriptionist received a raise.
7. Ramero made notes on a large legal pad.
8. Jane is a considerate generous person.
9. He was a well trained salesman.
10. Mr. Smith's account is past due.
11. The salesperson was well trained.
12. We will consider your suggestions of course.
13. Unfortunately the home was not insured.
14. I am sure that you will agree Mrs. Franklin that our offer is a generous one.
15. In addition we have included a bonus check for your excellent suggestion.

PART 2

1. I think therefore that you will be pleased with the results.
2. Nevertheless we will be happy to discuss the matter with you again if you do not agree with our decision.
3. We can I think resolve this matter on Friday at the meeting.
4. We will of course expect a refund for the damaged goods.
5. Furthermore we will exert a concentrated effort to conserve energy.
6. Our new advertising program will result I hope in an increase in our occupancy rate.

Name/Class____________________

7. We will be happy to exchange the defective machine for a new one however.
8. The new television has a sharper clearer picture than the old one.
9. Please check the last payment dates on all past due accounts.
10. John is a well dressed man.
11. Please submit a payment of at least $25 on your past due account.
12. Do you have a copy of an up to date calendar for Mr. Mitchell?
13. Please prepare a follow up study on the effects that the March procedural changes made in productivity.
14. The young performers were a well behaved group.
15. We will follow up on this problem in two weeks.

Word Study Exercises

DIRECTIONS: ***Highlight or underline the correct word choice in each of the following sentences.***

PART 1

1. The proposed Collinsville (cite, sight, site) for the new building is (farther, further) away from the city than the proposed Belleville (cite, sight, site).
2. When John (presence, presents) our proposal to the board, (it's, its) important that he be (allowed, aloud) at least 20 minutes on the agenda.
3. We suggest that you (farther, further) consider installing a fence to (envelop, envelope) the property.
4. Mr. Andrews will be prepared to (cite, sight, site) prices at the meeting on Friday.
5. The Finance Committee published (it's, its) budget for next year.
6. The rainbow was a beautiful (cite, sight, site).
7. Please order 10,000 No. 10 (envelops, envelopes).
8. The new security fence will (envelop, envelope) the parking lot reserved for (personal, personnel).
9. No one will be (allowed, aloud) (to, too, two) enter the parking lot without proper identification.
10. The (presence, presents) of a security guard will (farther, further) ensure the safety of our (personal, personnel).
11. The new lake will (envelop, envelope) the (cite, sight, site) of the old church.
12. Please give me a large (envelop, envelope).
13. We drove (farther, further) today than we did yesterday.

Name/Class____

14. The committee will consider your suggestion (farther, further) next week.

15. (It's, Its) my intention (to, too, two) apply for the opening in the Marketing Division.

PART 2

1. The planning committee will hold (it's, its) first meeting on Tuesday at 1:30 p.m.
2. Your (presence, presents) at the meeting is essential.
3. Have you bought all the (presence, presents) on your Christmas list?
4. Watch the jury while the defense (presence, presents) (it's, its) closing argument.
5. Please (cite, sight, site) the Pledge of Allegiance.
6. The sunset at the Grand Canyon is a breathtaking (cite, sight, site).
7. (It's, Its) the responsibility of this committee to choose the (cite, sight, site) for the new factory.
8. Persons younger than ten will not be (allowed, aloud) to go on this camping trip.
9. Talking (allowed, aloud) during the taping session is not (allowed, aloud).
10. Angie was very excited when she saw her birthday (presence, presents).
11. (It's, Its) the last meeting of the year.
12. The speaker planned to (cite, sight, site) Abraham Lincoln in his dinner speech.
13. You could smell the (presence, presents) of smoke in the air.
14. Only employees are (allowed, aloud) in the production area.
15. Do not talk (allowed, aloud) during the lecture.

Name/Class ____________________

EXERCISE

Proofreading Exercise 2-A

DIRECTIONS: ***Use proofreaders' marks to correct the following letter. A list of proofreaders' marks is in the Reference Handbook at the back of the textbook.***

January 19, 20__

Ms. Judy McIntosh
Office Manager
Ross Advertising Agency
1750 Branson Road
St. Louis, MO 63166

Dear Ms. McIntosh:

Enclosed is our knew catelog. You well find many new items from which to chose. Our new line if chairs illustrated on pages 49-57 should by of particular interest to you.

Inside the back cover, you will find order blanks and postage paid envelops for your use in placing a order. We look for ward to recieving an order from you soon.

Sincerely

Bob Miller

xxx

EXERCISE Name/Class ____________________

Proofreading Exercise 2-B

DIRECTIONS: ***Use proofreaders' marks to correct the following letter. A list of proofreaders' marks is in the Reference Handbook at the back of the textbook.***

June 10, 20__

Mrs. Georgia Macon
Yale Supply Company
7945 East Elm Street
Peoria, IL 61611

Dear Mrs. Macon:

We ordered 15,000 catalogs from you on April 9. However we have not recieved this order.

Our supply of these catelogs is now low. The branch at our Denver cite has only 50 catalogs remaining in it's inventory. We will be in a difficult position if we ran out of them.

Please let us know whether their is some problem in completing the order. We will be happy to supply any farther information that you may need. Its imperative that we receive these catalogs within the next ten days. Please send us an up to date status report on our order.

Sincerely yours,

Jill King

xxx

Name/Class____

Proofreading Exercise 2-C

DIRECTIONS: ***Use proofreaders' marks to correct the following letter. A list of proofreaders' marks is in the Reference Handbook at the back of the textbook.***

Januray 19, 20__

Garden City Real Estate Company
9547 Riverside Drive
Collinsville, IL 62234

Ladies and Gentleman

We will be relocating to your area in June and would like to fine an apropriate sight to build a new home. Its important that the building cite is located no further than 30 minutes from the center of the city.

We would also consider looking at homes that are for sale. We will require a home that has three bedrooms and at least two bathrooms. We would prefer a home that has a fence that envelopes the yard.

If we do not find a suitable home to buy, we will need to rent a home untill we are able to finish building our new home.

During the first week of March, we will be in your city and would like to look at any building sites and homes that would match our needs. Thank you for you assistants in relocating my family.

Sincerly

M. J. Olsen

xxx

Section 3

3.1 OBJECTIVES

In Section 3, you will work toward the following objectives:

- Correctly insert commas where appropriate in sentences containing introductory dependent clauses and introductory prepositional phrases.
- Correctly format delivery notations, subject lines, money, book titles, and fax cover sheets when transcribing the dictation for this section.
- Correctly complete Punctuation Exercises, Word Study Exercises, and Proofreading Exercises in preparation for transcription.
- Complete Spelling Test 3 with at least 80 percent accuracy.
- Select the appropriate words and the correct spelling according to the context of the dictation when transcribing this section's documents.

3.2 PUNCTUATION REVIEW

Use a comma after an introductory dependent clause. Dependent clauses begin with subordinating conjunctions such as *although, as, because, before, even though, if, since, unless, when,* and *whether*. A sentence containing an independent clause and one or more dependent clauses is called a complex sentence.

Example: When Mr. Carson calls, be sure to tell him about the change in the program for the sales conference.

"PAUL, AREN'T YOU THE ONE WHO SAID THAT YOU WOULDN'T RECOGNIZE A DEPENDENT CLAUSE IF ONE HIT YOU OVER THE HEAD?"

No comma is needed when the independent clause is stated before an essential dependent clause. However, if the dependent clause is nonessential, it should be set off by commas.

Examples: Be sure to tell Mr. Carson about the change in the program for the sales conference when he calls. The sales conference will take place in New York, which is an exciting city.

It is recommended that you use a comma after all introductory prepositional phrases. You should use a comma after an introductory prepositional phrase that contains a verb form or is five or more words long. If the introductory prepositional phrase is less than five words long and does not contain a verb form, you may omit the comma. However, use a comma if one is needed for clarity.

Introductory Prepositional Phrase Containing a Verb Form:

After hearing the news, we planned our sales strategy for the new marketing territory.

Introductory Prepositional Phrase Containing Five or More Words:

Between Angie's desk and the elevator, there is a spot marked for the new copy machine.

Introductory Prepositional Phrase Needing a Comma for Clarity:

For our committee, meetings will be scheduled every Wednesday at 9 a.m.

Introductory Prepositional Phrase Containing Fewer than Five Words and No Verb Form:

By five o'clock he had completed all the dictation.

OR

By five o'clock, he had completed all the dictation.

3.3 WORD STUDY

The words listed here are frequently confused in transcription because they sound alike when dictated but have different meanings. Study the words carefully so that you will be able to select the appropriate word according to the context of the dictation.

accept (verb) to receive; to give approval to

We will *accept* applications for this position tomorrow.

The representatives for the other company will *accept* the proposed changes.

except (preposition) with the exclusion or exception of

Everyone in the department attended the conference *except* John.

addition (noun) something added

The *addition* of the Iowa plant brings our total to 50.

edition (noun) one version of a publication

This is the latest *edition* of the book.

currant (noun) a kind of berry

He ate *currant* jam on his toast.

current (adjective) occurring at the present time; now in progress

Mr. Jamison obtained the loan at the *current* interest rate.

waive (verb) to give up something, such as a right, a claim, or a privilege

The corporation decided to *waive* the right to renew the option on the property.

waiver (noun) the act of giving up a right, a claim, or a privilege; a document containing a declaration of such an act

We received the *waiver* in the mail yesterday.

wave or waver (verb) to sway; to fluctuate in opinion

The only juror voting against the defendant was beginning to *waver*.

wave (noun) a sweeping movement of the hand used as a signal or a greeting

She motioned to the door with a *wave* of her hand.

your (possessive pronoun) belonging to you

This is *your* book.

you're contraction for *you are*

We hope *you're* planning to go to the lecture.

3.4 SPELLING REVIEW

The dictation for this section contains the words listed here. Study them carefully to help you transcribe more rapidly. If you hear other words in the dictation that you do not know how to spell, make a list of those words and learn their correct spellings. This practice will help you improve your transcription speed.

accept
addition
assuredly
authoritative
automatically
custom
distinctive
edition
enrollment
except
exclusive
financial
forecast
guaranteed
heritage
hesitant
knowledgeable
literary
luxurious
minimal
normally
permanent
prominent
pursuant
quality
receipt
separate
shipment
shipped
strictly
supplements
time-saver
unique
upkeep
volume
waive
waiver
waver

TRANSCRIPTION GUIDELINES

BOOK AND MAGAZINE TITLES. You may enter the titles of books and magazines in one of the following three ways:

1. Enter the titles in italics, and capitalize the first letter of each important word (preferred).
2. Underline titles, and capitalize the first letter of each important word.
3. Key the titles in all-capital letters.

Examples: *Angie's Secret* Angie's Secret ANGIE'S SECRET

DELIVERY NOTATION. The delivery notation is keyed at the left margin on the line after the enclosure notation (after the reference initials if there is no enclosure). See also *Copy Notation* and *Envelope* in the Reference Handbook.

Examples: By certified mail, By registered mail, By Express Mail, By Federal Express, By fax, By special delivery, By messenger

An alternate location for the delivery notation is a double space above the inside address. The notation placed in this position should be keyed in all capitals.

SUBJECT LINE. A subject line of a letter is keyed a double space below the salutation. The subject line is centered or indented the same amount as the paragraphs are indented. If you are using block style for the letter, you must key the subject line at the left margin. Double-space after the subject line before you start the first paragraph.

October 30, 20__

Mrs. Shirley Bronson
XYZ Corporation
6401 West Main Street
Belleville, IL 62223

Dear Mrs. Bronson:
↓2
Subject: National Management Conference
↓2
Would you serve as the master of ceremonies for the National Management Conference that will be held in Chicago on March 25-27?

MONEY. Do not use a decimal point and zeros when you type an even amount of money. Use a comma to separate dollar amounts of five figures or more. (The trend is to omit the comma in amounts of four digits unless they appear with larger amounts.) Amounts that are less than $1 are written in digits and words. Even amounts in millions or more may be expressed by combining digits and words for clarity.

Examples:	$12,500	$35.90	$534,827.65
	50 cents	$1400 or $1,400	
	$1 million	$3 billion	

FAX COVER SHEET. Your word processing software may have a template you can use to create a fax cover sheet. If you are creating a template for your use only, fill in any information that will remain constant. However, if you are creating a template that many different people will use, create a form with blank lines that can be filled in with the appropriate information. Try to create entry lines that have a common left margin to make the form easier to use. You may want to add graphics that include the firm name and address at the top of the form. The following is a sample form:

FAX COVER SHEET

Date: ______________________________
To: ______________________________
____
Fax Number: ______________________________
From: ______________________________
____
Fax Number: ______________________________
Number of pages (including this cover sheet): ______________
Message: ______________________________
____
____
____
____
____
____
____
____
____

If any part of this fax transmission is missing or not clearly received, please call:
Name: ______________________________
Phone number: ______________________________

ASSIGNMENTS

EXERCISE

Page 91

Complete the Punctuation, Word Study, and Proofreading Exercises that are located on pages 91–96 at the end of this section. The purpose of these exercises is to assist you with the transcription assignment. Tear the completed exercises out of the textbook, and give them to your instructor before you take Spelling Test 3 and before you transcribe the dictation for this section.

SPELLING TEST 3

Ask your instructor for Spelling Test 3. Complete this test before you transcribe the dictation for Section 3.

SECTION 3 DICTATION

Recording for Section 3

Transcribe all of the letters in modified-block style with mixed punctuation and indented paragraphs. Refer to the Reference Handbook for sample letter styles. Be sure to check your transcripts for mailability using the checklist in Section 1.

Use the following letterheads when you transcribe:

1. Pacific Life Insurance Company
2. Wilson Mutual Insurance Company
3. Arden Publishing Company
4. American Literary Association
5. Fax cover sheet

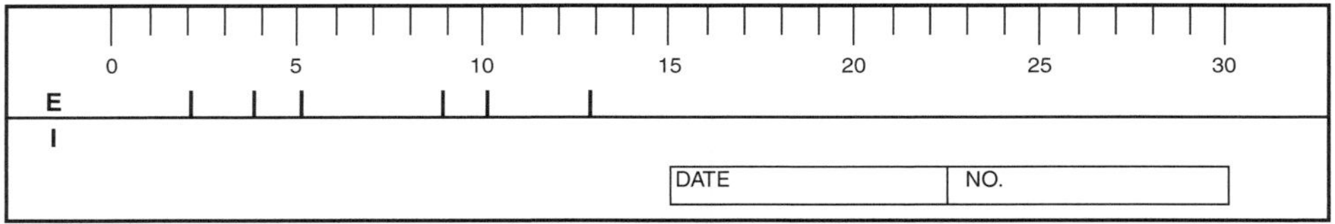

Name/Class ______________________________

Section 3 Exercises

When completed, tear these exercises out of the textbook and give them to your instructor.

Punctuation Exercises—Introductory Dependent Clauses and Introductory Prepositional Phrases

DIRECTIONS: ***Insert commas where needed in the following sentences.***

PART 1

1. In case your plans change call me before you leave.
2. By concentrating on the reports he can finish the project by noon.
3. After the monthly sales meeting we ate lunch in the hotel dining room.
4. On June 15 in the attorney's office at 115 East Main Street we will sign the final transfer papers.
5. During the next three weeks the committee will finalize the plans for the move to the new building.
6. In the past ten years we have paid similar claims.
7. After concluding our contract negotiations we had dinner at Sczblewski's restaurant.
8. Under the present club rules presidents may not succeed themselves.
9. On top of the building a new air-conditioning system has been installed.
10. After the test in American Government 131 Jane Mary and John discussed the questions.
11. After reading the notice of the meeting in Chicago I made a reservation at the Whitehall.
12. In accordance with the committee's recommendation we will repaint the offices.
13. In the four years that I have worked here the company has doubled in size.
14. After the presentation concerning the new personnel procedures Mr. Harris will answer questions from the audience.
15. On January 19 at the University Mall we will celebrate the grand opening of our new store.
16. By 5:30 p.m. she had completed her assignments in English keyboarding and business accounting.
17. With the danger in mind we proceeded with caution.
18. At the Snowmass Country Club down in the valley the people watched the avalanche.
19. At the time of the election we were sure that our candidate would win.
20. In spite of the recommendation of the salespeople we installed the smaller air-conditioning unit.
21. After we finished skiing for the day we dined at La Boheme.
22. Before October 30 you must file that case in the circuit court.
23. At the convention in Chicago we received several good ideas for improving production in the office.
24. Before the final deadline of November 9 we signed the new contract.
25. If you are unable to attend the meeting perhaps your assistant will be able to act on your behalf.

Name/Class ____

PART 2

1. Since the February sales promotion meeting almost all sales personnel have increased their monthly sales.
2. Unless we receive a payment by the tenth of next month we will be forced to turn your account over to our attorneys for collection.
3. Perhaps your assistant will be able to act on your behalf if you are unable to attend the meeting.
4. Almost all sales personnel have increased their monthly sales since the February sales promotion meeting.
5. We will be forced to turn your account over to our attorneys for collection unless we receive a payment by the tenth of next month.
6. When the package is delivered check the contents immediately to be sure that everything we ordered has been included.
7. When the alarm sounded the security police evacuated the building.
8. If I can be of any further assistance please let me know.
9. Before we can sign the purchase contract we must obtain the approval of the Board of Directors.
10. If you have any questions after you read the contract I will be happy to answer them.
11. Although Sarah has no experience I think she will make an excellent assistant.
12. As you know we will have a seminar on letter writing next Tuesday.
13. Even though we have written three letters requesting payment Mr. James has not paid his bill.
14. Because we are moving to our new location we are having a sale.
15. Whether you decide to join us or not we will have to proceed with our present plans.
16. Since our telephone conversation of last Friday we have received additional information.
17. Before you leave this evening please be sure that all the letters are in the mail.
18. Unless we can finish the construction before the end of the month we will have to pay a penalty.
19. If you will prepare a report illustrating your ideas I will arrange for you to present your suggestions to the committee.
20. If you cannot control your typing errors slow down and concentrate on accuracy.
21. If you do not hear from us by 3 p.m. go to the airport to meet Mrs. Perkins.
22. When the damage report is finished we will decide whether to repair the present building or to build on another site.
23. Since Mr. Collins is retiring the chief accountant's job is open.
24. Unless we receive the production report by 3:30 p.m. we will not be able to finish the production analysis before the meeting.
25. When she returns you may go to lunch.

Word Study Exercises

DIRECTIONS: ***Highlight or underline the correct word choice in each of the following sentences.***

PART 1

1. I believe all the employees will (accept, except) the new guidelines (accept, except) Karl Morris.
2. The (to, too, two) members of the committee were beginning (to, too,

two) (waiver, waver) on the issue after (your, you're) presentation.

3. According to the (currant, current) progress report, the new (addition, edition) to the building will be completed by October 27.
4. (Your, You're) assignment is to obtain a signed (waiver, waver) by January 19.
5. (Your, You're) sure to like the taste of our new (currant, current) jelly.
6. The new (addition, edition) of the office manual will replace the (currant, current) (addition, edition) on June 1.
7. The (currant, current) supplier of (currants, currents) for our (currant, current) jelly has informed us that the new contract will be (accepted, excepted).
8. We will (accept, except) the proposed changes in the (currant, current) contract (accept, except) those listed on page 7.
9. The plans for the (addition, edition) of a new manager, five sales (personal, personnel), and (to, too, two) assistants in the next six months make the (addition, edition) of office space a priority item.
10. You must sign the (waiver, waver) before you will be (allowed, aloud) to take the rafting trip down the Colorado River.
11. We cannot (accept, except) this check unless we are willing (to, too, two) sign a release.
12. Robert finished all his work (accept, except) the project for Mrs. Caldwell.
13. We must finish these (to, too, two) projects in (addition, edition) to those we already have.
14. Please obtain the latest (addition, edition) of this textbook.
15. Our (currant, current) jelly is just like the type Grandma used (to, too, two) make.

PART 2

1. John Nagle has the (currant, current) marketing report.
2. She decided (to, too, two) (waive, wave) her right (to, too, two) remain silent.
3. Judy signed the (waiver, waver) yesterday.
4. The opposition (to, too, two) House Bill 4975 is beginning to (waiver, waver).
5. Give me (your, you're) opinion of the report before Friday's meeting.
6. (Your, You're) invited (to, too, two) attend the party.
7. All regions will be represented at the meeting (accept, except) the North Central Region.
8. There are several (additions, editions) to the new (addition, edition) of the book.
9. You will soon receive (your, you're) order of five cases of (currant, curent) jelly.
10. Will you (accept, except) the (currant, current) offer?
11. Does this letter mean that (your, you're) willing to sign the (waiver, waver)?
12. He signaled with a (waive, wave) for us to continue.
13. (Your, You're) decision to (waive, wave) (your, you're) right (to, too, two) renew the contract was a wise one.
14. Once you have made up (your, you're) mind, don't (waiver, waver).
15. Please (accept, except) my apology for the delay in the shipment of (your, you're) merchandise.

Name/Class______________________________

Proofreading Exercise 3-A

DIRECTIONS: ***Use proofreaders' marks to correct the following letter. A list of proofreaders' marks is in the Reference Handbook at the back of the textbook.***

July 18, 20__

Mr. E. G. Mitchell
M & M Printing Company
109 East Poplar Street
West Frankfort, IL 62896

Dear Mr. Mitchell

Please send us 50 copies of you're brochure #25.

I understand the cost is 50¢ per copy. Since we receive a 10% discount we have enclosed a check for $22.50.

When you publish new additions of you're brochure #42 and brochure #79 please let us know.

Yours truly

George McCafferty

xxx
Enclosure

EXERCISE Name/Class ____________________

Proofreading Exercise 3-B

DIRECTIONS: ***Use proofreaders' marks to correct the following letter. A list of proofreaders' marks is in the Reference Handbook at the back of the textbook.***

(current date)

Mr. George A. Caughman
7814 Lake Road
Huntington, UT 84528

Dear Mr. Caughman

Your interest in our products is apreciated. Are designs were especially selected for durabilty, beauty, and quality. We have enclosed materials that we hope you will find usefull in chosing one or more of our artistic ceramic tile designs for any setting that you have in mind.

Since there is no McGee Tile distributor conviently close to you we have enclosed an order from for your use in ordering any materials that you desire. We assure you that you order will be filled shipped and received promtly and in good condition.

Thank you for selecting McGee Tile products They are the best that you can buy.

Sincerely

MCGEE TILE, INC.

J. P. Wilson, Jr.
Customer Relations

xxx
Enclosures

Name/Class______________________________

Proofreading Exercise 3-C

DIRECTIONS: ***Use proofreaders' marks to correct the following memorandum. A list of proofreaders' marks is in the Reference Handbook at the back of the textbook.***

MEMO TO: Eric Rushing

FROM: Wayne Justin

DATE: (current date)

SUBJECT: Building Project

Since you have agreed to except the responsibility for overseeing the building project you will be responsible for making all office decor decisions in the new addition to the building except for the executive office complex.

While you are working on the plans for this edition to our building your going to be reporting to Ed Bradley. If you find that you need additional support staff call the personal office for assistance.

Since this assignment will take most of your time some of your currant duties will be assigned to Marcus Williams. Could you arrange some free time around 1:00 p.m. on Thursday to discuss the responsibilities that need to be transfered to Marcus?

xxx

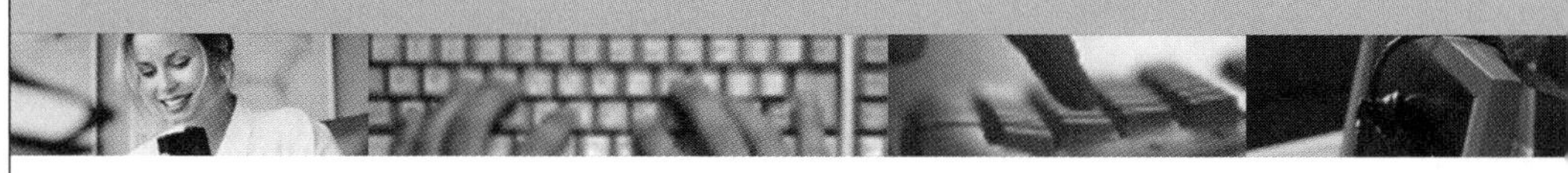

Section 4

4.1 OBJECTIVES

In Section 4, you will work toward the following objectives:

- Correctly format street numbers and Canadian postal abbreviations when transcribing the dictation for this section.
- Correctly complete Word Study Exercises and Proofreading Exercises in preparation for transcription.
- Complete Spelling Test 4 with at least 80 percent accuracy.
- Select the appropriate words and the correct spelling according to the context of the dictation when transcribing this section's documents.

4.2 WORD STUDY

The words listed here are frequently confused in transcription because they sound alike when dictated but have different meanings. Study the words carefully so that you will be able to select the appropriate word according to the context of the dictation.

appraise (verb) to decide the value of

The real estate agent will *appraise* our house on Thursday.

apprise (verb) to inform; to notify

I will *apprise* you of any change in the meeting time.

miner (noun) a person who works in a mine

The coal *miner* was tired after working all day in the mine.

minor (adjective) lesser in size, amount, extent, or importance

The *minor* problem did not cause a delay in the completion of the building.

minor (noun) a person who is under legal age

A *minor* is not admitted unless accompanied by an adult.

overdo (verb) to do too much

Don't *overdo* on your first day of jogging.

overdue (adjective) past the time for payment

Your account is *overdue*.

4.3 SPELLING REVIEW

The dictation for this section contains the words listed here. Study them carefully to help you transcribe more rapidly. If you hear other words in the dictation that you do not know how to spell, make a list of those words and learn their correct spellings. This practice will help you improve your transcription speed.

accompanied
accomplish
actually
appointment
appraise
apprise
appropriate
beneficial
departure
difficulty
engagement
gradually
importance
initial
interruption
investigation
lapse
magnificent
miner
minor
overdo
overdue
participate
perhaps
prolong
receive
reinstated
strenuous
supervisor
temporary
valuable
voyage

4.4 TRANSCRIPTION GUIDELINES

STREET NUMBERS. Spell out *one* through *ten* in street names. Use digits for higher numbers. Do not abbreviate direction designations such as *East* or *West* before the street name. Abbreviate compound direction designations when they appear after street names, and insert commas before them. Spell out *North, South, East,* and *West* following a street name, and omit the comma.

Examples: One East Fifth Street

2 West 78th Street

293 Oak Street, NW

161 Maple Avenue South

CANADIAN POSTAL ABBREVIATIONS. Use the following two-letter abbreviations in Canadian addresses:

AB	Alberta
BC	British Columbia
MB	Manitoba
NB	New Brunswick
NF	Newfoundland
NT	Northwest Territories
NS	Nova Scotia
NU	Nunavut
ON	Ontario
PE	Prince Edward Island
QC	Quebec
SK	Saskatchewan
YT	Yukon Territory

You may use the two-letter Canadian abbreviations for the provinces and territories, or you may spell out their names. The following are examples of Canadian addresses if you are mailing a letter from the United States. Key the name of any foreign country on the last line in all-capital letters.

Preferred Forms: Ms. R. G. Quinn

1473 Carling Avenue

Vancouver, BC V6C 1P8

CANADA

or

Mr. Robert Caswell

230 Slater Street

Ottawa, Ontario

CANADA K1P 5H6

You will be transcribing a few letters on Canadian letterheads to Canadian addresses. If you were mailing a letter in Canada to a Canadian address, you would not key the word *CANADA* in the address, just as you would not type the words *UNITED STATES* on a letter to be mailed from Chicago to New York. The following are examples for keying Canadian addresses on the Canadian letterheads you will be using:

NOTE:
Review the punctuation rules you studied in Sections 1 through 3, and be ready to apply them in the letters you transcribe for Section 4.

Preferred Forms: Ms. R. G. Quinn

1473 Carling Avenue

Vancouver, BC V6C 1P8

Mr. Robert Caswell

230 Slater Street

Ottawa, ON K1P 5H6

or

Ottawa, Ontario K1P 5H6

For your convenience and future reference, this information also appears in the Reference Handbook.

ASSIGNMENTS

Page 101

Complete the Word Study and Proofreading Exercises that are located on pages 101–104 at the end of this section. The purpose of these exercises is to assist you with the transcription assignment. Tear the completed exercises out of the textbook and give them to your instructor before you take Spelling Test 4 and before you transcribe the dictation for this section.

SPELLING TEST 4

Ask your instructor for Spelling Test 4. Complete this test before you transcribe the dictation for Section 4.

SECTION 4 DICTATION

Go To... Recording for Section 4

Transcribe all of the outgoing letters in block style with open punctuation. Refer to the Reference Handbook for sample letter styles. Be sure to check your transcripts for mailability using the checklist in Section 1.

Use the following letterheads when you transcribe:

1. Dennis Piper, M.D.
2. Pacific Life Insurance Company
3. No letterhead provided—e-mail
4. B & J Float Tours, Inc.
5. Madison Insurance Company

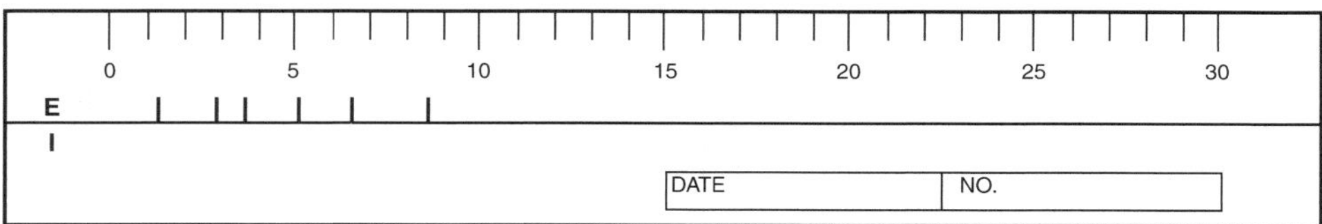

Name/Class____

Section 4 Exercises

When completed, tear these exercises out of the textbook and give them to your instructor.

Word Study Exercises

DIRECTIONS: ***Highlight or underline the correct word choice in each of the following sentences.***

1. This (miner, minor) change will not require us (to, too, two) get the board's approval.

2. (Your, You're) report is (overdo, overdue); it was supposed to be finished yesterday.

3. The (miner, minor) was cautioned not (to, too, two) (overdo, overdue) his activities until he recovers from his injury.

4. We must (appraise, apprise) the committee members of the (miner, minor) adjustment that is needed.

5. Once the adjustment is made, we will need to (appraise, apprise) (it's, its) effectiveness after a month.

6. Before you apply for a position, you should do research on the prospective firm to (appraise, apprise) yourself of as much information as possible.

7. The following explanation will (appraise, apprise) you of the differences between the (to, too, two) bids for installing a new computer.

8. We will (appraise, apprise) the effectiveness of the new advertising campaign at the meeting on November 9.

9. The plane was an hour (overdo, overdue).

10. Do not (overdo, overdue) your use of formatting techniques in your letters.

11. Irving Swartz will (appraise, apprise) the property.

12. Jane McIntosh will (appraise, apprise) us of the new policies.

13. Charles is a retired gold (miner, minor).

14. An adult is charged $3.50; a (miner, minor) child is admitted for $1.75.

15. The storm caused (miner, minor) damage.

16. The last job applicant seemed (to, too, two) (overdo, overdue) her makeup.

17. (Your, You're) payment is a week (overdo, overdue).

18. Exercise is good for you as long as you do not (overdo, overdue) it.

19. The football player received a (miner, minor) injury in the game.

20. A (miner, minor) is not permitted (to, too, two) have a library card until the age of six.

Name/Class____

21. (Your, You're) library book is (to, too, two) days (overdo, overdue).

22. We will have the jewelry from the estate (appraised, apprised) (to, too, two) resolve the (miner, minor) dispute.

23. Please be (appraised, apprised) of the fact that the new law does apply in this situation.

24. The retired coal (miner, minor) receives a pension.

25. The coal (miner, minor) noticed a (miner, minor) error in his paycheck.

Proofreading Exercise 4-A

DIRECTIONS: ***Use proofreaders' marks to correct the following letter. A list of proofreaders' marks is in the Reference Handbook at the back of the textbook.***

February 1, 20__

Atlas Manufacturing Company
2975 Fourth Avenue
Springfield, MA 01101

Attention Accounting Department

Ladies and Gentlemen

While reviewing are accounts recievable records we found that your account is two months overdo. We havenot recieved an answer to are inquires regarding your past due account. If their is some temporary financial difficulty we will be glad to work out a payment plan.

Your prompt payment will preserve you good credit rating. Please sent you check today.

Sincerely

Steve Shields

xxx

EXERCISE Name/Class____

Proofreading Exercise 4-B

DIRECTIONS: ***Use proofreaders' marks to correct the following letter. A list of proofreaders' marks is in the Reference Handbook at the back of the textbook.***

(current date)

Mr. Roy A. Bartlett
20 Garden Street
Rapid City, SD 57701

Dear Mr. Bartlett

It's our desire to serve every account promtly efficiently and courteously. Since we pay our bills promptly we expect our customers to do the same. However you have not responded to our resent letter reguarding the balance on your account. Therefore we must remind you that we cannot carry past due accounts on our books.

A reasonable length of time has been aloud and cannot be extended farther. Therefore, please send a check or money order in the amount of $ 985.17 to bring your account up to date.

Very truely yours

Delphia Mitchell
Accounting Department

xxx

EXERCISE Name/Class______________________________

Proofreading Exercise 4-C

DIRECTIONS: ***Use proofreaders' marks to correct the following memorandum. A list of proofreaders' marks is in the Reference Handbook at the back of the textbook.***

MEMO TO: Kathy Layman

FROM: Trina Maze

DATE: (current date)

SUBJECT: Computer System

We must evaluate our current computer system. I beleive a change is overdo. Please investigate the hardware and software needs of the departments and appraise me of your findings and your recomendations.

If possible please complete you report by the end of next month. If you do not think you will be able to meet this deadline please let me know.

xxx

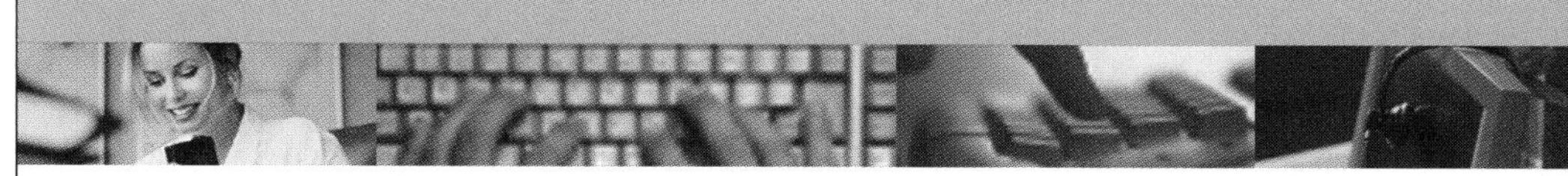

Section 5

5.1 OBJECTIVES

In Section 5, you will work toward the following objectives:

- Correctly insert commas where appropriate in sentences containing appositives and dates.
- Correctly format house numbers, attention lines, envelopes, and department and division names when transcribing the dictation for this section.
- Correctly complete Word Division Exercises, Punctuation Exercises, Word Study Exercises, and Proofreading Exercises in preparation for transcription.
- Complete Spelling Test 5 with at least 80 percent accuracy.
- Select the appropriate words and the correct spelling according to the context of the dictation when transcribing this section's documents.
- Complete Word Study Test 2 on the word study vocabulary in Sections 3, 4, and 5 with at least 80 percent accuracy.
- Complete the Practice Transcription Test (optional).

5.2 PUNCTUATION REVIEW

Use commas to set off an appositive. An appositive explains or identifies the noun or pronoun that precedes it.

Example: Mr. Loyd Jacobs, chairman of the board, will deliver the dinner address.

Insert a comma between the day and the year. If the sentence continues after the date, insert a comma after the year. If the date consists of only the month and year, do not use a comma to separate them.

Examples: Angela was born on June 26, 1980.

November 2002 is the projected completion date of the new facility.

5.3 WORD STUDY

The words listed here are frequently confused in transcription because they sound alike when dictated but have different meanings. Study the words carefully so that you will be able to select the appropriate word according to the context of the dictation.

ad (noun) an advertisement

The new *ad* will appear in the November issue of the magazine.

add (verb) to join or unite; to combine in one sum

Please *add* this letter to the Williams file.

She had to *add* many columns of numbers to finish the chart.

advice (noun) a recommendation; an opinion given about what to do

Paul did not heed his brother's *advice*.

advise (verb) to inform; to recommend

My attorney will *advise* me on the matter.

complement (verb) to complete or make complete; to fill out

A husband and wife *complement* one another in a marriage.

complement (noun) something that completes or fills up

The team does not have its full *complement* of players.

compliment (noun) an expression of courtesy or respect; a flattering remark

He received a *compliment* on his fine job.

device (noun) a thing created for some purpose; a plan

This *device* is used to open envelopes automatically.

devise (verb) to plan; to work out

Please *devise* a slogan for marketing the new product.

passed (verb) moved on; transferred

She *passed* the report around the conference table.

past (noun) a former time

I have attended the meetings in the *past*.

past (adjective) at a former time; gone by

I have been out of town on business for the *past* two weeks.

stationary (adjective) fixed; not movable

The flagpole is *stationary*.

stationery (noun) paper

He ordered new engraved *stationery* for the office.

5.4 SPELLING REVIEW

The dictation for this section contains the words listed here. Study them carefully to help you transcribe more rapidly. If you hear other words in the dictation that you do not know how to spell, make a list of those words and learn their correct spellings. This practice will help you improve your transcription speed.

advice	device	registration
advise	devise	representative
alternate	document	resolved
campaign	enthusiastic	resume
committee	modem	satisfactory
competitive	necessary	stationary
complement	nominal	stationery
compliment	operation	systematic
concentrated	patience	technical
conclude	personalized	tuition
demonstrating	prompt	

5.5 TRANSCRIPTION GUIDELINES

HOUSE NUMBERS. Always use digits to express house numbers; *One* is always spelled out, however. Do not use commas in house numbers.

Examples: 2475 East Main Street One West Hickory Avenue

ATTENTION LINE. The attention line is keyed as the first line of the inside address. The word *attention* should be followed by a colon. When an attention line is used, the appropriate salutation is *Ladies and Gentlemen*. The trend is to omit attention lines.

Examples: Attention: Mr. John Williams (Most efficient)

ATTENTION: MS. JOAN WILSON

An alternate location is a double space below the inside address at the left margin. Double-space between the attention line and the salutation. However, if you are using your word processing program to create the envelope, this location will not work.

June 26, 20__

Attention: Human Resources Manager
M & M Industries
115 East Main Stree
West Frankfort, IL 62896 ↓ 2

Ladies and Gentlemen

An illustration of attention line placement on an envelope appears in the next section.

NOTE:
It is common practice to accept the positioning of word processing programs when formatting envelopes.

ENVELOPES. On the envelope, place the attention line as the first line of the address.

The delivery notation should be placed on line 9. It should end about ½ inch from the right edge of the envelope. Delivery notations should be in all capitals.

Be sure to use the ZIP Code + 4 whenever you know the complete ZIP Code. Position the address as shown in the following illustrations:

NO. 10 ENVELOPE

9 1/2 by 4 1/8 inches

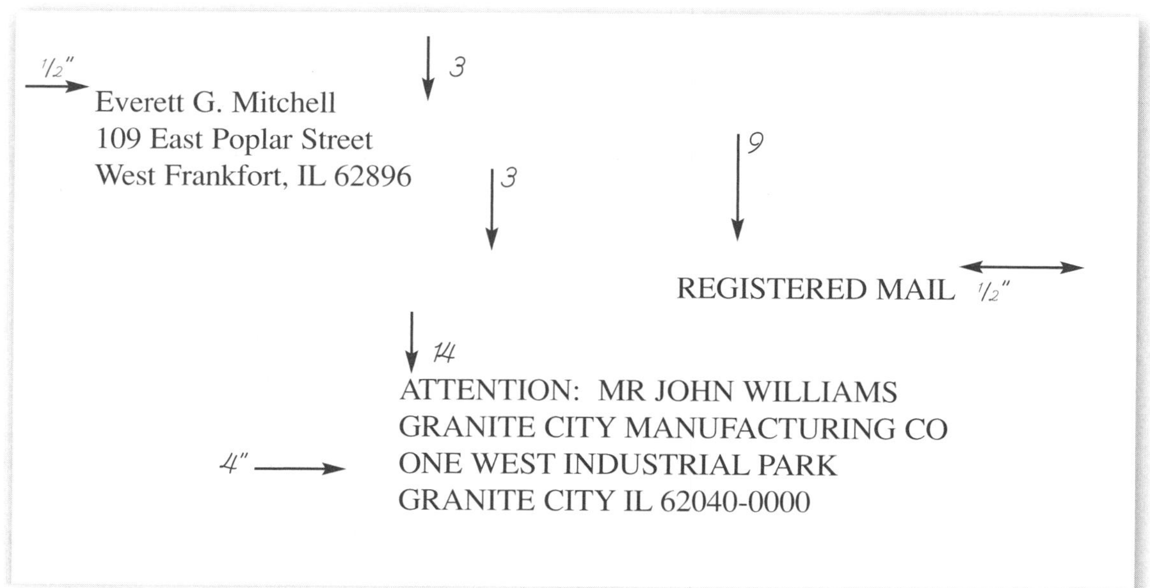

1/2"
3
Everett G. Mitchell
109 East Poplar Street
West Frankfort, IL 62896
3
9
REGISTERED MAIL
1/2"
14
ATTENTION: MR JOHN WILLIAMS
GRANITE CITY MANUFACTURING CO
4"
ONE WEST INDUSTRIAL PARK
GRANITE CITY IL 62040-0000

NO. 6 3/4 ENVELOPE

6 1/2 by 3 5/8 inches

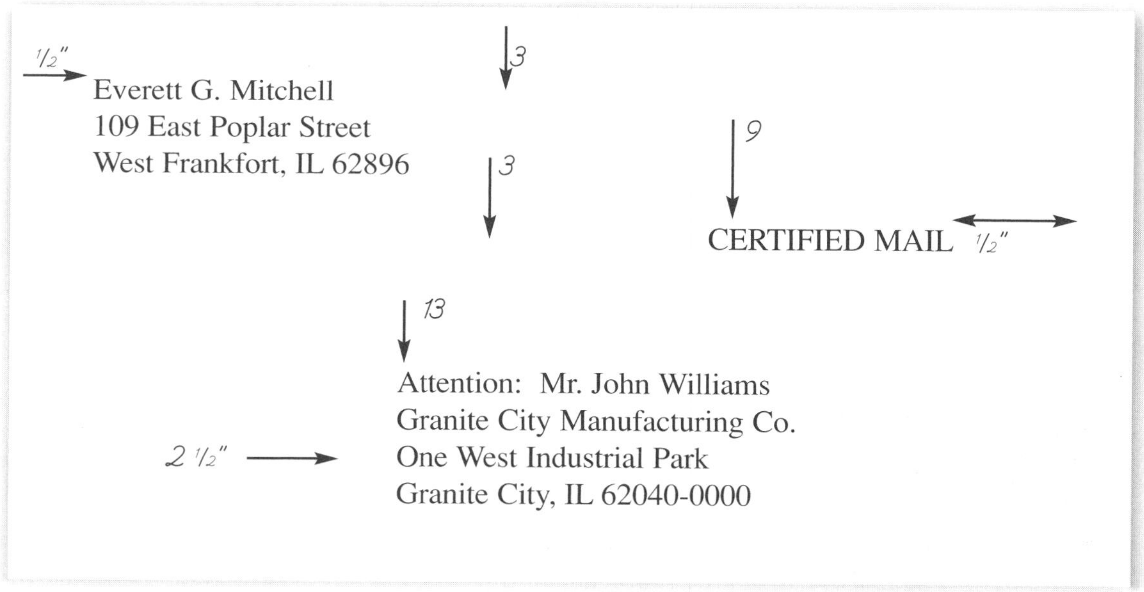

Figure 5.1
Dictation is useful when reports must be sent to a central office from the field. *Can you think of other work situations where dictation improves productivity?*

DEPARTMENT AND DIVISION NAMES. Capitalize the official name of a division or a department within your own firm.

Examples: Send this invoice to the Accounting Department.

Notify the Human Resources Department that we will need a part-time employee during November 1–20.

The Board of Directors must approve the budget for this year before we can approve this purchase order for the new word processing equipment.

Capitalize the names of divisions and departments in other firms only if you definitely know that they are the official names.

Examples: Your marketing department would benefit from our Star Sales Training Program.

The Department of Research and Development at Madison Manufacturing Company requested a copy of our report on chemical tolerances.

WORD DIVISION GUIDE. A divided word is harder to read than a word printed as a single unit. However, some formats require the division of words for a correct right margin. In most situations, the transcriptionist accepts the word-division decisions made by word processing programs. If word division decisions need to be made, follow these guidelines.

1. Always carry at least three keystrokes over to the next line.

2. Avoid dividing words of five letters or fewer. (You must have at least three keystrokes on each line. Some references allow one of these to be a punctuation mark.)

3. Divide only between syllables. If you are unsure of the syllabication, use a dictionary.

4. Avoid dividing a word at the end of the first line or last full line of a paragraph.

5. Do not divide a word at the end of the last line of a page.

6. Avoid dividing words at the end of more than two consecutive lines.

7. Do not divide one-syllable words.

8. Do not divide abbreviations.

   Examples: f.o.b. UMWA UNICEF

9. Do not divide contractions.

   Examples: doesn't o'clock wouldn't

10. Do not divide a one-letter syllable at the beginning or end of a word.

    Wrong: . . . a- . . . bacteri-

    mount a

11. Do not divide a two-letter syllable at the end of a word. Since a hyphen is required, only one space would be saved. At least three keystrokes should be carried over to the next line. (Some references allow you to count a punctuation mark as one of the three strokes.)

    Wrong: . . . apparent- . . . accura-

    ly cy

12. If possible, avoid dividing a two-letter syllable at the beginning of a word. (See also Rule 18.)

    Wrong: . . . be- . . . in-

    ginning troduce

13. Divide hyphenated words at the hyphen only.

    Examples: . . . self- . . . sister-

    control in-law

14. Divide a solid compound word between the elements of the compound.

    Examples: . . . business- . . . home-

    person owner

15. Divide after single-letter syllables.

    Examples: . . . para-

    lyze

. . . regu-

late

. . . sepa-

rate

16. Divide between two single-letter syllables.

Examples: . . . concili-

ation

. . . evalu-

ation

17. If possible, divide after the prefix.

Examples: . . . circum-

navigate

. . . super-

structure

18. Avoid word divisions that will be confusing to the reader.

Wrong:	. . . inter-	**Better:**	. . . in-
	pret		terpret
Wrong:	. . . read-	**Better:**	. . . re-
	just		adjust

19. Divide between the suffix and the root word. If the final consonant is doubled before adding a suffix, divide between the double letters. If the root word ends in a double letter, divide after the double letters.

Examples: . . . begin-

ning

. . . occur-

ring

. . . progress-

ing

. . . recall-

ing

20. Avoid dividing in the middle of word endings such as *able, ible,* and *ical.*

Correct:	. . . reach-	. . . vis-
	able	ible
Wrong:	. . . logi-	
	cal	

21. Avoid dividing proper names. If necessary, divide the name before the surname.

Examples: . . . Angela C. Mitchell   . . . Mr. Loyd V. Jacobs

22. Avoid dividing dates. If necessary, divide between the day and the year.

Example: . . . June 26,
2002

23. Avoid dividing numbers. When absolutely necessary, divide a long number after a comma. (Divided numbers are very difficult to read.)

Example: . . . 395,890,-
123,746

24. Avoid dividing street addresses. If necessary, divide a street address between the street name and the word *Street, Avenue,* or similar designation.

Example: . . . 414 Walnut
Street

25. Avoid dividing names of places. If necessary, divide between the city and the state or between the state and the ZIP Code. (Dividing at the comma is preferred.)

Examples: . . . Chicago,
Illinois 60606   . . . Chicago, Illinois
60606

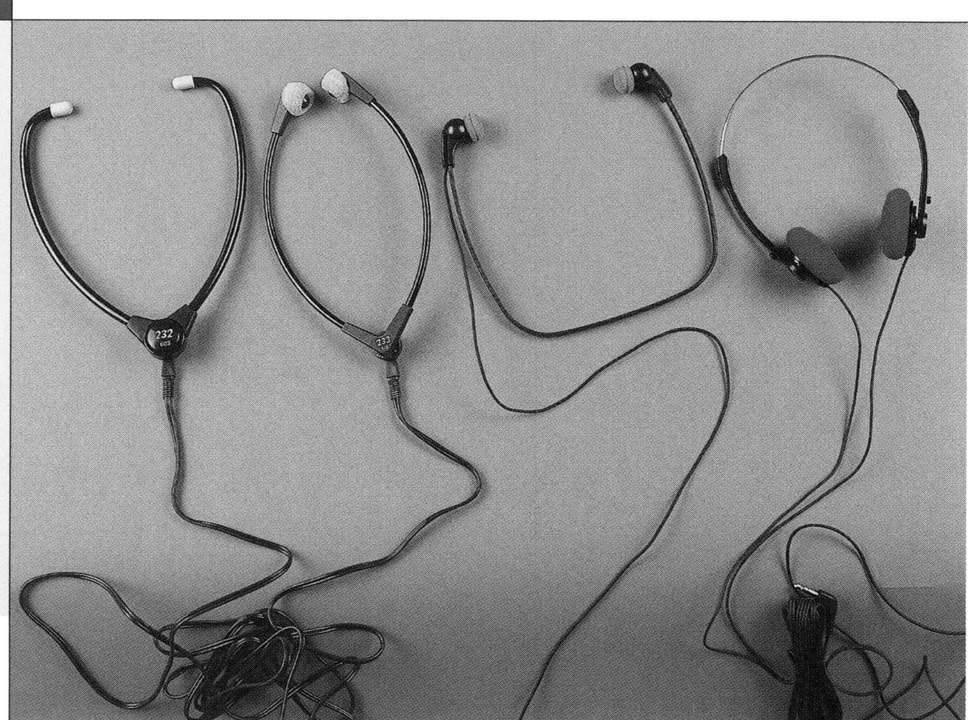

Figure 5.2
Various types of ear phones. (Phillips)

26. Divide an itemized list before any number or letter.

Example: . . . these items: (1) . . ., (2) . . .

Wrong: . . . these items: (1) . . ., (2) . . .

Assignments

Complete the Punctuation, Word Study, Proofreading, and Word Division Exercises that are located on pages 115–120 at the end of this section.The purpose of these exercises is to assist you with the transcription assignment. Tear the completed exercises out of the textbook, and give them to your instructor before you take Spelling Test 5 and before you transcribe the dictation for this section.

SPELLING TEST 5

Ask your instructor for Spelling Test 5. Complete this test before you transcribe the dictation for Section 5.

SECTION 5 DICTATION

Transcribe all of the outgoing letters in modified-block style with open punctuation and indented paragraphs. Refer to the Reference Handbook for sample letter styles. Be sure to check your transcripts for mailability using the checklist in Section 1.

Use the following letterheads when you transcribe the letters:

1. Madison Insurance Company
2. No letterhead provided—e-mail
3. Association of Office Managers
4. Cambell & Company
5. No letterhead provided—e-mail

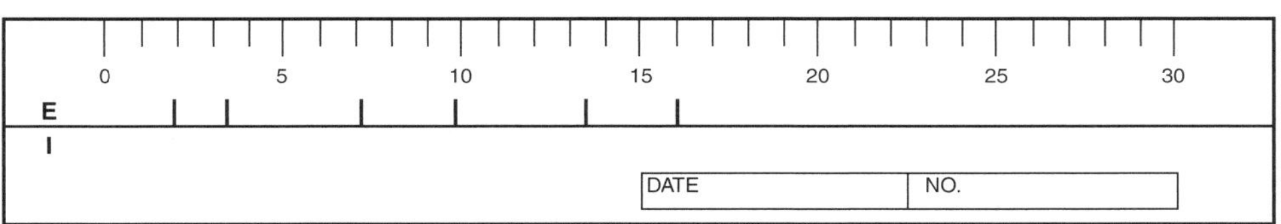

WORD STUDY TEST 2

Ask your instructor for Word Study Test 2. This test covers the word study information contained in Sections 3 through 5. The Word Study Review Summary in the Appendix will help you prepare for this test. Complete this test after you transcribe Section 5's dictation. The following is a list of words you should study before you take the test:

NOTE:
Review the Word Study portions of Sections 3 through 5 before you take this test. It is much easier to understand a word in context than to match a word with its definition.

accept	currant	passed
ad	current	past
add	device	stationary
addition	devise	stationery
advice	edition	waive
advise	except	waiver
appraise	miner	wave
apprise	minor	waver
complement	overdo	you're
compliment	overdue	your

PRACTICE TRANSCRIPTION TEST

This test is optional. If you decide to take the Practice Transcription Test, ask your instructor for the test. It contains items you have previously transcribed. You will transcribe for 15 minutes. Use a spelling checker or a dictionary to look up any words you do not know how to spell.

Relax! This one does not count as a grade. Do your best. Work on any problem areas before the next transcription test.

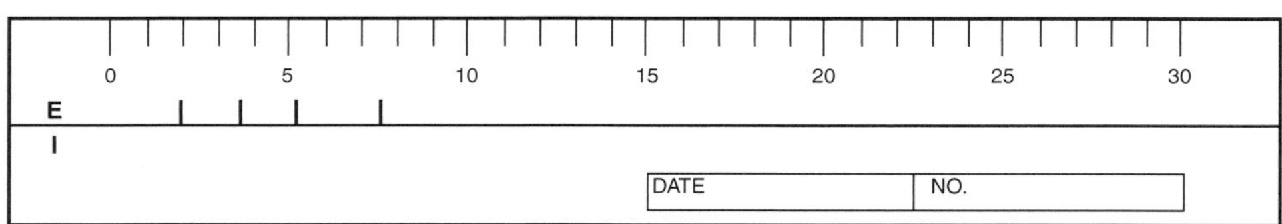

Name/Class ____________________

Section 5 Exercises

When completed, tear these exercises out of the textbook and give them to your instructor.

Punctuation Exercises—Appositives

DIRECTIONS: ***Insert the proper punctuation where needed in the following sentences.***

PART 1

1. The retirement dinner for Andrew Jacobs vice president of sales will be held at the Adams Mark on Friday October 30.
2. The Starlight Inn the site of our convention will provide free transportation to and from the airport.
3. The deadline for our report is Thursday June 26.
4. The general manager of the ABC Production Plant our most efficient plant will share the new methods they use with the general managers of our other plants at the meeting on Wednesday June 5.
5. The Bicentennial Celebration the biggest event of the year will last a full week.
6. Angie Miller the receptionist will direct you to my office when you arrive.
7. The deposition will be taken on Friday June 10.
8. Angela was born on Thursday June 26.
9. His first book *The Strongest Will* will be published in March.
10. Mrs. Janice Perry president of Smith Distributing Company will deliver the commencement address.
11. The committee will meet in the Conference Room Room 230.
12. Mrs. Gomez the company president will arrive for a visit on June 5.
13. Mason & Hall my employer will market a new product for your area soon.
14. Please send me a copy of your booklet *Redecorating Made Easy* as advertised in the April issue of *Homemaker's Monthly*.
15. Your flight Midwest Airlines 749 will leave the Marion Airport at 2:30 p.m. on Friday September 14.

PART 2

1. Did you see *Sarah Jane* a movie about a young girl who is on her own for the first time?
2. On Friday August 9 Ms. Carson has an appointment at 2:30 p.m. with Mr. Hines general manager of Hines Advertising Agency.

3. Ralph Smith zoning administrator issued the building permit.
4. My interview is with Mrs. Carol Davis manager of the division.
5. Mr. James Gibson a well known author will be our guest speaker.
6. We sent you a check on Friday July 10 for $1500 the amount of the original bill.
7. Hilda Carver our attorney is preparing a new will for us.
8. The antique car a Maxwell was still in running condition.
9. Martin Reed an aerobatic pilot will perform as part of the celebration.
10. We will meet at Crawford's the new department store in the mall.
11. We awarded the contract to renovate the Grand the theater on Pine Street.
12. Mrs. Lamas took the Chou presentation the committee's favorite to the meeting.
13. Angie took two classes computer applications and keyboarding.
14. This is Bob Martin my assistant.
15. The board meeting is scheduled for Friday April 23.

Word Study Exercises

DIRECTIONS: ***Highlight or underline the correct word choice in each of the following sentences.***

PART 1

1. My (advice, advise) (to, too, two) you is (to, too, two) do (your, you're) best on every job (your, you're) assigned.
2. The committee is asking for (your, you're) (advice, advise) regarding the best (stationary, stationery) (to, too, two) use for the (ad, add) mailing on November 9.
3. (Your, You're) committee assignment is (to, too, two) (device, devise) a new brochure that will (complement, compliment) the new (ad, add) campaign.
4. The fact that the committee unanimously (passed, past) the motion (to, too, two) (accept, except) the (advice, advise) of the consultant without any changes was a (complement, compliment) (to, too, two) the thoroughness of the report.
5. The attached questionnaire will be (passed, past) out (to, too, two) all (personal, personnel) at (their, there, they're) next department meetings.
6. Bob learned about the job through an (ad, add) in the newspaper.
7. We will (ad, add) this purchase (to, too, two) (your, you're) account.

Name/Class ____

8. (Your, You're) (advice, advise) (to, too, two) buy the (to, too, two) stocks proved (to, too, two) be correct.

9. I understand that (your, you're) going to (advice, advise) Loyd when you are finished.

10. The (to, too, two) pillows (complement, compliment) the couch.

11. (Your, You're) going to receive many (complements, compliments) on (your, you're) work.

12. This (device, devise) is used to collate paper.

13. Leroy will (device, devise) a way to make it work.

14. Jane (passed, past) out the paper.

15. We have been studying the Constitution for the (passed, past) (to, too, two) days.

PART 2

1. There have been many wars in the (past, passed).

2. The bench in the garden is (stationary, stationery).

3. The new employee is wasting (to, too, two) much (stationary, stationery).

4. Lisa sent application letters in reply to three employment (ads, adds).

5. When you reconcile (your, you're) bank statement, you must (ad, add) any deposits made after the statement date.

6. The salesperson's (advice, advise) was (to, too, two) purchase a (device, devise) for opening the mail automatically.

7. Our position on that matter will remain (stationary, stationery).

8. John will (device, devise) a new marketing plan for the product.

9. The color of the new drapes in the conference room (complements, compliments) the color of the material in the chairs.

10. Our attorneys will (advice, advise) us concerning which alternative is the better of the (to, too, two).

11. Our committee has met three times in the (past, passed).

12. We have received many (complements, compliments) on our new (stationary, stationery).

13. We must (ad, add) (to, too, two) more employees to (complement, compliment) the (personal, personnel) in the new office.

14. The new (stationary, stationery) bicycle will (complement, compliment) the other equipment in the workout center.

15. Paula (passed, past) the new (Personal, Personnel) Department offices on the way (to, too, two) the meeting.

EXERCISE

Name/Class ____________________

Proofreading Exercise 5

DIRECTIONS: ***Use proofreaders' marks to correct the following memorandum. A list of proofreaders' marks is in the Reference Handbook at the back of the textbook.***

MEMO TO: Brent Bullock

FROM: Alan Trescott

DATE: (current date)

SUBJECT: Letterhead

Our letterhead design needs to be updated, and we need to add our e-mail address. As a result, I have requested that the Art Department design a new letterhead. They have submited five possible designs for our new stationary. In the passed, we have relied on an outside agency to design our stationary.

Please advice me which design you think best projects the image we want to convey. We need to make a final dicision before our meeting with the design staff on Monday June 5.

xxx

EXERCISE Name/Class ______________________________

Word Division Exercise

DIRECTIONS: ***In the following exercises some words may be divided and some should not be divided. The words have been syllabicated for you. For the words that may be divided, draw a diagonal between the syllables in the syllabicated word to indicate the best place to divide. Use the Word Division Guide to assist you in completing the exercise. In the answer lines at the left, write the number of the rule that explains why the word is divided as you have it or why the word should not be divided.***

__________ **1.** around—a round

__________ **2.** strongly—strong ly

__________ **3.** strength—strength

__________ **4.** wheelbarrow—wheel bar row

__________ **5.** referring—re fer ring

__________ **6.** dairy—dair y

__________ **7.** geometry—ge om e try

__________ **8.** supervision—su per vi sion

__________ **9.** compatible—com pat i ble

__________ **10.** height—height

__________ **11.** positive—pos i tive

__________ **12.** couldn't—could n't

__________ **13.** omitting—o mit ting

__________ **14.** graduation—grad u a tion

__________ **15.** strenuous—stren u ous

__________ **16.** confessing—con fess ing

__________ **17.** thought—thought

__________ **18.** self-entertaining—self — en ter tain ing

__________ **19.** consecutive—con sec u tive

__________ **20.** economical—e co nom i cal

__________ **21.** permitted—per mit ted

__________ **22.** usually—u su al ly

__________ **23.** continuation—con tin u a tion

__________ **24.** YMCA—Y M C A

__________ **25.** 308 Monticello Drive—308 Mon ti cel lo Drive

EXERCISE Name/Class ____________________

______ **26.** expendable—ex pend a ble

______ **27.** submitting—sub mit ting

______ **28.** international—in ter na tion al

______ **29.** manageable—man age a ble

______ **30.** October 30, 1997—Oc to ber 30, 1997

______ **31.** reallocation—re al lo ca tion

______ **32.** trapezoid—trap e zoid

______ **33.** expelling—ex pel ling

______ **34.** hideous—hid e ous

______ **35.** humiliation—hu mil i a tion

______ **36.** Carbondale, Illinois 62901—Car bon dale, Il li nois 62901

______ **37.** dominate—dom i nate

______ **38.** negative—neg a tive

______ **39.** anticipate—an tic i pate

______ **40.** #3251—# 3 2 5 1

______ **41.** comical—com i cal

______ **42.** competitive—com pet i tive

______ **43.** Mrs. Alice K. Jacobs—Mrs. Al ice K. Ja cobs

______ **44.** expressing—ex press ing

______ **45.** situation—sit u a tion

______ **46.** congratulations—con grat u la tions

______ **47.** oxygen—ox y gen

______ **48.** forgetting—for get ting

______ **49.** circumstances—cir cum stances

______ **50.** handicap—hand i cap

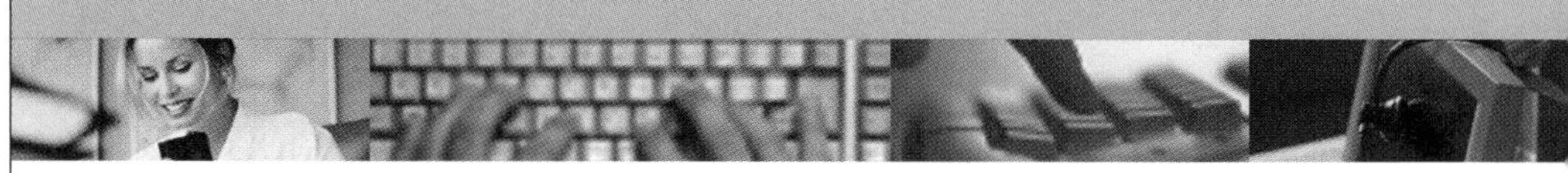

Section 6

6.1 OBJECTIVES

In Section 6, you will work toward the following objectives:

- Correctly complete Word Study Exercises and Proofreading Exercises in preparation for transcription.
- Complete Spelling Test 6 with at least 80 percent accuracy.
- Select the appropriate words and the correct spelling according to the context of the dictation when transcribing this section's documents.

6.2 WORD STUDY

The words listed here are frequently confused in transcription because they sound alike when dictated but have different meanings. Study the words carefully so that you will be able to select the appropriate word according to the context of the dictation.

NOTE:
Use ***whether***, not ***if***, to indicate which one of two. Did she indicate whether we made a profit or lost money?

air (noun) the atmosphere

The *air* is polluted around some industrial complexes.

heir (noun) a person who inherits property or a hereditary title

He is the sole *heir* to the Hamilton estate.

altar (noun) a raised structure that serves as a center for worship

They exchanged wedding vows at the *altar*.

alter (verb) to change; to modify

We must *alter* the plans.

weather (noun) the general condition of the atmosphere

The raincoat provided protection against the foul *weather*.

weather (verb) to endure exposure to the atmosphere

The siding will *weather* well.

whether (conjunction) used to introduce an indirect question with alternatives

Whether he arrives or not, I will be there.

6.3 SPELLING REVIEW

The dictation for this section contains the words listed here. Study them carefully to help you transcribe more rapidly. If you hear other words in the dictation that you do not know how to spell, make a list of those words and learn their correct spellings. This practice will help you improve your transcription speed.

adjourned	ceremony	emitting
advisers	compliance	evidence
altar	construction	excessive
alter	decide	execute
candidate	deteriorating	fortune

industrial	prospects	specific
instructions	qualifications	unanimously
municipal	recently	weather
observed	reception	whether
ordinance	scene	
pollution	scrubbers	

Assignments

Page 123

Complete the Word Study and Proofreading Exercises that are located on pages 123–126 at the end of this section. The purpose of these exercises is to assist you with the transcription assignment. Tear the completed exercises out of the textbook, and give them to your instructor before you take Spelling Test 6 and before you transcribe the dictation for this section.

SPELLING TEST 6

Ask your instructor for Spelling Test 6. Complete this test before you transcribe the dictation for Section 6.

SECTION 6 DICTATION

Go To... Recording for Section 6

The dictation recordings for Sections 6 through 18 and Section 20 contain dictated corrections. For example, the dictator will give you instructions by saying, "Operator, change Wednesday to Tuesday in the first paragraph." Review the corrections before you begin to transcribe.

Transcribe all of the outgoing letters in block style with open punctuation. Refer to the Reference Handbook for sample letter styles. Be sure to check your transcripts for mailability using the checklist in Section 1.

Use the following letterheads when you transcribe:

1. Municipal Pollution Control Board
2. Boyd Studio
3. Allan Kraft
4. Walter Rains
5. No letterhead provided—minutes

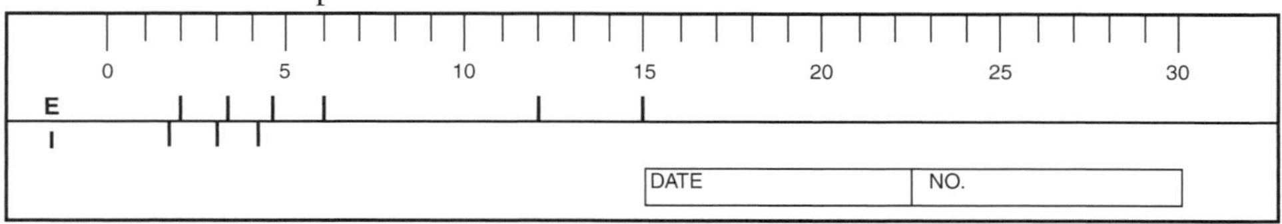

ALWAYS LISTEN TO MARKED INSTRUCTIONS FIRST!

Name/Class ____________________

Section 6 Exercises

When completed, tear these exercises out of the textbook and give them to your instructor.

Word Study Exercises

DIRECTIONS: ***Highlight or underline the correct word choice in each of the following sentences.***

1. She is one of (to, too, two) (airs, heirs) (to, too, two) the Land estate.
2. We must (altar, alter) the location because the (weather, whether) report predicts rain.
3. The bride and groom stood at the (altar, alter).
4. The dust in the (air, heir) has been reduced by our new electronic (air, heir) filter.
5. The Research Department must determine (weather, whether) or not the pollution in the (air, heir) is responsible for the failure of the paint to (weather, whether) well.
6. The city officials are very concerned about the increase in (air, heir) pollution during the last month.
7. Please (altar, alter) my will (to, too, two) include my (to, too, two) new (airs, heirs) who were born last month.
8. We must (altar, alter) our marketing plans (to, too, two) include the new chopping (device, devise).
9. The new (air, heir) filtration system will be installed in the mine next week.
10. If the (weather, whether) does not cooperate, we will have to (altar, alter) our plans for a reception in the open (air, heir).
11. The parishioners lined up to kneel at the (altar, alter).
12. We must (altar, alter) this dress as the buyer requested.
13. You will need an umbrella in this (weather, whether).
14. The shingles will (weather, whether) well.
15. We need to know (weather, whether) you will be at the meeting or not.
16. Frank was the only (air, heir) (to, too, two) the estate.
17. Let me know (weather, whether) you want (to, too, two) (altar, alter) the will as we discussed yesterday.
18. The (weather, whether) has been unusually cold this month.
19. Roof sample No. 25 is cheaper, but it will not (weather, whether) as well as sample No. 48.
20. (Weather, Whether) Jane goes or not, I will be there.

Name/Class____________________

Proofreading Exercise 6-A

DIRECTIONS: ***Use proofreaders' marks to correct the following letter. A list of proofreaders' marks is in the Reference Handbook at the back of the textbook.***

(current date)

Mr. J. P. Wynns
1155 East Sixth Street
Ashland, OK 74524

Dear Mr. Wynns:

Thank you very much for requesting information about Victor Automatic Garage Door Opener Systems. Enclosed is a copy of our brochure that illustrates our currant line of garage door openers.

For farther information concerning prices service and installation contact our dealer James Carson 1997 Main Street Askland Oklahoma.

Once again, thank you for you interest in Victor. If we can be of farther asistence to you please feel free to contact us.

Sincerely yours,

VICTOR MANUFACTURING

COMPANY

Georgia Calvin
Assistant Sales Manager
Consumer Division

xxx
Enclosure
c: James Carson

Name/Class ______________________________

Proofreading Exercise 6-B

DIRECTIONS: ***Use proofreaders' marks to correct the following letter. A list of proofreaders' marks is in the Reference Handbook at the back of the textbook.***

(current date)

Mrs. Wilma VanHorn
4013 North Hayden Road
Rosemont, IL 60018

Dear Mrs. Vanhorn

Thank you for inquiring about Madison's new Art Deco collection.
Enclosed is the folder you requested.

The folder illustrates a totaly new idea in decorating with coordinated hardware. You will see items form the Art Deco collection used in each room. The Art Deco collection is of the same carefull design and handcrafted quality that have made Madison the leader in fine decorative hardware. You will find that the outdoor hardware whethers very well.

In edition to the folder you requested the enclosed booklet will give you some idea of the scope of decorative hardware items available in our collections of coordinated hardware for the home. In case you altar your decorating plans you may want to consider decorative hardware items from the Old English, Colonal, Mediterranean, and French Provincial collections.

We have included a shoping list to make your hardware buying easy. Check the items you want before you visit you Madison dealer. Peter T. McClaron is the Madison Hardware dealer nearest you. McClaron Hardware Supply is located at 115 East Main in Rosemont.

Cordialy yours

MADISON HARDWARE CORPORATION

Gary L. Perfetti
Sales Promotion

xxx
Enclosures - 3

Name/Class ____________________

Proofreading Exercise 6-C

DIRECTIONS: ***Use proofreaders' marks to correct the following letter. A list of proofreaders' marks is in the Reference Handbook at the back of the textbook.***

(current date)

Ute City Balloon Company
No. 32 Sardy Field
Aspen, CO 81611

Ladies and Gentleman

We would like to make a reservation for 10 people to take a hot air balloon ride on Saturday October 30. Do you have a balloon big enough to accomodate ten people, or will we have to take two balloons?

What arrangements do you have for rescheduling the reservations if the whether is prohibitive?

If you cannot accommodate us on October 30 please let us knew so that we can altar our plans.

Sincerely

Michael Warner

xxx

Section 7

7.1 OBJECTIVES

In Section 7, you will work toward the following objectives:

- Correctly insert commas where appropriate in compound sentences.
- Correctly complete Punctuation Exercises, Word Study Exercises, and Proofreading Exercises in preparation for transcription.
- Complete Spelling Test 7 with at least 80 percent accuracy.
- Select the appropriate words and the correct spelling according to the context of the dictation when transcribing this section's documents.

7.2 PUNCTUATION REVIEW

A compound sentence contains two or more independent clauses connected by a coordinating conjunction (*and, but, for, nor,* or *or*). Use a comma before the coordinating conjunction in a compound sentence.

Example: The human resources manager interviewed four applicants for the job, but she hired only one.

Be sure not to confuse compound sentences with sentences that have only compound predicates. Do not use a comma before the conjunction if the sentence contains only a compound predicate.

Example: The human resources manager interviewed four applicants for the job but hired only one.

If you are unsure, look for the subject and verb in each clause before inserting the comma. If there is only one subject for both verbs, do not use a comma. If each verb has its own subject, use a comma before the conjunction.

If both independent clauses are imperative, insert a comma before the conjunction.

Example: Give the report to me on Friday, and give copies of the report to Mr. Martin and Mrs. Fuji.

7.3 WORD STUDY

You may not have realized that there are so many words that sound alike but have different meanings and are spelled differently. Distinguishing among them quickly is critical to developing good transcription skills.

The words listed here are frequently confused in transcription because they sound alike when dictated but have different meanings. Study each of the words carefully so that you will be able to select the appropriate word according to the context of the dictation.

accede (verb) to agree to; to give in

I will *accede* to your request.

exceed (verb) to go beyond; to be greater than

The cost will not *exceed* $100.

affect (verb) to influence

The information did not *affect* her decision.

effect (noun) a result; an outcome

What *effect* did the medicine have on your cold?

effect (verb) to bring about; to cause to happen; to accomplish

Prompt payment will *effect* a change in the status of your account.

consul (noun) an official in a foreign country appointed to look after his or her country's citizens and businesses

Send my mail in care of the American *Consul* in Paris.

council (noun) an advisory group

The town *council* will meet to vote on the mayor's proposal.

counsel (noun) advice; a lawyer who gives advice

I will seek *counsel* from my attorney concerning this matter.

He sought advice from *counsel* before talking with the police.

counsel (verb) to give advice to; to advise

The attorney will *counsel* you regarding your rights.

deposition (noun) a written statement made under oath by a witness

The *deposition* of the defendant will be taken at 1:30 p.m. on Friday.

disposition (noun) a proper arrangement; the power or authority to arrange, settle, or manage; temperament, natural attitude toward things

They agreed on the final *disposition* of the matter.

She has a pleasant *disposition*.

leased (verb) rented

The apartment was *leased* for three years.

least (adjective) smallest in size, degree, or importance

That was the *least* amount of work he could do under the circumstances.

principal (noun) an amount of money borrowed or invested in stocks or bonds on which interest is paid; the head of a school

John earned 12 percent on the *principal*.

The *principal* at Sally's school also taught an English class.

principal (adjective) main; first in importance

His *principal* income came from his job as a letter carrier.

principle (noun) a rule of action; a law of conduct; a fundamental truth

They studied the *principle* of democracy in their government class.

verses (noun) lines of a poem or song; short divisions of a chapter in the Bible

They sang all three *verses* of the song.

The sermon was based on the first four *verses* of Psalm 99.

versus (preposition) against; in contrast with

Battling the flood made the rescuers feel it was the town *versus* nature.

7.4 SPELLING REVIEW

The dictation for this section contains the words listed here. Study them carefully to help you transcribe more rapidly. If you hear other words in the dictation that you do not know how to spell, make a list of those words and learn their correct spellings. This practice will help you improve your transcription speed.

accede	disposition	least
accessories	docket	Louisiana
applicable	effectively	lounges
assume	emergency	miracle
attached	exceed	paid
authority	excursions	plaintiff
client	expectations	possibility
consul	extremely	principal
council	Guadalupe	principle
counsel	hemp	pyramids
defendant	instructor	sponsor
deposition	itinerary	techniques
discontinue	leased	

ASSIGNMENTS

Page 131

Complete the Punctuation, Word Study, and Proofreading Exercises that are located on pages 131–136 at the end of this section. The purpose of these exercises is to assist you with the transcription assignment. Tear the completed exercises out of the textbook, and give them to your instructor before you take Spelling Test 7 and before you transcribe the dictation for this section.

SPELLING TEST 7

Ask your instructor for Spelling Test 7. Complete this test before you transcribe the dictation for this section.

SECTION 7 DICTATION

This recording contains dictated corrections. Be sure to review the corrections before you begin to transcribe.

Transcribe all of the outgoing letters in modified block style with mixed

punctuation and blocked paragraphs. Refer to the Reference Handbook for sample letter styles. Be sure to check your transcripts for mailability by using the checklist in Section 1.

Use the following letterheads when you transcribe:

1. Interoffice Memo 1
2. Rogers Video Theater
3. Holden & Holden
4. Kocher & Kocher
5. No letterhead provided—e-mail message

You will use the following computer printout when you transcribe the first item:

WIDGET SALES

(Figures show units sold.)

Division	Widget Accessories	Widget 274B	Widget 565C	Digital Widget DW1
Central	143,949	100,209	234,101	334,212
Northern	145,037	92,105	197,947	297,849
Northwest	101,324	94,113	205,778	300,123
Pacific	124,645	89,203	198,345	305,229
South Central	99,784	99,887	212,111	221,237
Southeast	100,712	121,123	206,949	275,495
Southwest	50,275	79,266	89,791	87,465
Western	100,948	100,123	245,478	325,695

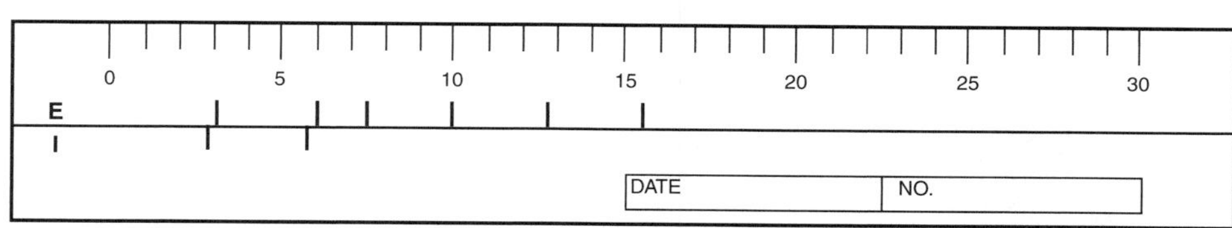

Name/Class____

Section 7 Exercises

When completed, tear these exercises out of the textbook and give them to your instructor.

Punctuation Exercises—Compound Sentences

DIRECTIONS: ***Insert the proper punctuation where needed in the following sentences.***

PART 1

1. The site of the new building has been purchased and construction will begin on June 1.
2. The payroll checks are ready and are being distributed this morning.
3. The employees will be pleased with the new proposal but the new procedure needs to be explained thoroughly.
4. Angela did well on her transcription test and will receive an A.
5. The depositions are scheduled to begin at 1 p.m. but the defendant has not yet arrived.
6. The vacation schedule must be completed by March 1 and the requirements for part-time employees must be calculated by March 15.
7. The main office on Jefferson Street will close on April 29 and it will reopen on May 1 in the new building at 141 Morgan Plaza.
8. The showroom will open at 9 a.m. but the service department will open at 8 a.m.
9. Susan was a conscientious student and I can recommend her for the job without reservation.
10. We will mail the finished report to you or you may pick it up Friday afternoon.
11. The main office on Jefferson Street will close on April 29 and will reopen on May 1 in the new building at 141 Morgan Plaza.
12. We are now revising our catalog and we will send you a copy as soon as it is printed.
13. I will meet you at the airport or I will send someone else to meet you and take you to your hotel.
14. There is no point in your returning to help with this project but we will need your help on Thursday on the Willis project.
15. Doctor Smith examined the patient and told him he could leave the hospital on Tuesday.

PART 2

1. The new office building will be completed on April 2 and we will move in on April 3.
2. You may look for another job or you may wish to investigate the possibility of promotion within your present firm.
3. I have not answered the letter from Mr. James but I will answer it as soon as I receive the information that I requested from the Marketing Division.
4. We called the credit office and received the information necessary to complete the application.

Name/Class ____________

5. The union members voted to accept the contract and the plant will reopen tomorrow.
6. They had looked forward to their vacation for three months and they were not disappointed.
7. We will have to rent additional space for expansion or we will have to build a new building.
8. We can hire one additional full time employee for the summer or we can hire the Miller Personnel Service to provide replacements for employees who are on vacation.
9. Mr. Watson ordered a phone for his car and it will be installed on Tuesday.
10. It will be necessary for you to complete a credit information sheet and send it to my attention before we can process your order.
11. James received a bank statement but he could not reconcile it with his records.
12. We have written you three letters requesting payment but you have not answered any of them.
13. The new advertising campaign will commence on October 1 and we will be able to determine its effectiveness by December 1.
14. It normally takes two months to process these loans but we may be able to cut the red tape under these circumstances.
15. We have received the financial analysis from the Accounting Department and we will make the final decision at the meeting next Thursday.
16. Our plane was delayed for mechanical reasons and we missed our connecting flight.
17. The sheets we received were the wrong size and we have returned them to the department store for credit to our account.
18. The jurors deliberated for two hours and they returned a verdict for the plaintiff.
19. Julie attended a seminar concerning new equipment for the office and she received some very helpful information.
20. The car needs a new transmission and needs a new set of tires.

Word Study Exercises

DIRECTIONS: *Highlight or underline the correct word choice in each of the following sentences.*

PART 1

1. The composer wrote three (verses, versus) to the song.
2. List the advantages and disadvantages of Proposal 29 (verses, versus) Proposal 35.
3. James read ten (verses, versus) in the Bible every day.
4. The basketball game at 7 p.m. will be the Volunteers (verses, versus) the Patriots.
5. The lawyer told his client he had a strong case (verses, versus) the absentee property owner.
6. The defense decided to (accede, exceed) to the plaintiff's demand.
7. The settlement will (accede, exceed) $75,000.

 Name/Class

8. (Your, You're) decision will (affect, effect) the outcome of the meeting.
9. What (affect, effect) did John's decision have on you?
10. We can (affect, effect) a change in the computer program by entering this information.
11. What is the address of the American (Consul, Council, Counsel) in Mexico City?
12. The change in the program was recommended by our Advisory (Consul, Council, Counsel).
13. You should seek (consul, council, counsel) from an attorney before signing the agreement.
14. (Your, You're) attorney will (consul, council, counsel) you about protecting (your, you're) interest in the business.
15. The doctor's (deposition, disposition) is scheduled for 3 p.m., but he will be late.

PART 2

1. The (deposition, disposition) of the problem took longer than we anticipated.
2. The warehouse has not been (leased, least) for three months.
3. Of the three projects we are working on, this one will require the (leased, least) amount of work.
4. The (principal, principle) of Central High School announced the names of the scholarship winners.
5. The (principal, principle) and interest are due on August 9.
6. Our (principal, principle) objective is to manufacture a quality product.
7. The scientist explained the (principal, principle) involved.
8. If the other side will (accede, exceed) to our request for an additional $5000, we will be able to (affect, effect) a settlement.
9. Our attorney will (consul, council, counsel) you regarding what (affect, effect) your action will have on the outcome of the lawsuit.
10. This information will (affect, effect) my actions in the future.
11. The members of the Budget (Consul, Council, Counsel) will not allow our expenditures to (accede, exceed) the approved amount.
12. We contacted the Italian (Consul, Council, Counsel) about immunization requirements.
13. The Grievance (Consul, Council, Counsel) will handle the (deposition, disposition) of the problem.
14. The Grievance (Consul, Council, Counsel) will meet with (consul, council, counsel) to discuss the legal ramifications of the alternative solutions.
15. I will seek (consul, council, counsel) from my attorney concerning the upcoming (deposition, disposition).
16. The (principal, principle) explained the (principals, principles) to be followed by the group while working on the project.
17. Alternative 3 is the (leased, least) desirable of all those available to us.
18. We made an extra payment on the (principal, principle) this month.
19. We (leased, least) an additional 6000 square feet of office space.
20. Please schedule the (deposition, disposition) of Dr. Jane Morgan.

EXERCISE

Name/Class____

Proofreading Exercise 7-A

DIRECTIONS: ***Use proofreaders' marks to correct the following letter. A list of proofreaders' marks is in the Reference Handbook at the back of the textbook.***

July 9, 20__

Mrs. Carol Jacobs
Attorney at Law
1528 East Oak Street
Bridgeport, IL 62417

Dear Mrs. Jacobs:

The discovery deposition of R. J. Harris is scheduated to be taken on August 9 at the Lawrence County Courthouse in room 7. Would you be able to appear for me, and take this testimony? I have a conflicting jury trail on that date. The council for the defense is John Reese and the court reporter will be Beth Redman.

The settlement offers made thus far have been insufficient to affect a settlement of the case. Hopefully we will be able to make a rapid deposition of the matter after this disposition.

Sincerely,

Elliott Crane

xxx

Name/Class ____________________

Proofreading Exercise 7-B

DIRECTIONS: ***Use proofreaders' marks to correct the following memorandum. A list of proofreaders' marks is in the Reference Handbook at the back of the textbook.***

MEMO TO: Executive Counsel Members

FROM: J. R. Minton, Chair

DATE: March 25, 20__

SUBJECT: Applications and Interviews

The Executive Counsel will meet on Thrusday to review the applications we have received for the postions of sceince instructor and principle for the upcoming school year.

In order to be consistent and fair to all canidates, we must draw up a list of questions that we plan to ask each canidate for each position.

I understand that the number of applications we will be reviewing accedes 50. We will plan to interview at leased five people for each position. It we feel the applications are promising we may interview as many as ten for each position.

xxx

Name/Class______________________________

Proofreading Exercise 7-C

DIRECTIONS: ***Use proofreaders' marks to correct the following memorandum. A list of proofreaders' marks is in the Reference Handbook at the back of the textbook.***

MEMO TO: Eric Keaton

FROM: Adam Solinski

DATE: (current date)

SUBJECT: Management Council

The newly appointed Management Counsel will determine the principals to be followed in the acquisition of all new property purchases or leases. It will be there responsibility to make certain that the amounts paid for property acquisitions do not accede the limits set up be the Board of Directors.

The Search Committee will report directly to the Management Council. The Search Committee will submit a analysis of additional purchased space verses additional leased space. This report should be finished by the end of next week.

xxx

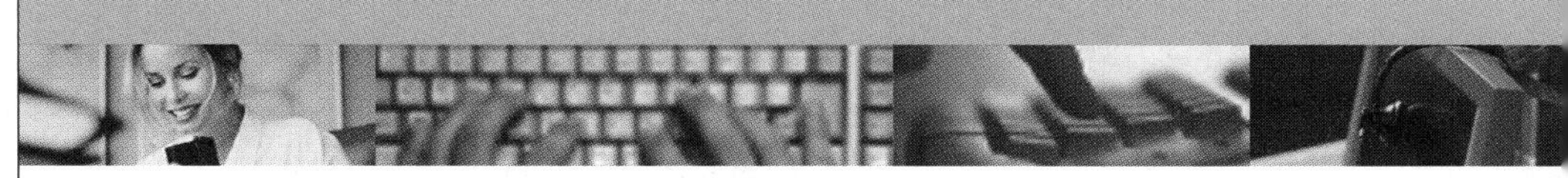

Section 8

8.1 OBJECTIVES

In Section 8, you will work toward the following objectives:

- Correctly complete Word Study Exercises and Proofreading Exercises in preparation for transcription.
- Complete Spelling Test 8 with at least 80 percent accuracy.
- Select the appropriate words and the correct spelling according to the context of the dictation when transcribing this section's documents.
- Complete Word Study Test 3 on the word study vocabulary in Sections 6, 7, and 8 with at least 80 percent accuracy.
- Complete Transcription Test 1.

8.2 WORD STUDY

The words listed here are frequently confused in transcription because they sound alike when dictated but have different meanings. Study the words carefully so that you will be able to select the appropriate word according to the context of the dictation.

biannual (adjective) twice a year

He makes *biannual* insurance premium payments.

biennial (adjective) every two years

Our *biennial* celebration will be held on August 8.

calendar (noun) a table that shows the months and days of the year

I will check my *calendar* to see whether I am free on that date.

calender (noun) a machine with rollers used to process paper or cloth

The paper finishing stopped when the *calender* broke down.

cent (noun) a penny; a unit of money equaling 1/100 of a dollar

The candy costs 1 *cent* at the school fair.

scent (noun) a smell; an odor

The perfume's *scent* was pleasant.

sent (verb) caused to go (past tense of send)

She *sent* the letter yesterday.

sense (noun) normal intelligence and judgment; an agreement with such intelligence and judgment; meaning

He is a person of good *sense*.

This solution makes *sense*.

Can you make any *sense* of the situation?

sense (verb) to become aware of

The dog could *sense* his fear.

employ (verb) to provide work for; to make use of

The new plant will *employ* 300 people.

employee (noun) a person hired by another

She has been an *employee* of the company for ten years.

8.3 SPELLING REVIEW

The dedication for this section contains the words listed here. Study them carefully to help you transcribe more rapidly. If you hear other words in the dictation that you do not know how to spell, make a list of those words and learn their correct spellings. This practice will help you improve your transcription speed.

NOTE:
This is a good time to review the punctuation rules you have been studying in preparation for the first transcription test that comes at the end of this section.

absenteeism
amendment
authorization
biannual
biennial
blossoms
brilliant
calendar
conscientious
convenience
costumes
decorations
delicate
disease
dissatisfied
electronic
emphasize
employ
employee
especially
excellent
foxglove
hybrid
identify
incomparable
occasionally
overlooked
promotion
quantity
souvenir
transmission
unconditionally
underwriters
widespread

ASSIGNMENTS

EXERCISE

Complete the Word Study and Proofreading Exercises that are located on pages 141–144 at the end of this section. The purpose of these exercises is to assist you with the transcription assignment. Tear the completed exercises out of the textbook, and give them to your instructor before you take Spelling Test 8 and before you transcribe the dictation for this section.

Page 141

SPELLING TEST 8

Ask your instructor for Spelling Test 8. Complete this test before you transcribe the dictation for Section 8.

Figure 8.1
Portable dictation units are used to record messages when traveling.
What do you think are the most important features of portable units?

SECTION 8 DICTATION

Recording for Section 8

Be sure to review the corrections before you begin to transcribe. Transcribe all of the outgoing letters in modified block style with open punctuation and indented paragraphs. Refer to the Reference Handbook for sample letter styles. Be sure to check your transcripts for mailability by using the checklist in Section 1.

Use the following letterheads when you transcribe:

1. Chamber of Commerce
2. Madison Insurance Company
3. Sunset Garden Center
4. Interoffice Memorandum 2
5. Fax cover sheet

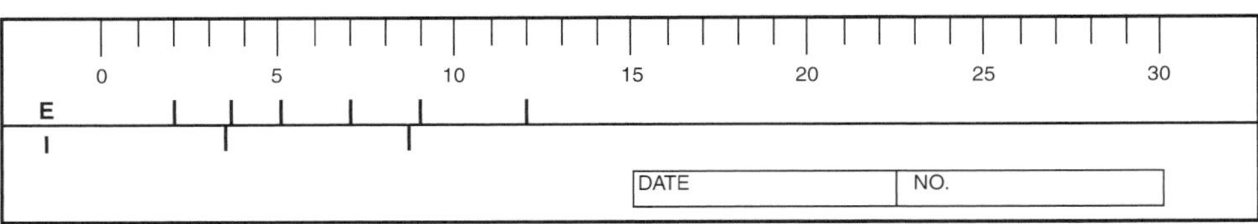

WORD STUDY TEST 3

Ask your instructor for Word Study Test 3. This test covers the word study information contained in Sections 6 through 8. The Word Study Review Summary in the Appendix will help you prepare for this test. Complete this test after you transcribe the dictation for Section 8. The following is a list of words that you should study before you take the test:

accede
affect
air
altar
alter
biannual
biennial
calendar
calender
cent
consul
council
counsel
deposition
disposition
effect
employ
employee
exceed
heir
leased
least
principal
principle
scent
sent
sense
verses
versus
weather
whether

TRANSCRIPTION TEST 1

Ask your instructor for Transcription Test 1. This test contains items you have previously transcribed. You will transcribe for 30 minutes. Use a spelling checker or a dictionary to look up any words you do not know how to spell. The first letter begins at 0 on the indication slip scale.

RELAX! There are no dictated corrections on this test. Just confidently apply what you have been learning, and you will do well. You can do this!

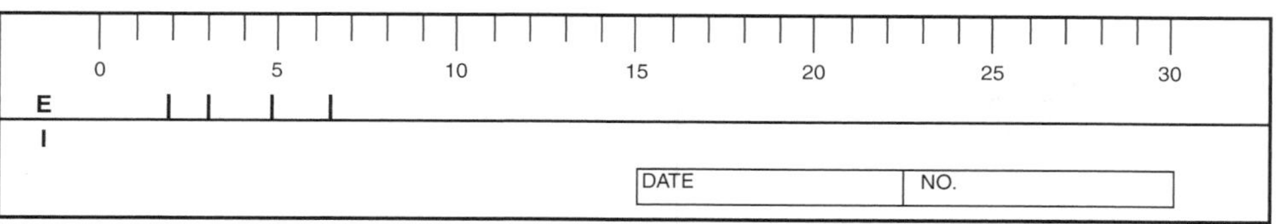

EXERCISE Name/Class ____________________

Section 8 Exercises

When completed, tear these exercises out of the textbook and give them to your instructor.

Word Study Exercises

DIRECTIONS: ***Highlight or underline the correct word choice in each of the following sentences.***

PART 1

1. Please mark (your, you're) (calendar, calender) so that the notice will be (cent, scent, sent) in a timely manner.
2. Postage will increase by (to, too, two) (cents, scents, sense) on January 1.
3. The wage schedule provides for (biannual, biennial) raises in July and December.
4. Please (employ, employee) (to, too, two) additional (employs, employees) for the Word Processing Center.
5. Proofread carefully; (your, you're) transcripts must make (cents, scents, sense).
6. Please (employ, employee) (to, too, two) temporary (employs, employees) (to, too, two) serve as replacements for vacationing (employs, employees) during the summer months.
7. We have purchased a new software program for maintaining our (calendar, calender).
8. Before the (biannual, biennial) report is (cent, scent, sent) in July, we need to compare it with the one we (cent, scent, sent) in December to be sure we are making (cents, scents, sense).
9. Your suggestion (to, too, two) (employ, employee) color-coded folders makes (cents, scents, sense) as a way of helping us identify information at a glance.
10. The (employ, employee) was injured while operating the (calendar, calender).
11. A (biannual, biennial) plant blooms twice a year.
12. A (biannual, biennial) celebration occurs once every two years.
13. Mark the date on (your, you're) (calendar, calender).
14. This machine is called a (calendar, calender).
15. The appointment (calendar, calender) costs 99 (cents, scents, sense).

PART 2

1. The (cent, scent, sent) of this perfume has made it a top seller.
2. Judy (cent, scent, sent) the letter by certified mail.
3. We could (cents, scents, sense) his excitement as soon as he entered the room.
4. John's answers didn't make any (cents, scents, sense).
5. We must (employ, employee) three more people.
6. Bob is one of our best (employs, employees).
7. A machine with rollers used to process paper or cloth is called a (calendar, calender).

Name/Class____

8. The pens cost 75 (cents, scents, sense) each.
9. The (employs, employees) in the Perfume Production Department were asked (to, too, two) choose the five (cents, scents, sense) they liked the best.
10. Yesterday we (cent, scent, sent) a memo (to, too, two) all (employs, employees) informing them that this year we will schedule the (biannual, biennial) sales for January and June.
11. Pansies are (biannual, biennial) flowering plants; therefore, they will bloom next year.
12. Since the hollyhocks you ordered are (biannuals, biennials), they will not produce blossoms until next year.
13. The (biannual, biennial) premium payment on the new (employ, employee) group insurance policy will be $175 for each (employ, employee), payable in January and July.
14. Please (employ, employee) some common (cents, scents, sense) when you are dealing with clients.
15. Mary (cent, scent, sent) a copy of the (calendar, calender) for the month with Sam when he went (to, too, two) court.

Proofreading Exercise 8-A

DIRECTIONS: ***Use proofreaders' marks to correct the following memorandum. A list of proofreaders' marks is in the Reference Handbook at the back of the textbook.***

MEMO TO: R. G. North, District Sales Manager

FROM: Angela Childers, President

DATE: March 30, 20__

SUBJECT: Biennial Sales Conferences

Our biennial sales conferences are scheduled for July 9, 10, and 11 in Chicago and January 15, 16, and 17 in Miami. Please mark these dates on your calender.

Since all sales employs are required to attend at leased one of the conferences you will need to make arrangements for approximately 50% of your sales employs to attend each conference. Please employee the attached chart when assigning personal to the conferences. A copy of this completed chart should be scent to this office before April 30.

If you have any questions or suggestions regarding the topics covered at these biennial sales conferences please let me know.

xxx
Attachment

Name/Class______________________________

Proofreading Exercise 8-B

DIRECTIONS: ***Use proofreaders' marks to correct the following memorandum. A list of proofreaders' marks is in the Reference Handbook at the back of the textbook.***

MEMO TO: All Divison Managers

FROM: Angela C. Jacobs, Personel Manager

DATE: March 25, 20__

SUBJECT: Biennial Training Seminars

Beginning in May and November, all our employs will be scent to biannual training seminars. The sessions will be repeated on too consecutive days so that all employees will be able to attend all the sesions. These seminars will be held in our conference center.

Please employee the attached calender to schedule attendence times. Please schedule half your employs on each day of the seminars. There must be someone covering the offices at all times.

These seminars should be profitable for both the employees and the firm. The speakers that we are scheduling are recognised experts in their fields.

We will provide a buffet lunch for all employs who attend the training seminars.

xxx
Attachment

Name/Class____

Proofreading Exercise 8-C

DIRECTIONS: ***Use proofreaders' marks to correct the following letter. A list of proofreaders' marks is in the Reference Handbook at the back of the textbook.***

(current date)

Mrs. Jessica Ling
8011 Oak Avenue
Rome, GA 30161

Dear Mrs. Ling

You will find a wide selection of clothing at our biennial clearance sale. Take advantage of our special discount on shirts. If you buy three you get one free.

This notice is being scent to our charge customers a week before the notice will be published for the general public to see. Just show this letter to one of our employs to receive the discount price before the general public receives notice of the sale on October 30.

Mark you calender today. Buying while you have the best selection makes good scents.

Sincerely

Austin Parks
Sales Manager

xxx

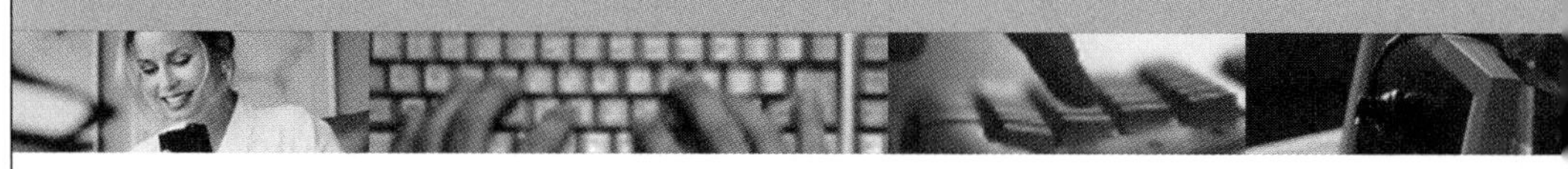

Section 9

9.1 OBJECTIVES

In Section 9, you will work toward the following objectives:

- Insert appropriate semicolons and commas in sentences containing conjunctive adverbs.
- Correctly format room numbers when transcribing the dictation for this section.
- Correctly complete Punctuation Exercises, Word Study Exercises, and Proofreading Exercises in preparation for transcription.
- Complete Spelling Test 9 with at least 80 percent accuracy.
- Select the appropriate words and the correct spelling according to the context of the dictation when transcribing this section's documents.

9.2 PUNCTUATION REVIEW

NOTE:
No comma is needed after ***hence, so, then, thus,*** and ***yet*** unless you want the reader to pause at that point.

The independent clauses in a compound sentence may be connected by a conjunctive adverb rather than by a coordinating conjunction. Use a semicolon before and a comma after the conjunctive adverb. The following are examples of conjunctive adverbs: *accordingly, consequently, furthermore, hence, however, moreover, nevertheless, otherwise,* and *therefore.*

Example: My car is in the garage; consequently, we will have to take your car to Chicago.

9.3 WORD STUDY

The words listed here are frequently confused in transcription because they sound alike when dictated but have different meanings. Study the words carefully so that you will be able to select the appropriate word according to the context of the dictation.

brake (noun) a device used to slow or stop the motion of a vehicle or machine
The accident was caused by a defective *brake* on the machine.

brake (verb) to slow down or to stop
He knew not to *brake* too hard on an icy road.

break (verb) to cause to come apart
The Board of Directors voted to *break* off the merger negotiations.

break (noun) a broken place; a separation; a crack
The Water Department repaired the *break* in the water line.

capital (adjective) chief; principal; main
Our *capital* concern was the completion of the project before the deadline.

capital (noun) money; a city or town that is the official seat of government of a state
Jennifer provided 51 percent of the *capital* to start the business.
Denver is the *capital* of Colorado.

capitol (noun) a statehouse; the building in which the state legislature meets

We will meet with State Representative Green at 8 a.m. at the *Capitol*.

precede (verb) to be, come, or go before

A coffee break will *precede* the final afternoon session.

proceed (verb) to advance or go on

We will *proceed* with negotiations as soon as Howard arrives.

9.4 SPELLING REVIEW

The dictation for this section contains the words listed here. Study them carefully to help you transcribe more rapidly. If you hear other words in the dictation that you do not know how to spell, make a list of those words and learn their correct spellings. This practice will help you improve your transcription speed.

abandoned
accessibility
accordingly
acoustical
associate
brake
break
capital
capitol
consequently
coordinate
describe
disruption
distributor
dramatic
economical
efficiency
erupting
evaluation
frequency
furthermore
geothermal
geysers
gondola
hospital
interrogatories
kangaroo
koala
leisure
luge
occurring
opinion
periodically
precede
proceed
renovation
routine
settlement
smorgasbord
specialty
sumptuous
traditional
updated

" DID YOU WANT A PERIOD AFTER THE WORD SEMI-COLON ? "

© Cartoon by Johns

9.5 TRANSCRIPTION GUIDELINES

All room numbers are expressed in digits. Do not use a comma in a room number.

Examples: The meeting will be held in Room 5.

The office is in Room 2003.

Figure 9.1

Dictation is used in many different work settings.

What types of information might the engineer pictured here record for transcription?

[Sanyo Fisher (USA) Corporation]

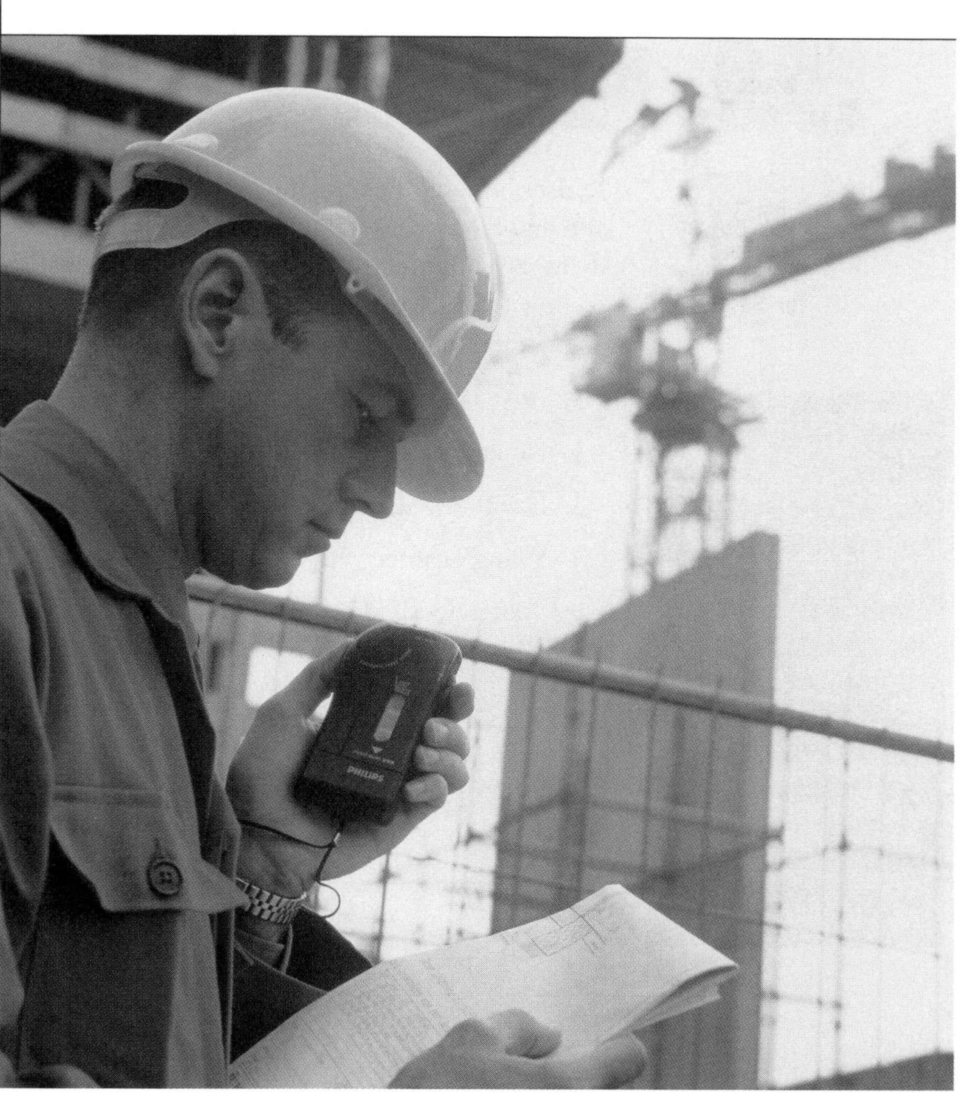

ASSIGNMENTS

Page 149

Complete the Punctuation, Word Study, and Proofreading Exercises that are located on pages 149–154 at the end of this section. The purpose of these exercises is to assist you with the transcription assignment. Tear the completed exercises out of the textbook, and give them to your instructor before you take Spelling Test 9 and before you transcribe the dictation for this section.

SPELLING TEST 9

Ask your instructor for Spelling Test 9. Complete this test before you transcribe the dictation for Section 9.

SECTION 9 DICTATION

Recording for Section 9

Transcribe all of the outgoing letters in modified-block style with open punctuation and blocked paragraphs. Refer to the Reference Handbook for sample letter styles. Be sure to check your transcripts for mailability by using the checklist in Section 1.

Use the following letterheads when you transcribe:

1. Adventure Tours
2. No letterhead provided—itinerary
3. Hawthorne Equipment, Inc.
4. Young & Price
5. Walter Todd, Mayor

Always be on the lookout for gender bias in the language of the documents you transcribe. It is easy for a dictator to concentrate so much on the content of the message that words containing gender bias slip in. Communicating Without Gender Bias in the Reference Handbook will help you identify such words and provide nongender-biased words to replace them.

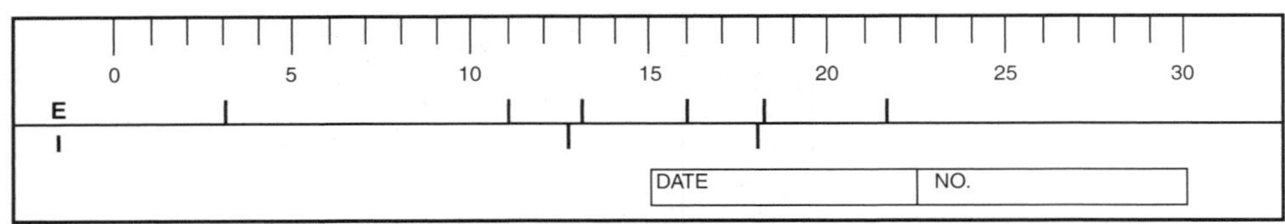

Name/Class

Section 9 Exercises

When completed, tear these exercises out of the textbook and give them to your instructor.

Punctuation Exercises—Conjunctive Adverbs

DIRECTIONS: ***Insert the proper punctuation where needed in the following sentences.***

PART 1

1. The Central Division increased sales by 20 percent this month moreover they increased the customer base by 10 percent.
2. The material presented at the meeting was really quite good however the presentation was too long.
3. If the market projection is correct we need to start interviewing applicants to hire four new people furthermore we need to make arrangements to lease the vacant space on the third floor.
4. After the production analysis is complete we will call a meeting of all department managers to discuss problem areas however we must meet with the manager of the Shipping Department before Thursday.
5. We must ask the employees in the Shipping Department to work on Saturdays until the first of the year otherwise we will not be able to fill all the orders by Christmas.
6. The Roberts Moving Company will be in charge of transporting all furniture and records to the new building on April 30 therefore all records must be sorted and packed prior to April 29.
7. Jason plans to meet you at the airport however he has a meeting at 4:30 p.m. and may be a few minutes late.
8. I must speak at a conference in New York on November 9 otherwise I would be happy to meet with you on that date.
9. I informed Richard of the meeting time however he did not attend.
10. You ordered 25 chairs however we have only 15 in stock.
11. We must receive your check by September 1 otherwise we will have to cancel your credit card.
12. I plan to attend the seminar moreover my assistant will accompany me.
13. They refuse to pay their bill consequently we must file suit against them.
14. We believe this is the best machine on the market furthermore it costs less than the competitor's model.
15. We offer a full service agreement on our new machines furthermore we will lend you a machine to use if we cannot repair yours within one day.

PART 2

1. In our telephone conversation you requested that we send you a copy of our lease agreement accordingly we have enclosed copies of the one-year lease agreement and the three year lease agreement.

Name/Class____

2. We do not have time to award all the scholarships today therefore we will meet again tomorrow at 3 p.m. to award the remaining ones.
3. Angie my assistant was promoted to assistant office manager consequently I must look for a new assistant to take her place.
4. Betty has more experience than Jane consequently I believe that we should hire Betty for the job.
5. We do not have the specific pen you ordered in stock therefore we have shipped a pen of equal quality instead.
6. The Board of Directors cut the budgets for each division by 5 percent accordingly we must establish priorities among our budget requests.
7. We are running a month behind in filling our orders therefore next week we are going to start working three shifts rather than two.
8. We have promoted from within the organization in the past moreover we expect to continue to do so in the future.
9. We expect our credit sales to increase appreciably in November and December consequently we plan to add several part time employees to handle the extra billing load.
10. Tina Reed's sales were down in June and July however her sales figures for August and September are up considerably.
11. John's car needs major repairs therefore he has decided to buy a new one.
12. If you can get to the airport by 6:15 p.m. we will be able to take the same flight however if you cannot be there by that time there is another flight to Denver at 8:45 p.m.
13. After the vacation schedule is made out the office manager will contact the employment agency for some temporary employees however he should check with our own part time employees first to see whether they might be able to work additional hours during the vacation season.
14. Our original plans called for completion of the building by August 1 however the heavy spring rains have caused so many construction delays that we may not be able to meet that date.
15. If you can find another investor before the end of the month we will be able to proceed with our plans furthermore we will be able to take advantage of the present low interest rates.

Word Study Exercises

DIRECTIONS: ***Highlight or underline the correct word choice in each of the following sentences.***

PART 1

1. The (capital, capitol) concern was to (brake, break) the deadlock so that the committee could (precede, proceed) with (it's, its) deliberation.
2. The students' tour of the (Capital, Capitol) in Nashville will (precede, proceed) lunch.
3. The parade will (precede, proceed) in front of the (Capital, Capitol).

Name/Class ____________________

4. Ted took the car to the garage to get the (brakes, breaks) repaired.
5. The construction project will not (precede, proceed) without additional (capital, capitol).
6. The renovation project of the (Capital, Capitol) building will begin in June.
7. A feasibility study must (precede, proceed) any (farther, further) (capital, capitol) investment.
8. Lack of studying usually (precedes, proceeds) a failing grade.
9. In some cars, you must depress the (brake, break) to shift from park to drive.
10. Attempting to move the gearshift lever from park to drive without depressing the (brake, break) will cause the gearshift lever to (brake, break).
11. Please adjust the (brakes, breaks) on my automobile.
12. Never (brake, break) hard on ice.
13. The bowl will (brake, break) if you put it on the hot stove.
14. I mended the (brake, break) in the vase.
15. (Their, There, They're) (capital, capitol) idea won the race.

PART 2

1. We do not have enough (capital, capitol) to start our own business.
2. Springfield is the (capital, capitol) of Illinois.
3. The state legislature meets in the (Capital, Capitol).
4. Professor Marani will (precede, proceed) me on the program.
5. (Their, There, They're) planning to (precede, proceed) with the construction on June 26.
6. Use low gear when driving down steep mountain roads (to, too, two) avoid continuously using your (brakes, breaks).
7. The people in the valley are afraid they will lose (their, there, they're) homes if the dam (brakes, breaks).
8. (Their, There, They're) (preceding, proceeding) (to, too, two) evacuate the village in the valley in anticipation of a (brake, break) in the dam.
9. (Their, There, They're) moving the office staff the week (preceding, proceeding) Thanksgiving.
10. (Their, There, They're) tour of the (Capital, Capitol) will (precede, proceed) (their, there, they're) visit (to, too, two) the Washington Monument.
11. Unless we hear from you before November 9, we will (precede, proceed) with our plans for the dinner meeting.
12. (Their, There, They're) required (capital, capitol) investment for the expansion project was prohibitive.
13. They notified the architect not (to, too, two) (precede, proceed) with the plans.
14. After you turn right on Market Street, (precede, proceed) five blocks (to, too, two) 342 Olive Street.
15. We must (brake, break) our contract with you.

EXERCISE Name/Class______________________________

Proofreading Exercise 9-A

DIRECTIONS: ***Use proofreaders' marks to correct the following letter. A list of proofreaders' marks is in the Reference Handbook at the back of the textbook.***

June 26, 20__

Mrs. Lucinda Busch
1749 Quail Run Drive
San Antonio, TX 78209

Dear Mrs. Busch:

The merger negotiations will brake down unless we precede to offer additional consessions.

The opposition's capitol concern seems to by the wage reduction demands that are pending. It is my opinion that we will by able to affect the merger if we modify our demand by approximately 3%, moreover I think we can attain all our other goals it we make this one modification immediately.

Discuss this with John and let me know how you want me to precede. Our next meeting is scheduled for July 9.

Sincerely,

Edna Asbury

xxx

Name/Class ______________________________

Proofreading Exercise 9-B

DIRECTIONS: ***Use proofreaders' marks to correct the following memorandum. A list of proofreaders' marks is in the Reference Handbook at the back of the textbook.***

MEMO TO: David Fisher

FROM: A. C. Barnfield

DATE: June 26, 20__

SUBJECT: Feasibility Study for Memphis Plant

I believe we must altar our original plan to expand the present facility in this area.

Please organize a feasibility study for a new production plant in the Memphis area. Please set up a tenative calender for the proposed planing steps and for the construction of the new facility.

In order to convince the Board of Directors of the need for this plant, we must gather as much supporting information as possible concerning costs and increased marketing potential.

This study must preceed any efforts to obtain capitol committments for the proposed building project. If we do a through job on our background work, we will be able to precede without any farther brakes in our progress toward expansion.

Please give me a progress report within three weeks.

xxx

Name/Class____

Proofreading Exercise 9-C

DIRECTIONS: ***Use proofreaders' marks to correct the following memorandum. A list of proofreaders' marks is in the Reference Handbook at the back of the textbook.***

MEMO TO: Jeffery Hanson

FROM: J. M. Lopez

DATE: (current date)

SUBJECT: House Bill 775

We expect that their will be lengthy debate in the Appropriations Committee on House Bill 775. We will precede on the asumption that the vote will be favorable however we must be prepared to present a strong alternate position in case there is a brake in the support of the bill.

The schools in our district need the capitol support this bill will provide. Please outline some talking points that illustrate the positive impact that a favorable vote would have on our schools.

xxx

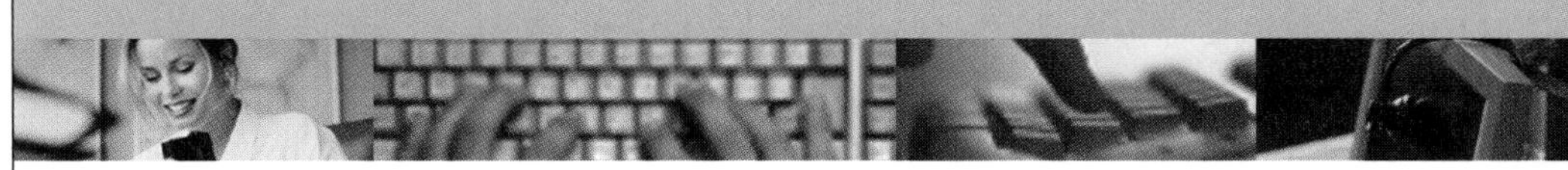

Section 10

10.1 OBJECTIVES

In Section 10, you will work toward the following objectives:

- Correctly format a news release when transcribing the dictation for this section.
- Correctly complete Word Study Exercises and Proofreading Exercises in preparation for transcription.
- Complete Spelling Test 10 with at least 80 percent accuracy.
- Select the appropriate words and the correct spelling according to the context of the dictation when transcribing this section's dictation.

10.2 WORD STUDY

The words listed here are frequently confused in transcription because they sound alike when dictated but have different meanings. Study the words carefully so that you will be able to select the appropriate word according to the context of the dictation.

command (verb) to give an order to
In an hour the general will *command* his troops to break camp.

command (noun) an order
She issued the *command* to march.

commend (verb) to praise; to entrust
We *commend* your act of bravery.
Julie's grandfather will *commend* his rare-book collection to her when she turns 21 years old.

fiscal (adjective) having to do with financial matters
The *fiscal* year is the 12-month period between settlements of financial accounts.

physical (adjective) of the body as opposed to the mind
He has a *physical* examination every year.

quiet (adjective) calm; motionless; not noisy
It was a *quiet* library.

quit (verb) to stop
He *quit* his job.

quite (adverb) completely; entirely
He was *quite* surprised.

weak (adjective) not strong
He was still *weak* from his long illness.

week (noun) seven days
This was her first *week* of work.

10.3 SPELLING REVIEW

The dictation for this section contains the words listed here. Study them carefully to help you transcribe more rapidly. If you hear other words in the dictation that you do not know how to spell, make a list of those words and learn their correct spellings. This practice will help you improve your transcription speed.

acquire	difficult	managerial
alleviate	diligence	obedience
analysis	diminish	optimism
analyzing	discouraged	physical
anticipate	dissemination	prescribed
appreciable	eligible	professional
aspects	exceptional	quiet
audience	familiar	quit
cognizant	fiscal	quite
command	imagination	relief
commend	implementation	surgery
consensus	innovative	tenure
controlling	irreparable	weak
controversial	jeopardize	week

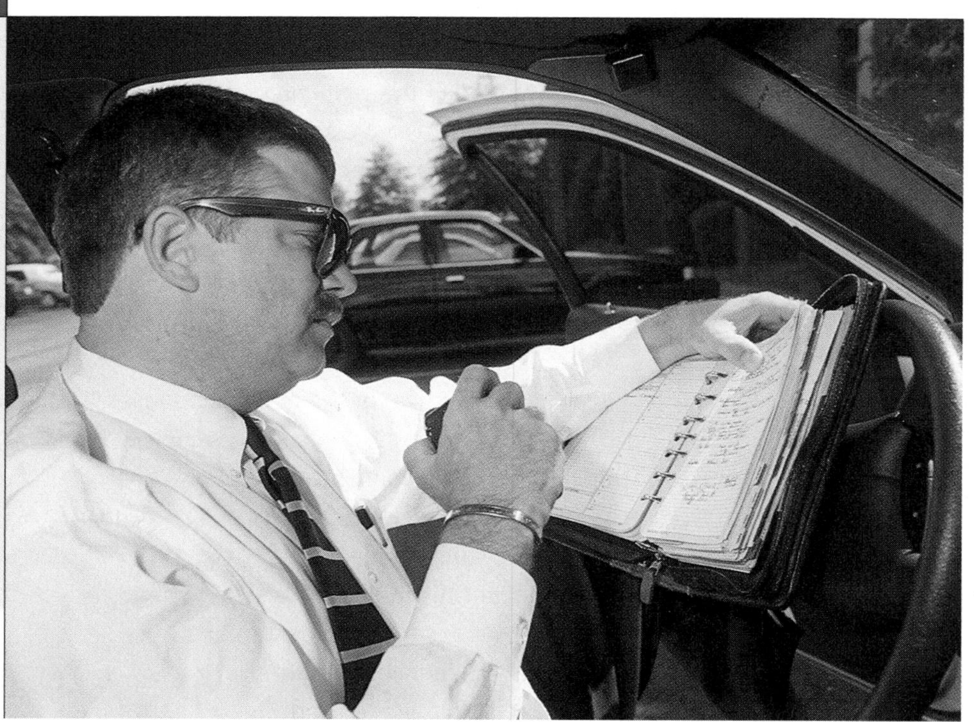

Figure 10.1
Portable dictation equipment can be used to communicate timely information.
Do you think this salesperson might dictate the results of customer visits in the field?

10.4 TRANSCRIPTION GUIDELINES

NEWS RELEASE

The author suggests using the following format from *The Gregg Reference Manual*, Ninth Edition, by William A. Sabin (Glencoe/McGraw-Hill, New York, 2001, pp. 512–513).

HEADING. The heading should indicate the name and address of the organization sponsoring the news release. It should also show the name and phone number of the person to contact in case more information is needed.

The heading should also indicate when the information contained in the news release may be distributed to the public. In many cases the phrase *For immediate release* is sufficient. If the information is to be kept confidential until a specific time and date, the heading should carry a notation like this:

For release 9 a.m. EST, May 7, 2001

HEADLINE. The text of the news release should begin with a descriptive title and, if desired, a subtitle.

CONTENT CONSIDERATIONS. The first paragraph should begin with a bold run-in head that indicates the city and state of origin and the date on which this material is to be released. This run-in head is usually followed by a colon or a dash (typical newspaper practice) rather than by a period.

At the end of the text, leave 1 blank line and type one of the following notations, centered: three spaced pound signs (# # #) or the phrase -30-. These notations, derived from long-standing newspaper practice, signify "the end."

Illustration of Press Release

News Release Griffin Hospital

233 Lakeland Ave.
Coventry, CT 08765

Contact: Ahmed Aradian
Phone: 203-555-1294
Fax: 203-555-1295

FOR IMMEDIATE RELEASE

GRIFFIN HOSPITAL OFFERS NEW PROCEDURE

Noninvasive Procedure Relieves Angina Symptoms and Pain

Coventry, Connecticut, December 5, 2002: Griffin Hospital today announced a new, noninvasive procedure to relieve angina symptoms and pain. Enhanced External Counterpulsation, or EECP, is a nonsurgical procedure that can reduce or eliminate symptoms of angina, according to hospital officials. Angina is characterized by agonizing chest pain brought on by exercise or emotional stress. Many candidates for EECP have had angioplasty and/or open heart surgery, and there are no other medical options available to them.

The Centers for Medicare and Medicaid Services (CMS) announced that EECP will be covered for Medicare patients effective October 1. Many other insurers cover the procedures based on the individual member's insurance plan.

# # #

Assignments

Page 159

Complete the Word Study and Proofreading Exercises that are located on pages 159–164 at the end of this section. The purpose of these exercises is to assist you with the transcription assignment. Tear the completed exercises out of the textbook, and give them to your instructor before you take Spelling Test 10 and before you transcribe the dictation for this section.

SPELLING TEST 10

Ask your instructor for Spelling Test 10. Complete this test before you transcribe the dictation for Section 10.

SECTION 10 DICTATION

Be sure to review the corrections before you begin to transcribe. Transcribe all of the outgoing letters in modified block style with open punctuation and indented paragraphs. Refer to the Reference Handbook for sample letter styles.

Use the following letterheads when you transcribe:

Recording for Section 10

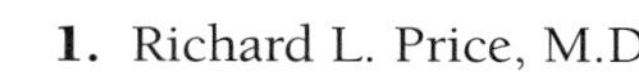

1. Richard L. Price, M.D.
2. Davis Command Training Center
3. News Release
4. Empire Manufacturing Company
5. Kingston Furniture Company

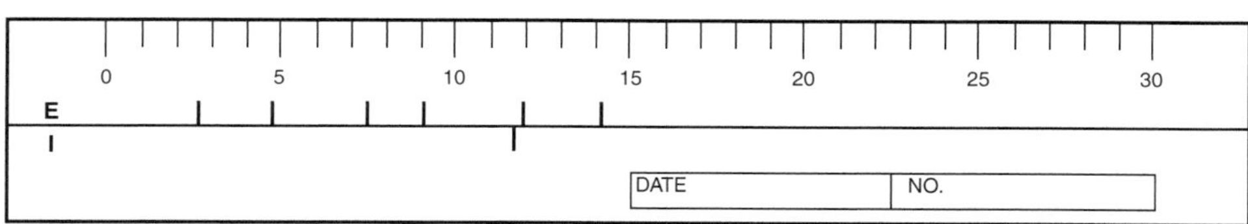

Name/Class ____________________

Section 10 Exercises

When completed, tear these exercises out of the textbook and give them to your instructor.

Word Study Exercises

DIRECTIONS: ***Highlight or underline the correct word choice in each of the following sentences.***

PART 1

1. The (fiscal, physical) plan is due next (weak, week).
2. We (command, commend) the athletes on (there, their, they're) (fiscal, physical) conditioning program.
3. He was (quiet, quit, quite) serious when he (commanded, commended) the students to be (quiet, quit, quite).
4. The report was (to, too, two) (weak, week) (to, too, two) support his position.
5. The patient was (quiet, quit, quite) (weak, week); it will take several (weaks, weeks) for him (to, too, two) regain his former (fiscal, physical) strength.
6. We (command, commend) the effort you made (to, too, two) complete the (fiscal, physical) report last (weak, week).
7. You will gain weight if you (quiet, quit, quite) exercising.
8. After your surgery, you will be (quiet, quit, quite) (weak, week); therefore, you should limit your (fiscal, physical) efforts to (quiet, quit, quite) endeavors.
9. We want to (command, commend) the team on (there, their, they're) victory.
10. A great deal of (fiscal, physical) effort went into the training of the team.
11. General Smith will (command, commend) the troops during the invasion.
12. General Smith issued that (command, commend) yesterday.
13. Jack was (commanded, commended) for his heroism in the battle.
14. (Their, There, They're) (fiscal, physical) year ended on June 30.
15. The general (fiscal, physical) condition of our staff is excellent.
16. They all take steps to ensure a (quiet, quit, quite) work environment.

Name/Class________________________________

17. Several staff members (quiet, quit, quite) smoking last year.

18. They were (quiet, quit, quite) happy about the new contract.

19. Since his accident, Bill has had a (weak, week) knee.

20. Stacey has missed a (weak, week) of work this month.

PART 2

1. After being wounded, General Armstrong was (to, too, two) (weak, week) (to, too, two) (command, commend) the troops in the battle.

2. The merger was (quiet, quit, quite) a surprise.

3. The nurse evaluated the (fiscal, physical) condition of the (weak, week) patient.

4. The family (commanded, commended) the whole medical staff for saving Julie's life.

5. General Armstrong (cent, scent, sent) a (command, commend) (to, too, two) the forces at the river.

6. The (personal, personnel) in the Accounting Department were hoping for a (quiet, quit, quite) (weak, week) while they prepared the (fiscal, physical) reports.

7. The (employs, employees) are supposed to (quiet, quit, quite) working at five o'clock.

8. The North Central Region's sales figures for this (fiscal, physical) period are (quiet, quit, quite) impressive.

9. We were (quiet, quit, quite) surprised when the computer did not implement our footnote (commands, commends).

10. The firm installed a (fiscal, physical) fitness center for the (employs, employees).

11. The jury examined the (fiscal, physical) evidence as they deliberated the facts of the case.

12. The vice president considered the report that was written by the new (employ, employee) to be (quiet, quit, quite) (weak, week).

13. Our deadline is one (weak, week) from June 26.

14. The group was very (quiet, quit, quite) as the speaker made her presentation.

15. The singer was (quiet, quit, quite) nervous as she prepared for a (command, commend) performance before Queen Elizabeth.

16. A strong (command, commend) of the English language will help you become successful in your career.

Name/Class ______________________________

17. The president (commanded, commended) the committee for their excellent solution to the problem.

18. The Board of Directors voted to make changes in the policy for the next (fiscal, physical) year.

19. It (quiet, quit, quite) raining five minutes before we left to go to the airport.

20. You will find a list of the computer (commands, commends) in the manual.

Name/Class____

Proofreading Exercise 10-A

DIRECTIONS: ***Use proofreaders' marks to correct the following letter. A list of proofreaders' marks is in the Reference Handbook at the back of the textbook.***

March 25, 20__

Mr. L. R. Rogers
Rogers Distributing Company
24 Chestnut Street
Chicago, IL 60610

Dear Mr. Rogers

It was a pleasure talking with you today. I expect the advertising aproach that you outlined during the meeting Thursday will be quit successfull it if can be implimented prior too the introduction of the new line from General Mechanics Company.

We have ordered the changes in the design that you requested. You should receive the first shippment of hte new models by June 15.

Your Truely

Fred Rains

xxx

Name/Class____

Proofreading Exercise 10-B

DIRECTIONS: ***Use proofreaders' marks to correct the following memorandum. A list of proofreaders' marks is in the Reference Handbook at the back of the textbook.***

MEMO TO: Kirk Krausman

FROM: J. B. Bleyer

DATE: October 30, 20__

SUBJECT: Expansion of Employee Exercise Facility

You are to be commanded for your organization of the new exercize facility for employs. Although it has been open for only six months we have already seen quit a significant drop in absenteism. By encouraging our employes to improve there personnal fiscal-exercise programs you have done a great service to the employees and the company as well.

In fact, you plan has been so successfull that we are approving phase two of your original porposal. When you have determined exactly how much capitol will be required to implement phase two let me know.

Congradulations on a job well done.

xxx

Name/Class ____________________

Proofreading Exercise 10-C

DIRECTIONS: ***Use proofreaders' marks to correct the following memorandum. A list of proofreaders' marks is in the Reference Handbook at the back of the textbook.***

MEMO TO: Audrey Mason

FROM: George Hillman

DATE: (current date)

SUBJECT: Presentation to the Board of Directors

The report concerning your projections on the next physical year was quit interesting furthermore, I am sure the Board of Directors will command your effort when they meet next weak.

Your projections provide support for the fiscal plant expantion that we will be proposing at the next board meeting.

Are you available to have lunch with me on Thursday so that we can review the details of you projections and their impact on our presentation to the Board of Directors?

xxx

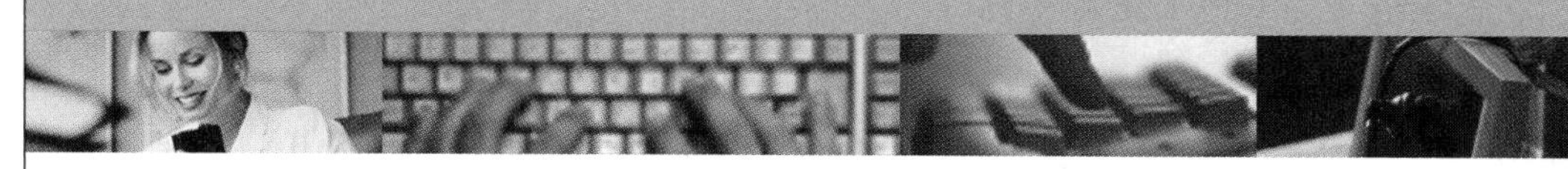

Section 11

11.1 OBJECTIVES

In Section 11, you will work toward the following objectives:

- Insert semicolons where appropriate in compound sentences containing other commas and in compound sentences where the coordinating conjunction has been omitted between independent clauses.
- Correctly complete Punctuation Exercises, Word Study Exercises, and Proofreading Exercises in preparation for transcription.
- Complete Spelling Test 11 with at least 80 percent accuracy.
- Select the appropriate words and the correct spelling according to the context of the dictation when transcribing this section's documents.
- Complete Word Study Test 4 on the word study vocabulary in Sections 9, 10, and 11 with at least 80 percent accuracy.
- Complete Transcription Test 2.

11.2 PUNCTUATION REVIEW

Use a semicolon instead of a comma to separate independent clauses when other commas appear in either independent clause and misreading might occur.

Example: **Andrew Jacobs, chairman of the board, will preside over the meeting; and the seminar, which follows immediately, will be introduced by Francesca Jamison, president.**

Use a semicolon to separate two independent clauses when the coordinating conjunction has been omitted.

Example: **It's the only answer; sell the business.**

11.3 WORD STUDY

The words listed here are frequently confused in transcription because they sound alike when dictated but have different meanings. Study the words carefully so that you will be able to select the appropriate word according to the context of the dictation.

access (noun) approach; admittance; entrance

He gained *access* through the west door.

excess (noun) an amount that is more than enough; a surplus

An *excess* of water in the stream caused a flood.

excess (adjective) more than needed; extra

The *excess* merchandise will go on sale Saturday.

bare (adjective) exposed; revealed; uncovered

The walls were *bare* in the new office.

bear (verb) to carry; to transport; to withstand; to endure

The porters will *bear* the supplies to base camp.

Let him *bear* the expense of the trip.

choose (verb) to select; to make a choice

She decided to *choose* the first applicant for the job.

chose selected (past tense of choose)

He *chose* to postpone the meeting.

eminent (adjective) outstanding; remarkable; distinguished

She is an *eminent* scientist.

imminent (adjective) near at hand; likely to happen without delay

The completion of the new building is *imminent*.

11.4 SPELLING REVIEW

The dictation for this section contains the words listed here. Study them carefully to help you transcribe more rapidly. If you hear other words in the dictation that you do not know how to spell, make a list of those words and learn their correct spellings. This practice will help you improve your transcription speed.

access
approximately
bare
bear
community
completion
confirm
discussed
eminent
excess
extension
finalized
glimpse
imminent
impression
incurring
introductory
memorabilia
merchandise
minute
neighbors
original
population
preferred
prior
probably
professor
strangers
subscription
success

ASSIGNMENTS

EXERCISE

Complete the Punctuation, Word Study, and Proofreading Exercises that are located on pages 169–174 at the end of this section. The purpose of these exercises is to assist you with the transcription assignment. Tear the completed exercises out of the textbook, and give them to your instructor before you take Spelling Test 11 and before you transcribe the dictation for this section.

Page 169

SPELLING TEST 11

Ask your instructor for Spelling Test 11. Complete this test before you transcribe the dictation for Section 11.

Recording for Section 11

SECTION 11 DICTATION

This recording contains dictated corrections. Be sure to review the corrections before you begin to transcribe. Transcribe all of the outgoing letters in block style with open punctuation. Refer to the Reference Handbook for sample letter styles.

The following photograph is to be removed and attached to your transcript of the News Article that is the second item on the dictation for Section 11.

Figure 11.1
Wilkey's Cafe, Belle Rive, Illinois

Use the following letterheads when you transcribe:

1. Plant Life
2. News Article
3. S. J. Smith
4. Interoffice Memorandum 1
5. Rainbow Department Store

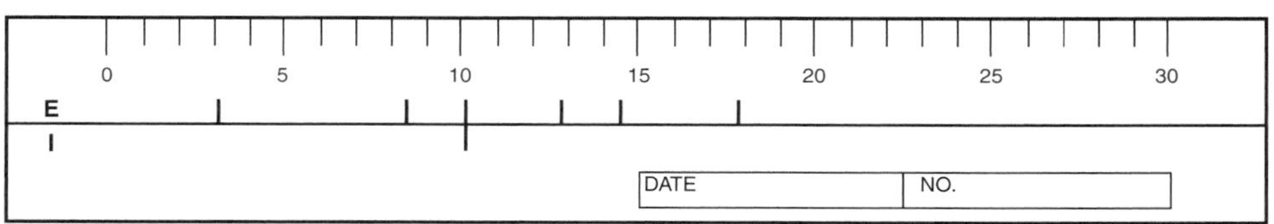

WORD STUDY TEST 4

Ask your instructor for Word Study Test 4. This test covers the word study information contained in Sections 9 through 11. The Word Study Review Summary in the Appendix will help you prepare for this test. Complete this test after you transcribe the dictation for Section 11. The following is a list of words you should study before you take the test:

access	chose	precede
bare	command	proceed
bear	commend	quiet
brake	eminent	quit
break	excess	quite
capital	fiscal	weak
capitol	imminent	week
choose	physical	

TRANSCRIPTION TEST 2

Ask your instructor for Transcription Test 2. This test contains items you have transcribed previously. You will transcribe for 30 minutes. Use spelling checker or a dictionary to look up any words you do not know how to spell.

Relax! You have transcribed these items before. You *can* do well!

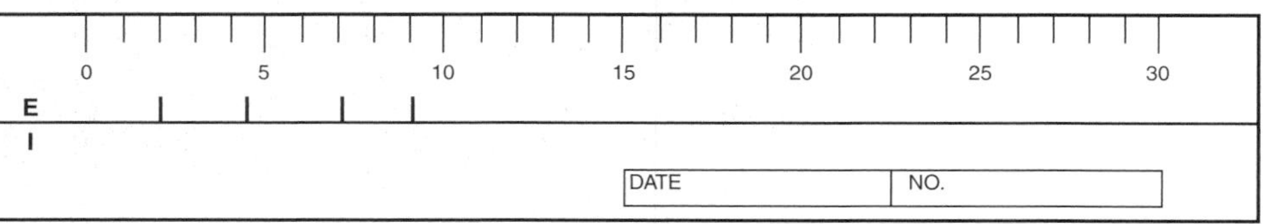

Name/Class ______________________________

Section 11 Exercises

When completed, tear these exercises out of the textbook and give them to your instructor.

Punctuation Exercises—Semicolons With Other Commas, Conjunction Omitted

DIRECTIONS: ***Insert the proper punctuation where needed in the following sentences.***

PART 1

1. The speaker Carl Hayden will arrive for the seminar on Tuesday and in the afternoon we will meet him at the airport.
2. We will buy the property we need it for the expansion of our building.
3. If the meeting ends before noon I will be able to meet your plane but take a taxi to the hotel if it lasts longer.
4. Act now send your registration today.
5. When Ms. Jacobs received the award she commended her colleagues and her staff and the president also gave her a raise.
6. After Gina was named president she made changes in the organizational chart and operations manager Troy was promoted to vice president of operations.
7. Before Matt took off in the Seminole he went through his checklist and the control tower told him that he was third in line for takeoff.
8. Please enter this information as fast as you can I need it for the two o'clock meeting.
9. Jack turned his assignment in late Jason still has not turned in his assignment.
10. We must hurry we are late for the sales meeting.
11. After her presentation of the new policies Betty the vice president invited the audience to ask questions and as a result there was quite a discussion among the members present concerning the new retirement policy.
12. When the new merchandise arrives check it carefully to be sure we received the correct items and the correct quantity and when you are finished take the invoice to the Accounting Department.
13. The meeting began at 3 p.m. in Kansas City Missouri we arrived at 3:30 p.m.
14. If you are hired for this position you will attend a one-week training class if you apply yourself diligently you will be considered for promotions.
15. Interviews were conducted by Ms. Carol Jacobs the human resources manager and Mr. John Moore the division head and only three people were invited to come for a second interview.

EXERCISE Name/Class

PART 2

1. If we take Route 41 we will arrive in five hours and will be late but if we take Route 57 we will arrive in four hours and will be on time.
2. When we receive the current sales figures we can evaluate our new advertising program we will be able to make a decision concerning any changes that may be needed in that program.
3. Failure to respond to this letter will be taken to mean that you do not intend to pay your bill and are defaulting on your obligations and we will contact our attorney regarding collection of your account.
4. We are unable to ship the desks file cabinets and credenzas and our store will ship them as soon as they arrive.
5. When Ms. Zimmerman returns from her business trip she will handle this matter personally please acknowledge the request immediately.
6. As you mentioned at the last meeting we will have to increase our prices I think that we should have two small increases rather than one large one.
7. Ms. Wong was willing to accept the compromise Mr. Gilula was not.
8. Drive north on Interstate 57 until you reach Salem then turn east on Route 50.
9. The meeting will start promptly at 9 a.m. be on time.
10. It's going to rain be sure you take your umbrella.
11. Don't delay mail the enclosed card today.
12. As soon as we receive the signed contract we will begin working on the new designs for the executive offices parking garage courtyard and production plan and a model should be ready for your approval by January 1.
13. Bring your textbook to class you will need it every day.
14. The file folder contains the signed contract the project plan and the contract addendum and Jim asked to be given a copy of it.
15. The proposal was presented by Anthony Mazzio Patricia Stone and Lee Jones and the ramifications of implementing the plan were put to a vote.

Word Study Exercises

DIRECTIONS: ***Highlight or underline the correct word choice in each of the following sentences.***

PART 1

1. You may (choose, chose) what to put on the (bare, bear) wall behind your desk.
2. You will have (access, excess) to the new building on or before June 1.
3. The (access, excess) supplies will be stored in the closet in the library.
4. The (eminent, imminent) scientist may (choose, chose) to allow questions at the end of her presentation.

Name/Class________________________________

5. The due date for completion of the report is (eminent, imminent).
6. Since we did not know the password, we were denied (access, excess) to the documents.
7. Please (bare, bear) in mind that you must (choose, chose) the option you want soon because the deadline is (eminent, imminent).
8. Harold was driving in (access, excess) of the speed limit.
9. Einstein was an (eminent, imminent) physicist.
10. Andrew (choose, chose) Marie as his partner to work on the design project.
11. After you (choose, chose) the alternative that appeals to you, you must (bare, bear) the consequences of your selection.
12. The (eminent, imminent) scientist presented his theories to the members attending the convention.
13. Please put the (access, excess) supplies in the storeroom.
14. You may have (access, excess) to the files between the hours of 8 a.m. and 5 p.m.
15. The completion of the building is (eminent, imminent).

PART 2

1. You must go through the gym to gain (access, excess) to the exercise room.
2. Many employees are on a diet to lose (access, excess) weight.
3. These are the (bare, bear) facts.
4. He must (bare, bear) the consequences of his actions.
5. You may (choose, chose) the color scheme for your new office.
6. Roy (choose, chose) the blue suit.
7. She is an (eminent, imminent) professor of law.
8. A storm is (eminent, imminent).
9. (Bare, Bear) in mind that Erte, the (eminent, imminent) artist, will attend the reception.
10. You will have (access, excess) to the third floor from the parking garage.
11. Since the walls of your new office are (bare, bear), you may (choose, chose) whatever artwork appeals to you.
12. Alice (choose, chose) to go to Dallas.
13. Because the deadline was (eminent, imminent), she rushed to finish the report.
14. They put the (access, excess) (capital, capitol) in an interest-bearing account.
15. Beverly (choose, chose) to take her vacation in July.

Name/Class ____________________

Proofreading Exercise 11-A

DIRECTIONS: ***Use proofreaders' marks to correct the following letter. A list of proofreaders' marks is in the Reference Handbook at the back of the textbook.***

October 1, 20__

Mr. Victor Collins
3344 Every Avenue
Scottsbluff, NE 69361

Dear Mr. Collins:

This winter we are offering an exciting variety of vacation packages that provide a relaxing escap from your busy work routine. You can enjoy scuba diving in the warm Caribbean waters, skiing in scenic Aspen, or viewing ancient ruins in Mexico.

You can enjoy the comradeship of one of our many group trips or the peacefull soletude of a vacation package created especially for you. Each of these vacation packages are designed for relaxation and enjoyment.

You deserve a vacation call us today at 239-2062 for additional details about you dream vacation.

Cordialy yours,

Holiday Travel Agency

Joyce Edmund
Manager

xxx

Name/Class____

Proofreading Exercise 11-B

DIRECTIONS: ***Use proofreaders' marks to correct the following memorandum. A list of proofreaders' marks is in the Reference Handbook at the back of the textbook.***

MEMO TO: Marsha Reynolds

FROM: Bruce Segal

DATE: April 2, 20__

SUBJECT: Move to Cleveland

The closing of the Toledo office is eminent. Please arrange to transfer the access inventory to the Cleveland office. Bare in mind that the employees who choose to transfer to the Cleveland office will be moving on May 25.

If you need assistence in accomplishing this task you may use the services of my assistent, Ellen Bradley, during the week of April 10. I will be our of the office on business during that week. She is quit familar with the Cleveland facility and will be able to help you. You will find her to be a capable efficient assistant.

xxx

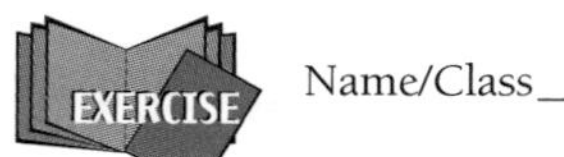

Name/Class________________________________

Proofreading Exercise 11-C

DIRECTIONS: ***Use proofreaders' marks to correct the following memorandum. A list of proofreaders' marks is in the Reference Handbook at the back of the textbook.***

MEMO TO: Bill Roberts

FROM: Harold Land

DATE: (current date)

SUBJECT: Employee Records

The results of the study you are proposing could be a valuable tool in future hiring dicisions.

Since Jack Hamilton's eminent retirment will leave our department understaffed our office will not be able to search the employ files for the information that you are requesting however, we will be glad to provide you with access to the files. If you chose to take advantage of this opportunity, bare in mind that all information must be kept confidential.

If you want to conduct the search yourself please let me no. I will make certain that you have adequate desk space while you are searching for the information you need.

I look forward to reading the results of your research.

xxx

Section 12

12.1 OBJECTIVES

In Section 12, you will work toward the following objectives:

- Correctly format foreign addresses when transcribing the dictation for this section.
- Correctly complete Word Study Exercises and Proofreading Exercises in preparation for transcription.
- Complete Spelling Test 12 with at least 80 percent accuracy.
- Select the appropriate words and the correct spelling according to the context of the dictation when transcribing this section's documents.
- Complete Transcription Test 3.

12.2 WORD STUDY

The words listsed here are frequently confused in transcription because they sound alike when dictated but have different meanings. Study the words carefully so that you will be able to select the appropriate word according to the context of the dictation.

collaborate (verb) to work together, especially in reference to literary, artistic, or scientific work

They will *collaborate* on the book.

corroborate (verb) to strengthen; to make more certain; to confirm; to support

The witness will *corroborate* his story.

right (adjective) correct

Her answer was *right*.

right (noun) privilege under the law

He has a *right* to an attorney.

rite (noun) a ceremonial or solemn act

The old book contained the *rite* that we had been discussing.

write (verb) to form or inscribe words on a surface

She will *write* a letter.

suit (noun) a set of clothes; a legal procedure

He wore a blue *suit*.

He will bring *suit* against the company.

suit (verb) to please; to adapt

We will change the paint color to *suit* you.

The orchestra will *suit* its music to the occasion.

suite (noun) a series or group of rooms occupied as a unit

We reserved a *suite* in the hotel.

sweet (adjective) having a taste like sugar or honey; having any agreeable taste, smell, sound, appearance; pleasant

The dessert was *sweet*.

She is a *sweet* girl.

12.3 SPELLING REVIEW

The dictation for this section contains the words listed here. Study them carefully to help you transcribe more rapidly. If you hear other words in the dictation that you do not know how to spell, make a list of those words and learn their corrrect spellings. This practice will help you improve your transcription speed.

achievement
adequate
advocate
allocated
alternative
arrival
boutique
cathedral
challenge
collaborate
concur
congratulations
corroborate
definitely
disappeared
executive
fascinating
florist
hospitality
hurricane
incidentally
manifest
manuscript
mutually
right
rite
salon
satisfactorily
suit
suite
superb
sweet
transferred
treasure
wreckage
write

Figure 12.1
Handheld units may be digital or cassette-based. (Sony)

12.4 TRANSCRIPTION GUIDELINES

When you are addressing a letter to a foreign country, the name of that foreign country should be keyed in all-capital letters as the last line of the address on the envelope and as the last line of the inside address on the letter. The following example illustrates the address for a letter being sent to England:

Example: Mr. Jerome Swanson
Lancaster Apartments
36 Queen's Gate
London SW7 5JA
ENGLAND

ASSIGNMENTS

Page 179

Complete the Word Study and Proofreading Exercises that are located on pages 179–182 at the end of this section. The purpose of these exercises is to assist you with the transcription assignment. Tear the completed exercises out of the textbook, and give them to your instructor before you take Spelling Test 12 and before you transcribe the dictation for this section.

SPELLING TEST 12

Ask your instructor for Spelling Test 12. Complete this test before you transcribe the dictation for Section 12.

SECTION 12 DICTATION

Recording for Section 12

Be sure to review the corrections before you begin to transcribe. Transcribe all of the outgoing letters in modified block style with mixed punctuation and indented paragraphs. Refer to the Reference Handbook for sample letter styles.

Use the following letterheads when you transcribe:

1. Holiday Travel Agency
2. Anchor Tool Company, Inc.
3. Columbia Hotel
4. News Release
5. Gordon L. Perry
6. Holden & King

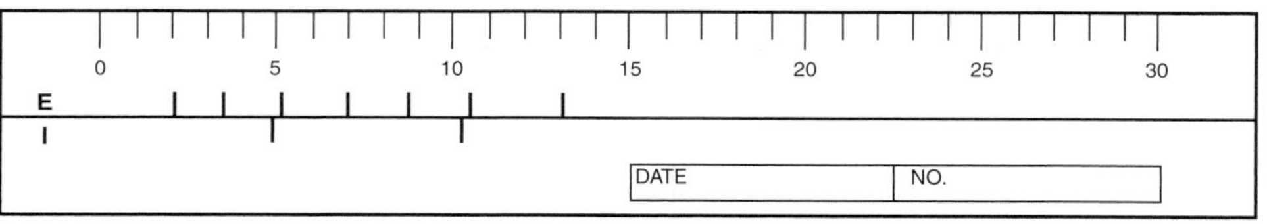

TRANSCRIPTION TEST 3

Ask your instructor for Transcription Test 3. This test and the future tests contain items you have not transcribed previously. You will transcribe for 30 minutes. Use the spelling checker or a dictionary to look up any words you do not know how to spell.

In the classroom and on the job, a professional attitude includes cooperation, the ability and willingness to communicate with others, good attendance, and the best use of time (productivity). Don't forget to maintain your work area and equipment. Read or listen to directions carefully.

Relax! Apply what you have learned, and do your best.

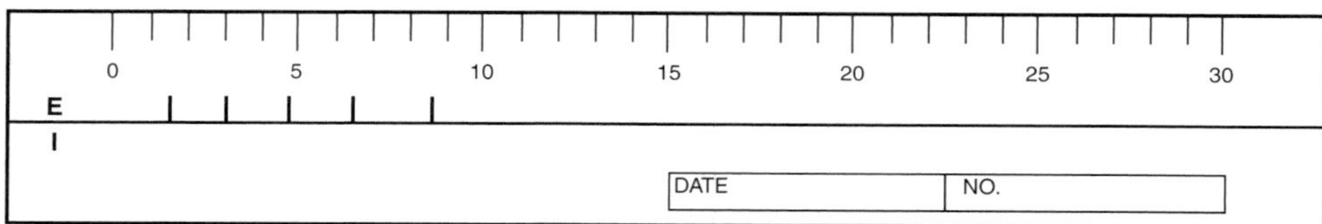

Name/Class____________________

Section 12 Exercises

When completed, tear these exercises out of the textbook and give them to your instructor.

Word Study Exercises

DIRECTIONS: ***Highlight or underline the correct word choice in each of the following sentences.***

PART 1

1. The executive (suit, suite, sweet) of offices is being remodeled.
2. The physical evidence did (collaborate, corroborate) the statements made by the district attorney.
3. The lemonade was not (quiet, quit, quite) (suit, suite, sweet) enough.
4. What (right, rite, write) do you have to make that decision?
5. The employees believe (their, there, they're) (rights, rites, writes) will be protected by the new contract.
6. The statement of the witness (collaborated, corroborated) the story of the suspect.
7. The (to, too, two) authors (collaborated, corroborated) (to, too, two) (right, rite, write) the screenplay.
8. The hotel (suit, suite, sweet) was on the top floor.
9. According to the contract, David has a (right, rite, write) (to, too, two) (choose, chose).
10. The owners of the building said that they would remodel to (suit, suite, sweet) the new tenant.
11. The (to, too, two) doctors will (collaborate, corroborate) on (their, there, they're) cancer research.
12. The results of the most recent test (collaborate, corroborate) our earlier findings.
13. Dean made the (right, rite, write) choice.
14. According to her contract, Janet has the (right, rite, write) to withdraw before the end of the year.
15. The congregation listened silently as Jerry read the (right, rite, write).
16. Please (right, rite, write) the (ad, add) for the newspaper.
17. Please send my black (suit, suite, sweet) to the cleaners.
18. (Their, There, They're) are three defendants in the (suit, suite, sweet).
19. The property owner will build to (suit, suite, sweet) the lessee.
20. (Their, There, They're) are three rooms in our hotel (suit, suite, sweet).

PART 2

1. This coffee cake is (to, too, two) (suit, suite, sweet) for our customers.
2. The decision was (right, rite, write).
3. The (to, too, two) authors will (collaborate, corroborate) on the article.
4. The testimony presented in court was (collaborated, corroborated) by the (depositions, dispositions) taken previously in the (suit, suite, sweet).

5. Do the alterations (suit, suite, sweet) you?
6. We will (right, rite, write) the report together.
7. You have the (right, rite, write) to have an attorney present.
8. The candy at the reception was (quiet, quit, quite) (suit, suite, sweet).
9. Our office occupies a (suit, suite, sweet) on the top floor.
10. Can you (right, rite, write) a poem that will (suit, suite, sweet) the occasion?
11. Dr. Yount (collaborated, corroborated) with Dr. Hanson on the research project.
12. Did you find the (right, rite, write) solution to the problem?
13. The new research (collaborated, corroborated) our earlier findings.
14. The ancient (right, rite, write) was re-enacted for the tourists.
15. Please exercise your (right, rite, write) to vote.
16. Please (right, rite, write) your report before Thursday.
17. The new (suit, suite, sweet) of offices will be ready for occupancy by August 9.
18. The owner will remodel the building to (suit, suite, sweet) your needs.
19. Wear a (suit, suite, sweet) to the interview.
20. The tea was too (suit, suite, sweet).

Proofreading Exercise 12-A

DIRECTIONS: ***Use proofreaders' marks to correct the following memorandum. A list of proofreaders' marks is in the Reference Handbook at the back of the textbook.***

MEMO TO: Monica Brock

FROM: Amy Foster

DATE: July 15, 20__

SUBJECT: Advertising Program

The results of the survey seem to collaborate our idea that we should change our advertising approach. With the write advertising program I believe we can increase our sales by 10 to 20 percent within the next 6 months.

Please be prepared to present your new advertising proposal at the meeting on August 9. I think we should chose at least six new adds for our campaign.

xxx

Name/Class______________________________

Proofreading Exercise 12-B

DIRECTIONS: ***Use proofreaders' marks to correct the following letter. A list of proofreaders' marks is in the Reference Handbook at the back of the textbook.***

(current date)

Mr. Randy McKeehan
439 North Fifth Street
Cameron, AZ 86020

Dear Mr. McKeehan:

Enclosed is your copy of the Conley Home Planning Book. We apologise for the delay in getting this book to you but an overwhelming demand for this new book exhausted our original supply. We appreciate your patients.

While you are trying to make all of those exciting decisions about colors fixtures appliances furnishings and floor plans, your going to enjoy browsing through the Conley Home Planning Book and find many fascinating ideas for your new home. This book will provide up to date guidance rite at your fingertips.

You and your family will especially appreciate the scale furniture and grid sheets. These will help you make realistic dicisions concerning room size.

Enclosed is a list of additional books that contain decorating ideas. If you wish to order any of these books simply indicate your choices on the enclosed postage-paid card.

Sincerely yours,

Julie Anderson
Consumer Relations

xxx
Enclosures

EXERCISE Name/Class________________________________

Proofreading Exercise 12-C

DIRECTIONS: ***Use proofreaders' marks to correct the following letter. A list of proofreaders' marks is in the Reference Handbook at the back of the textbook.***

(current date)

Mrs. Carol Quinn
925 East Meadow Street
Carbondale, IL 62901

Dear Mrs. Quinn:

I will be attending the convention on Chicago next month. I have reserved a suit at the convention hotel so that we may study you proposal to corroborate on the new electronics textbook without interuption.

The resent market projections collaborate are belief that the time is rite for a new textbook in this area. If we decide to write this new textbook we must work quickly.

Our academic backgrounds should compliment one another quiet effectively. I look forward to the possibility of collaborating with you on this new endeavor.

Sincerely,

Karen J. Blackwell

xxx

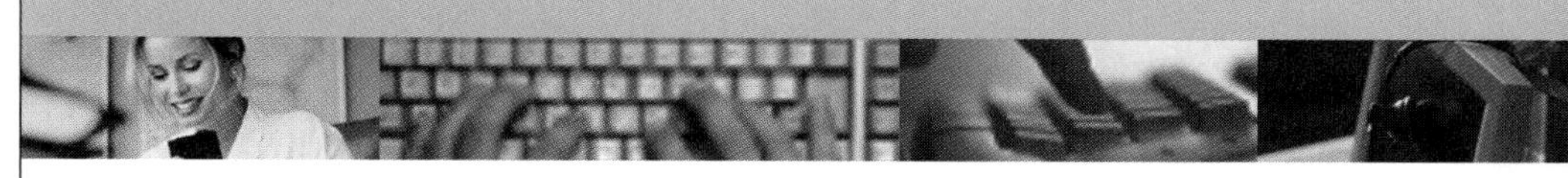

Section 13

13.1 OBJECTIVES

In Section 13, you will work toward the following objectives:

- Insert commas and colons where appropriate in sentences containing quotations or enumerated items.
- Correctly complete Punctuation Exercises, Word Study Exercises, and Proofreading Exercises in preparation for transcription.
- Complete Spelling Test 13 with at least 80 percent accuracy.
- Select the appropriate words and the correct spelling according to the context of the dictation when transcribing this section's documents.
- Complete Transcription Test 4.

13.2 PUNCTUATION REVIEW

Use a comma before a *short* quotation.

Example: She said, "Be at work on time every day."

Remember: Periods and commas always go inside quotation marks. Semicolons and colons always go outside quotation marks.

Use a colon to introduce a long one-sentence quotation or a quotation of more than one sentence. If a quotation takes up four or more printed lines, key it single-spaced and indented ½ inch from each margin. Double-space above and below the quoted material. Quotation marks are unnecessary; the indention takes the place of the quotation marks.

Example: In the conclusion of the report, he wrote:

The proposed new plant location at Centerville appears to be ideal for our purposes. The power supply is sufficient. After talking with city officials and various other members of the community, I believe the local work force can meet our demands for employees. The proposed site includes adequate space for future expansion.

Use a colon before an enumeration or when the items in a series are listed on separate lines. Indent the numbered items that are written on separate lines if the paragraphs are indented; block them if the paragraphs are blocked. Double-space between numbered items.

Examples: At lunch, we ate the following: shrimp cocktails, club sandwiches, cheesecake, and iced tea.

The meetings will be held in the following cities:

1. Chicago
2. New York
3. Seattle
4. St. Louis

Do not use a colon if the series is immediately preceded by a verb or a preposition, unless the items are listed on separate lines.

Examples: He took courses in math, word processing, and English.

The last ones to arrive were John, Betty, and Karl.

13.3 WORD STUDY

The words listed here are frequently confused in transcription because they sound alike when dictated but have different meanings. Study the words carefully so that you will be able to select the appropriate word according to the context of the dictation.

> NOTE:
> You differ ***with*** someone. One thing differs ***from*** another thing.

defer (verb) to postpone; to submit in opinion or judgment

The school will *defer* his fees until he receives his check.

He will *defer* to his father on this matter.

differ (verb) to disagree; to be unlike

They *differ* on the resolution of the matter.

They *differ* with your decision.

This book cover *differs* from the other book cover.

disburse (verb) to pay out; to expend

It is Jane's responsibility to *disburse* the profits.

disperse (verb) to break up and scatter in all directions

The police officers were there to *disperse* the crowd.

formally (adverb) in a customary form; with regard to form, fixed customs, and rules

The new constitution was *formally* adopted by the organization.

> NOTE:
> If you are referring to a series of more than two, use ***first*** rather than ***former.***

formerly (adverb) previously; in the past

Formerly the company name was Quinn, Mason & Peabody, but it was changed to Mason & Peabody.

former (adjective) previous; occurring in the past; the first in a series of two

She was a *former* employee.

Of the two spellings, the *former* is preferred.

The chairs are available in brown, blue, and green; but I prefer the *first.*

latter (adjective) the second in a series of two

The chairs are available in blue and in green, but I prefer the *latter.*

imply (verb) to suggest; to hint; to intimate

She went on to *imply* that she did not approve.

infer (verb) to draw a conclusion

I *infer* from your statements that you do not approve.

13.4 SPELLING REVIEW

The dictation for this section contains the words listed here. Study them carefully to help you transcribe more rapidly. If you hear other words in the dictation that you do not know how to spell, make a list of those words and learn their correct spellings. This practice will help you improve your transcription speed.

accountants	dissolve	memorandum
adjournment	dynamic	numerous
administration	expenditures	organization
bookkeeping	formally	pamphlet
capacity	former	proxy
considerably	formerly	ratify
conversion	implied	secretarial
defer	imply	subsidiary
differ	independent	transition
disburse	infer	vacancy
disbursement	inquiries	
disperse	luncheon	

"SHE SAYS SHE'S GOING TO HIRE THE FIRST PERSON THAT TELLS HER THE SIGNS MISSPELLED!"

© Cartoon by Johns

ASSIGNMENTS

Page 187

Complete the Punctuation, Word Study, and Proofreading Exercises that are located on pages 187–192 at the end of this section. The purpose of these exercises is to assist you with the transcription assignment. Tear the completed exercises out of the textbook, and give them to your instructor before you take Spelling Test 13 and before you transcribe the dictation for this section.

SPELLING TEST 13

Ask your instructor for Spelling Test 13. Complete this test before you transcribe the dictaton for Section 13.

SECTION 13 DICTATION

Be sure to review the corrections before you begin to transcribe. Transcribe all of the outgoing letters in modified-block style with mixed punctuation and indented paragraphs. Refer to the Reference Handbook for sample letter styles.

Use the following letterheads when you transcribe:

Recording for Section 13

1. Grayson & Wilson
2. Secretarial Association
3. Interoffice Memorandum 2
4. Interoffice Memorandum 1
5. Second National Bank

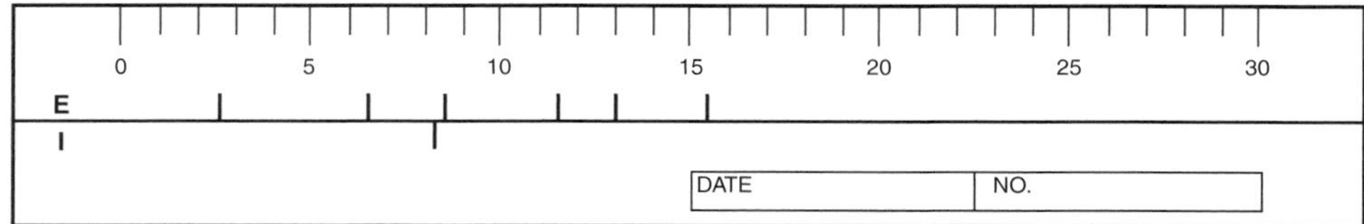

TRANSCRIPTION TEST 4

Ask your instructor for Transcription Test 4. This test contains items you have not transcribed previously. You will transcribe for 30 minutes. Use a spelling checker or a dictionary to look up any words you do not know how to spell.

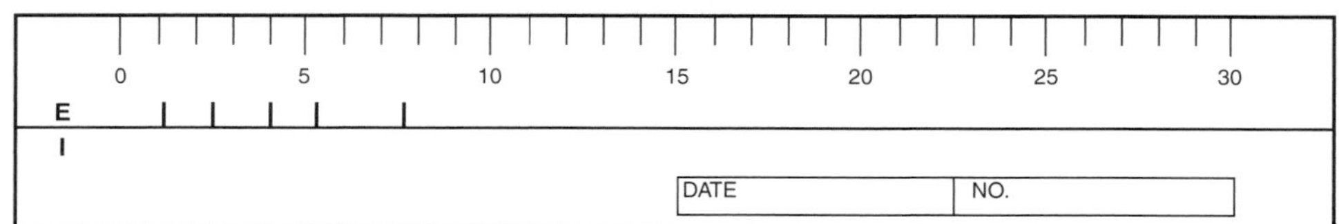

Name/Class ____________________

Section 13 Exercises

When completed, tear these exercises out of the textbook and give them to your instructor.

Punctuation Exercises—Quotations and Colons

DIRECTIONS: ***Insert the proper punctuation where needed in the following sentences.***

1. The guard said No photographs are allowed.

2. Mr. Davis said Send this report to James Reed.

3. Please send this information to our offices in the following cities

1. Aspen

2. Chicago

3. Nashville

4. New York

5. San Francisco

4. You will get a raise starting next week Mr. Grebe said.

5. When you print the new menu remove the following items

1. liver and onions

2. oysters

3. stuffed peppers

6. The waiting room chairs come in three colors brown rust and beige.

7. The position requires the following skills the ability to key at least 70 words a minute the ability to transcribe dictation at 35 words a minute and the ability to key digits accurately.

8. How fast can you key 50 60 70 or more?

9. Remember this when you start a new job Don't be afraid to ask questions.

10. Before Friday complete these lessons 10 11 12 and 13.

11. Add these fractions $^1/_2$ $^1/_4$ $^1/_8$ and $^1/_{12}$.

12. We suggest that you substitute one of the following models 1214 2905 3415 or 7986.

13. The company policy manual contains the following statement

Each salesperson will be furnished an automobile that is to be used for business purposes only. In addition, each salesperson will be furnished a company credit card for use in paying the automobile expenses.

14. Mrs. Pennington said Please forward these customer requests to Wayne Reed in Chicago.
15. The following employees are qualified for the promotion
    1. Carrie Aston
    2. Joan Benson
    3. James Remington
    4. Ahmed Rutan
16. A student who develops a high transcription rate
    1. Is an accurate typist.
    2. Makes undetectable corrections.
    3. Is a good speller.
    4. Proofreads carefully.
    5. Transcribes a mailable copy on the first draft.
17. Mrs. Dorney said Write a report contrasting the strategies of both parties.
18. Order the following supplies for the office
    1. Ten reams of paper
    2. Two boxes of blue medium-point pens
    3. One box of red medium-point pens
    4. Six boxes of paper clips
    5. One three-hole paper punch
19. Mr. Davis made the following statement

    We have met our sales goals for the last six months. Each division has surpassed its sales figures for last year. As a result, we are announcing a new bonus incentive program. You will receive more details next week.
20. Read these chapters 12 13 14 15 and 16.

Word Study Exercises

DIRECTIONS: ***Highlight or underline the correct word choice in each of the following sentences.***

PART 1

1. Mr. Mason's opinion (defers, differs) from Mr. Robert's opinion.
2. Before the committee members (disbursed, dispersed), they (formally, formerly) (passed, past) the proposal that (formally, formerly) they had tabled.
3. I (imply, infer) from your report that you are against the vice president's suggestion.
4. Jacob Henry (implied, inferred) that he would not attend the conference.
5. They will (disburse, disperse) the grant funds next week.

 Name/Class ____________________

6. The business office will (defer, differ) its fees until the scholarship funds have been (disbursed, dispersed).
7. I (imply, infer) from the letter that they do not like the proposed contract changes.
8. José (implied, inferred) that he will (accept, except) the changes.
9. Mrs. Carol Mitchell was (formally, formerly) Miss Carol Jacobs.
10. The judges will (formally, formerly) announce the winner of the contest at the final meeting before we (disburse, disperse).
11. The bank agreed to (defer, differ) the repayment of his loan until June 30.
12. Your opinion (defers, differs) from Robert's opinion.
13. Since payday falls on a holiday, Mr. Collins will (disburse, disperse) the payroll one day early.
14. The clouds began to (disburse, disperse) about noon.
15. Peter Crystal will be (formally, formerly) charged tomorrow.

PART 2

1. (Formally, Formerly) the address was 507 Madison Avenue, but we moved to 308 Monticello Drive.
2. Joe (implied, inferred) that prices will increase next week.
3. We can (imply, infer) from the evidence that he is innocent.
4. Since she had been in the hospital, the instructor agreed to (defer, differ) the grade until she finished the report.
5. The Scholarship Committee will (disburse, disperse) the available scholarship funds.
6. My answer (defers, differs) from Harry's by $15.25.
7. She (implied, inferred) that her visitors would be late.
8. After studying (their, there, they're) financial statements, we (implied, inferred) that the company was having financial difficulty.
9. The merger will be (formally, formerly) announced on October 30.
10. After the service, the congregation (disbursed, dispersed).
11. (Formally, Formerly) John Alden was the president; Rita Perry is now the president.
12. We were all (former, latter) students of Harry Brown.
13. We had to (choose, chose) between Proposal 294 and Proposal 307. I (choose, chose) the (former, latter), Proposal 294. Patricia (choose, chose) the (former, latter), Proposal 307.
14. The attorney read the provisions in Mr. Wilson's will for (disbursing, dispersing) the property in the estate.
15. As the crowd (disbursed, dispersed), we heard several people say that the movie was the best one they had seen this year.

Name/Class____

Proofreading Exercise 13-A

DIRECTIONS: ***Use proofreaders' marks to correct the following memorandum. A list of proofreaders' marks is in the Reference Handbook at the back of the textbook.***

MEMO TO: Clark Roberts

FROM: Charles Lewis

DATE: June 26, 20__

SUBJECT: Employee Suggestion Bonuses

I think we should defer our decision to disperse the funds for employ suggestions until we have had time to discuss further the suggestions from Sarah Whittington and John Collins. Upon rereading there proposals, I think that the dicision of are commitee was a bit hasty.

If we were to combine their ideas and modify them slightly I think we would realize a significent savings of the capitol needed to accomplish our objective. Let me know whether your opinion defers from mine.

xxx

EXERCISE Name/Class ______

Proofreading Exercise 13-B

DIRECTIONS: ***Use proofreaders' marks to correct the following letter. A list of proofreaders' marks is in the Reference Handbook at the back of the textbook.***

June 25, 20__

Mrs. Lola Mead
789 South Columbia Avenue
Oak Harbor, WA 98277

Dear Ms. Mead:

Now is the time to plan ahead for those cool Fall days when everyone will be spending more time at home. At the House of Distinction you will find trained experienced interior designers to help with your decorating needs. There services are free of charge. Look at some examples of savings you will enjoy during the annual summer sale:

1. Save fifteen percent on beautiful real-leather Wilson sofas.

2. Save fifteen percent on upholstered furniture from Reed House.

3. Save twenty percent on a select group of beautiful Redford upholstered furniture. Their our sofas, love seats, and chairs that have been superbly tailored and styled for total livability.

4. Save up to twenty percent on living room, dining room, and bedroom groups from Woodville.

5. Save fifteen percent on Miller patio furniture, the ultimate in wrought iron furniture.

6. Take advantage of special prices on our carpet clearence sale.

The unique, the unusual, and the finest in home furnishings await you at the House of Distinction. Come in soon to take advantage of the big discounts during our annual summer sale.

Yours truly,

HOUSE OF DISTINCSION

Robert Jackson

xxx

EXERCISE Name/Class______________________________

Proofreading Exercise 13-C

DIRECTIONS: ***Use proofreaders' marks to correct the following memorandum. A list of proofreaders' marks is in the Reference Handbook at the back of the textbook.***

MEMO TO: Jane Hamilton

FROM: John H. Downs

DATE: (current date)

SUBJECT: Program Funds

The board will announce it's plans for dispersement of the funds for the women's physical education program for the next physical year at the upcoming meeting with department heads.

Mr. Johnson resently circulated a memo stating "The women's physical education program is overfunded when compared to the relative needs for equipment in the men's program." In light of Mr. Johnson's position, I think that it is imperetive that you be prepared to defend the proposed expendetures for the following items: tennis rackets, exercise and training equipment, basketball uniforms, and tumbling mats.

xxx

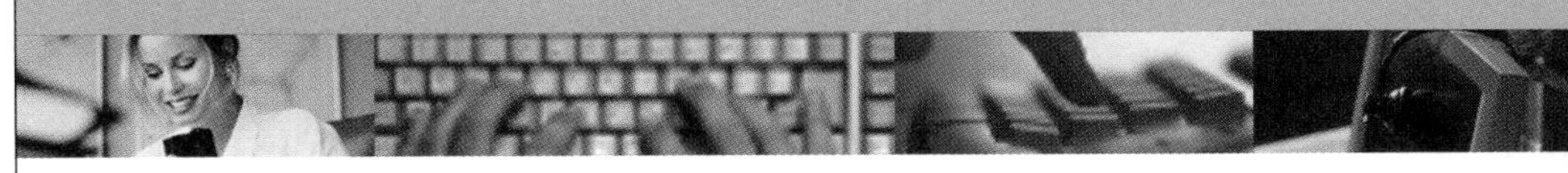

Section 14

14.1 OBJECTIVES

In Section 14, you will work toward the following objectives:

- Insert semicolons where appropriate in sentences containing transitional words or items in series.
- Correctly complete Punctuation Exercises, Word Study Exercises, and Proofreading Exercises in preparation for transcription.
- Complete Spelling Test 14 with at least 80 percent accuracy.
- Select the appropriate words and the correct spelling according to the context of the dictation when transcribing this section's documents.
- Complete Word Study Test 5 on the word study vocabulary in Sections 12, 13, and 14 with at least 80 percent accuracy.

14.2 PUNCTUATION REVIEW

When transitional words or phrases such as *for example, namely,* or *that is* link two independent clauses or introduce an explanation or an enumeration, use a semicolon before the word or phrase and a comma after it.

Examples: Tell me what you can about the new employee; that is, her training, her previous experience, her personality, and her appearance.

We have many tasks to complete before we can turn the project over to the Production Department; for example, we must perform stress tests on the frame.

Use a semicolon to separate items in a series when the individual items contain commas or when the individual items are complete sentences.

Examples: The sites of the division headquarters are located in Chicago, Illinois; Baltimore, Maryland; Phoenix, Arizona; Portland, Oregon; and Sarasota, Florida.

Before you leave today, please do the following: arrange for the conference room for our meeting on Wednesday; schedule an appointment with Mr. Benton for Thursday; call the printer to approve the proof copy; and cancel the meeting with Mrs. Monroe.

14.3 WORD STUDY

The words listed here are frequently confused in transcription because they sound alike when dictated but have different meanings. Study the words carefully so that you will be able to select the appropriate word according to the context of the dictation.

adapt (verb) to make suitable; to conform

She will *adapt* to her new position and her new employer.

adept (adjective) highly skilled; expert

They are *adept* downhill skiers.

adopt (verb) to take and use as one's own

We have voted to *adopt* the new designs.

among (preposition) in company or association with; use *among* when you are referring to one of three or more persons or things

Mr. Kennedy was *among* the three applicants called for a second interview.

between (preposition) in relation to; one or the other; use *between* when you are referring to two persons or things.

Mr. Kelly was seated *between* the president and the treasurer.

can (auxiliary verb) implies ability or power

Can you finish the report by Tuesday?

The police *can* arrest that man for stealing.

may (auxiliary verb) implies permission or possibility

You *may* present your report at the meeting.

It *may* rain this afternoon.

credible (adjective) believable

His version of the story was *credible*.

creditable (adjective) praiseworthy

The plans for marketing the new product are *creditable*.

hear (verb) to become aware of something through your sense of hearing

Do you *hear* his voice?

here (adverb) in this place

The meeting will be *here* at 9 a.m.

interstate (adjective) between or among states

The firm is involved in *interstate* commerce within a three-state area.

intrastate (adjective) within a state

The firm confines its activities solely to *intrastate* commerce. (one state only)

14.4 SPELLING REVIEW

The dictation for this section contains the words listed here. Study them carefully to help you transcribe more rapidly. If you hear other words in the dictation that you do not know how to spell, make a list of those words and learn their correct spellings. This practice will help you improve your transcription speed.

acquisition
adapt
adept
adopt
among
audition
between
category
commerce

NOTE:
If you are transcribing a lengthy report that will require several hours of hard work, what can you do to prevent or get rid of fatigue and still make the best use of your time?

conclusion
credible
creditable
decline
eventually
exterior
flexible
hear
here
interstate
intrastate
monetary
officers
opposition
perimeter
pertinent
policies
prospective
refusal
reluctant
summary
temperature
unparalleled

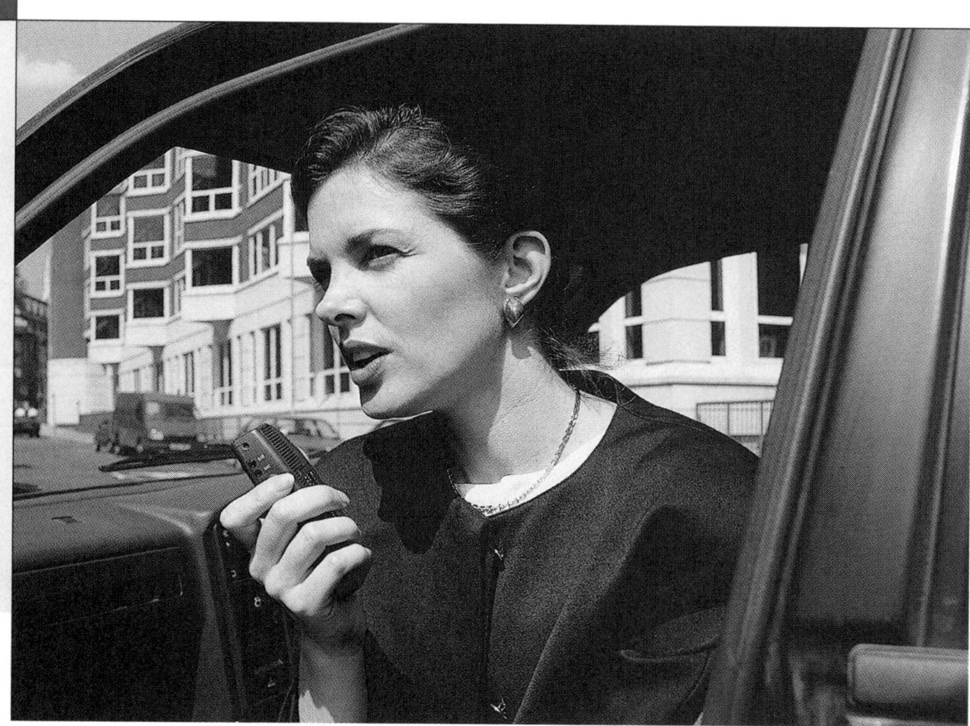

Figure 14.1
Real estate agents use dictation to report on listing activities.
What transcription guidelines and formats might apply in this situation?

ASSIGNMENTS

Page 197

Complete the Punctuation, Word Study, and Proofreading Exercises that are located on pages 197–202 at the end of this section. The purpose of these exercises is to assist you with the transcription assignment. Tear the completed exercises out of the textbook, and give them to your instructor before you take Spelling Test 14 and before you transcribe the dictation for this section.

SPELLING TEST 14

Ask your instructor for Spelling Test 14. Complete this test before you transcribe the dictation for Section 14.

SECTION 14 DICTATION

Recording for Section 14

Be sure to review the corrections before you begin to transcribe. Transcribe all of the outgoing letters in modified-block style with mixed punctuation and blocked paragraphs. Refer to the Reference Handbook for sample letter styles.

Use the following letterheads when you transcribe:

1. York Enterprises, Inc.
2. Steinheimer Advertising Agency
3. O'Brien Paints, Inc.
4. No letterhead provided–e-mail message
5. York Enterprises, Inc.
6. Mead Corporation
7. Interoffice Memorandum 2

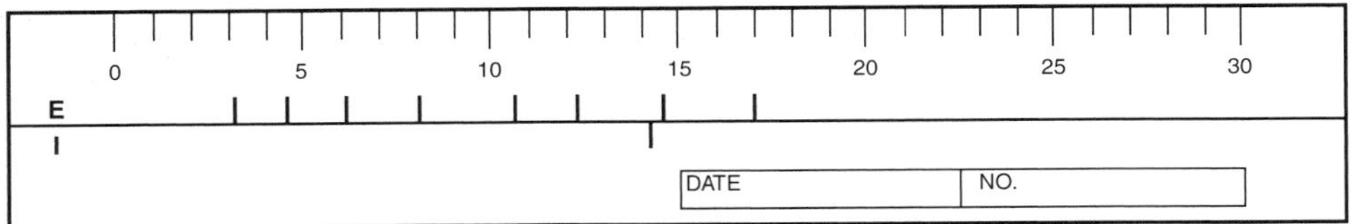

WORD STUDY TEST 5

Ask your instructor for Word Study Test 5. This test covers the word study information contained in Sections 12 through 14. The Word Study Review Summary in the Appendix will help you prepare for this test. Complete this test after you transcribe the dictation for Section 14. The following is a list of words you should study before you take the test:

adapt	defer	infer
adept	differ	interstate
adopt	disburse	intrastate
among	disperse	may
between	formally	right
can	former	rite
collaborate	formerly	suit
corroborate	hear	suite
credible	here	sweet
creditable	imply	write

Name/Class____

Section 14 Exercises

When completed, tear these exercises out of the textbook and give them to your instructor.

Punctuation Exercises—Semicolon with Series and Transitional Words

DIRECTIONS: ***Insert the proper punctuation where needed in the following sentences.***

1. The following employees will retire in May: Carol Jacobs 35 years Betty Land 33 years and Linda Morningstar 30 years.
2. The new additions to the landscaping are doing well namely the cherry tree the dogwood tree and the oak tree.
3. Sarah has had a very productive day for example she has finished the Jackson proposal prepared the agenda for the marketing meeting completed the arrangements for the annual sales meeting in Chicago and delivered the annual reports to the printer.
4. Please order the following items: three staplers Model 2975 four chair mats Model 247 two filing cabinets Model 7349 and eight conference room chairs Model 5618.
5. Paul is an excellent employee for example he is always on time uses his time efficiently makes good suggestions for improvements and works well with clients.
6. Please accomplish the following tasks while I am in Dallas arrange an appointment with Joe Adams the marketing manager prepare the final draft of the brochure for the printer mail the meeting notice to all the district managers and call Angela Jacobs regarding her presentation at the meeting in October.
7. We have four new employees namely Karen Barnfield assistant advertising manager Howard Matthews salesperson Darren Peters administrative assistant to the Sales Department and Michael Childers vice president of the Transportation Division.
8. The convention tour will include Grant Company a pharmaceutical firm Taylor & Jackson an advertising agency and Dynomatic an appliance manufacturer.
9. The classified ad listed the following requirements for the job: transcription ability 35 wpm typing skill 70 wpm WordPerfect knowledge database experience and telephone skills.

Name/Class ____________________

10. Sally seems quite serious about improving her grade for example she turned in two bonus transcripts today.

11. Jane Miller was absent on the following dates: June 10 2001 February 9 2002 March 20 2002 and April 10 2003.

12. The election committee nominated the following people: Sarah Jones president Jim Smith vice president Roger Morris secretary and Karen Jacobs treasurer.

13. He is an excellent race driver for example he has placed at least third in every race except one this year.

14. There are three candidates for the office namely Ralph Jones Ruth Matthews and Joe Martinez.

15. Mrs. Jones has an extremely heavy schedule this week for example she has to be in three cities in the next three days.

16. The report indicates what we expected that is our profits are up 5 percent as a result of our new promotion program.

17. We will hold sales meetings in the following cities: Dallas Texas New York New York Chicago Illinois Miami Florida Tulsa Oklahoma and Los Angeles California.

18. He is an unreliable employee for example he has been absent six times during the past month.

19. The following personnel attended the conference at the home office: Jim Brown Central Division Paul Marks Southern Division Julie Kelly Western Division and Darrell Yale Eastern Division.

20. Allison summarized the reasons that the project would not succeed namely lack of funds lack of trained personnel and lack of community support.

Word Study Exercises

DIRECTIONS: ***Highlight or underline the correct word choice in each of the following sentences.***

PART 1

1. We informed the client that we (can, may) (adapt, adept, adopt) our presentation to (their, there, they're) needs.

2. Martin must (choose, chose) (among, between) the two alternative courses of action.

3. The president will (choose, chose) the executive assistant from (among, between) the four division managers.

4. Everyone who worked on the project did a (credible, creditable) job.

5. We should (hear, here) by tomorrow whether the proposal will be (adapted, adepted, adopted) by Madison & Jones.

Name/Class ____________________

6. The agreement will be (formally, formerly) (adapted, adepted, adopted) at the board meeting in May.
7. The work on the quarterly report was divided evenly (among, between) the three members of the team.
8. The jury will (hear, here) (credible, creditable) testimony that he is innocent.
9. The racing skiers were (adapt, adept, adopt) at negotiating the moguls on the (quiet, quit, quite) morning.
10. We will (adapt, adept, adopt) our present plans to the new circumstances.
11. The plumber will have to (adapt, adept, adopt) the fitting to make it work.
12. Sam is an (adapt, adept, adopt) pilot.
13. Andrea and Robert Martin will (adapt, adept, adopt) the twin girls.
14. You will have to (choose, chose) one from (among, between) the four items shown.
15. Jane must (choose, chose) (among, between) the (to, too, two) job offers.

PART 2

1. We (can, may) see the water tower from our sunroom.
2. You (can, may) have an appointment next Tuesday at 1:30 p.m.
3. Jack had a (credible, creditable) excuse for being late.
4. The team made a (credible, creditable) showing at the tournament.
5. Terry moved closer so that he could (hear, here) the speaker.
6. Chan will meet us (hear, here) at 10 a.m.
7. We plan to expand our (interstate, intrastate) commerce to a six-state area.
8. M & M Industries confines (it's, its) business to the (interstate, intrastate) commerce of Illinois only.
9. Did you (hear, here) the news?
10. We must (choose, chose) (among, between) taking the (deposition, disposition) (hear, here) at our office or at (their, there, they're) office.
11. (Can, May) we have your answer before December 15?
12. We (can, may) (adapt, adept, adopt) the plans to (suit, suite, sweet) your needs.
13. We must (adapt, adept, adopt) the new policy so that we can expand our present (interstate, intrastate) business in Colorado to (interstate, intrastate) business (among, between) all the states.
14. Don was (quiet, quit, quite) (adapt, adept, adopt) at creating (credible, creditable) excuses for not having finished the assignment on time.
15. Everyone in the play gave a (credible, creditable) performance.

Name/Class____________________

Proofreading Exercise 14-A

DIRECTIONS: ***Use proofreaders' marks to correct the following memorandum. A list of proofreaders' marks is in the Reference Handbook at the back of the textbook.***

MEMO TO: All Department Managers

FROM: Henry Rush, Office Manager

DATE: July 15, 20__

SUBJECT: Effective Letter Writing Workshop

After reviewing a sample of the letters written in each of our departments I have come to the conclusion that many of our employees need instruction in writing effective letters. Not all of our employees fall into this category, in fact, some members of our staff are adapt letter writers. However, I believe all of us can benefit from a workshop on effective letter writing.

Mr. Marshall Reed, imminent professor of English at State College, has agreed to develop a workshop designed to help us become more effective letter writers. Mr. Reed will be here on Wednesday August 9. So that normal business operations can continue, Mr. Reed will conduct one workshop from 8 a.m. to 11:30 a.m. and another workshop from 1 p.m. to 4:30 p.m.

Please request that any employs in your department who are regularly required to right letters attend the workshop. When you device the attendance schedule for your department, please divide your employees evenly between the morning and afternoon sessions.

Please cooperate with Mr. Reed in any way that you can while he is hear.

xxx

EXERCISE Name/Class ____________________

Proofreading Exercise 14-B

DIRECTIONS: ***Use proofreaders' marks to correct the following memorandum. A list of proofreaders' marks is in the Reference Handbook at the back of the textbook.***

MEMO TO: Julia Coreman

FROM: Matthew Reed

DATE: October 30, 20__

SUBJECT: Selection of Vice President

I have schedualed a meeting on Teusday at 9:30 a.m. for you, John, and myself hear in my office. We must select the canidates for interviews from amoung the applicants for the new vice presidential position.

As we are considering these applicants, we need to keep in mind that this positon requires someone who is adapt at preparing budgets.

Jenny Mings has substancial experience with budgets however I am not sure how easily she will adapt to our management style.

From Roy Crawford's resume, I think that we can imply that he has some previous budget experience; however, he did not specificaly list budget experience.

George Slater's application looks quiet good, however, he is presently earning within $2,000 of what we are offering for this position. I am not sure he would be willing to make the move for the amount we will offer.

If you want to review the resumes before our meeting my assistant will be happy to get them for you.

xxx

Name/Class________________________________

Proofreading Exercise 14-C

DIRECTIONS: ***Use proofreaders' marks to correct the following memorandum. A list of proofreaders' marks is in the Reference Handbook at the back of the textbook.***

MEMO TO: S. D. Childers

FROM: Eliza Flowers

DATE: (current date)

SUBJECT: New Product Line

At the annual sales meeting, I was quite impressed with the presentation by the Research and Development Division concerning the new line of communication products that they have developed. The Advertising Department has also presented a number of additional creditable suggestions about the points we should stress when trying to sell these revolutionary new products.

I think we can increase our profits substantially if we introduce this new line of products. If we adept an aggressive sales campaign our research would suggest that we may be able to substantialy improve our relative sales position in the industry.

I think we should introduce these products in a limited test area first before expanding our efforts to intrastate markets. After we here from our sales staff concerning the market reaction we can adopt our limited intrastate efforts to the broader market.

When we expand to interstate markets I suggest that our initial advertising efforts be concentrated in major population centers; for example, Chicago, Illinois, Phoenix, Arizona, Dallas, Texas, Miami, Florida, Los Angeles, California, and Philadelphia, Pennsylvania.

Please work with John Davis to prepare advertising copy for our Internet sales effort. These new products should sell quite well through our Internet cite. Please let me hear your thoughts on these new products and your ideas for preceding. We must move rapidly if we want to have a national sales campaign ready for the Christmas holiday demand.

xxx

Section 15

15.1 OBJECTIVES

In Section 15, you will work toward the following objectives:

- Correctly complete Proofreading Exercises in preparation for transcription.
- Complete Spelling Test 15 with at least 80 percent accuracy.
- Select the appropriate words and the correct spelling according to the context of the dictation when transcribing this section's documents.
- Complete Transcription Test 5.

15.2 SPELLING REVIEW

The dictation for this section contains the words listed here. Study them carefully to help you transcribe more rapidly. If you hear other words in the dictation that you do not know how to spell, make a list of those words and learn their correct spellings. This practice will help you improve your transcription speed.

acquainted
align
apologize
apparatus
ascertain
auxiliary
capability
collateral
difference
error
exorbitant
expedite
integrity
interim
notifying
platform
readily
reciprocating
reconcile
regarding
reinforcement
reputable
research
similar
specifications
statistics
turbine
unforeseen
vacuum
versatile
vicinity

ASSIGNMENTS

Complete the Proofreading Exercises that are located on pages 205–208 at the end of this section. The purpose of these exercises is to assist you with the transcription assignment. Tear the completed exercises out of the textbook, and give them to your instructor before you take Spelling Test 15 and before you transcribe the dictation for this section.

Page 205

SPELLING TEST 15

Ask your instructor for Spelling Test 15. Complete this test before you transcribe the dictation for Section 15.

SECTION 15 DICTATION

This recording contains dictated corrections. Be sure to review the corrections before you begin to transcribe. Transcribe all of the outgoing letters in block style with open punctuation. Refer to the Reference Handbook for sample letter styles.

Recording for Section 15

Use the following letterheads when you transcribe:

1. No letterhead provided—e-mail message
2. Acme Manufacturing Company
3. Carol A. Thompson
4. Sullivan Production Company
5. Masters, Mayfield & Wilson
6. Sam C. Mitchell

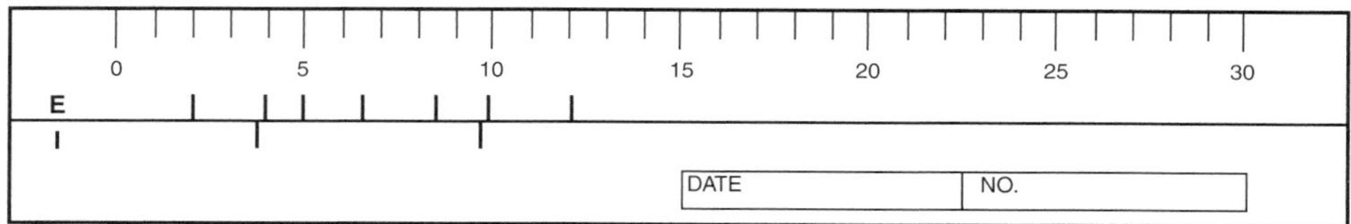

TRANSCRIPTION TEST 5

Ask your instructor for Transcription Test 5. This test contains items you have not transcribed previously. You will transcribe for 30 minutes. Use a spelling checker or a dictionary to look up any words you do not know how to spell.

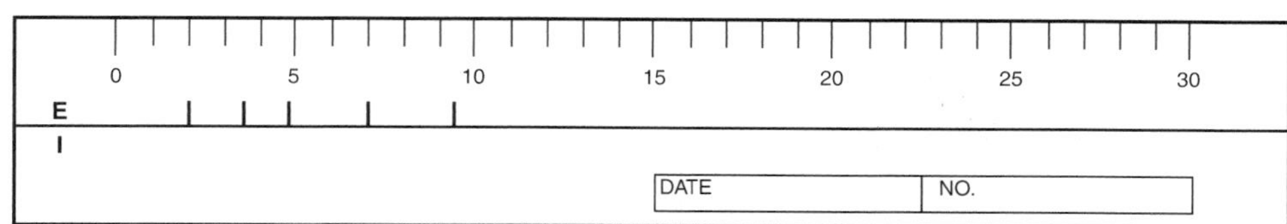

Name/Class ______________________

Section 15 Exercises

When completed, tear these exercises out of the textbook and give them to your instructor.

Proofreading Exercise 15-A

DIRECTIONS: ***Use proofreaders' marks to correct the following table. A list of proofreaders' marks is in the Reference Handbook at the back of the textbook. The unit prices listed are correct amounts.***

STAINLESS STEEL TABLEWARE

Pattern: Snowflake

Quantity	Individual Pieces	Price	Total
12	soup spoon	$12.00	144
12	dinner fork	12.00	144
12	dinner knife	12.00	144
12	salad frok	12.00	144
12	teaspoon	12.00	144
12	desert spoon	10.50	126
12	desert fork	10.50	126
12	desert knife	10.00	120
12	fish fork	12.50	144
12	fish knife	12.50	144
12	osyter fork	8.50	102
12	snail fork	8.50	102
3	soup ladel	28.00	84
8	serving spoon	15.00	180
3	serving fork	15.00	45
2	gravy ladle	30.00	60
6	cheese knife	10.50	53
2	multiple server	25.00	50
2	butter knife	12.00	24
		Total	$2,080

Name/Class

Proofreading Exercise 15-B

DIRECTIONS: ***Use proofreaders' marks to correct the following memorandum. A list of proofreaders' marks is in the Reference Handbook at the back of the textbook. Be sure to check the new prices for accuracy.***

MEMO TO: Margaret Fisher

FROM: Harold Legg

DATE: April 21, 20__

SUBJECT: Proposed Price Changes

After our meeting on Tuesday I realized that we had left several items off are list of price changes. Please reveiw the porposed price changes listed below:

Model	Description	Present Price	Increase	New Price
4579	Shirt	$ 29.85	$2.00	$ 31.85
6341	Tie	19.75	1.50	21.35
7822	Joging Suite	120.00	9.95	129.95
9034	Sweater	63.98	8.00	71.98
5703	Tennis Shorts	22.89	3.25	26.04

Are their other items that should be added to the list? Please let my have your reaction to these increases be Monday.

xxx

Name/Class ______________________________

Proofreading Exercise 15-C

DIRECTIONS: ***Use proofreaders' marks to correct the following expense report. A list of proofreaders' marks is in the Reference Handbook at the back of the textbook. Be sure to check the totals for accuracy.***

Name N. B. Davis, Vice President
Department Sales

Account Number 0754-125-342

EXPENSE REPORT

Date	Location	Travel	Lodging	Meals	Misc. Item	Amount	Daily Total
8/9	Chicago	155	200	10.85	Cab	35	
				30.35			431.20
8/10			200	6.95			
				12.20			
				32.20			250.35
8/11					Cab	35	35.00
8/15	Orlando	282	195	11.25	Cab	35	
				35.10			558.35
8/16			195	5.50			
				12.50			
				33.45			236.35
8/17					Cab	35	35.00
TOTALS		$437	$790	$180.35		$140	$1,547.35

EXERCISE Name/Class________________________________

Proofreading Exercise 15-D

DIRECTIONS: ***Use proofreaders' marks to correct the following letter. A list of proofreaders' marks is in the Reference Handbook at the back of the textbook.***

(current date)

Mr. N. B. Chapman
219 Princess Street
Dawson City, YT Y0B 1G0
Canada

Dear Mr. Chapman:

After many letters, delays, and broken promises, our supplier has admitted his enability to fell our purchasing requirements. Therefore, we must cancel you order for the soil tester. Thank you for your patients and understanding. We apologise for the inconvience. Your refund check is enclosed.

We are searching for an alternate source, and will offer the product in a future catelog when successful.

Enclosed is our latest catalog. As you will notice many items have been included for the first time. The new Weathermaster thermometer on on page 76 includes a cable-free sensor for remote readout. The inside display shows time, relative humidity, whether forecast, and both indoor and outdoor temperatures. Since both the indoor and outdoor units operate on batteries they can be placed anywhere.

The enclosed envelop requires no postage. We look forward to receiving your next order.

Sincerely,

Martin Wells
Order Supervisor

xxx
Enclosures

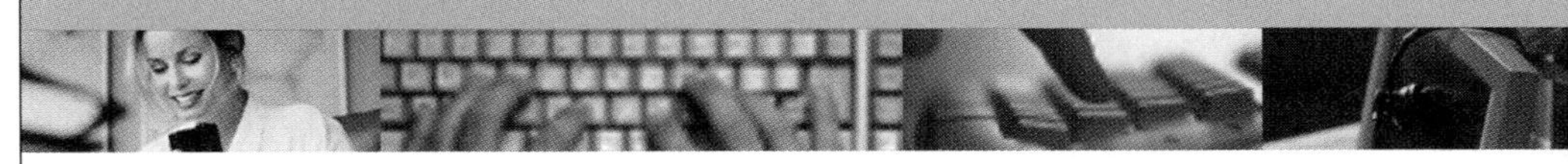

Section 16

16.1 OBJECTIVES

In Section 16, you will work toward the following objectives:

- Correctly complete Proofreading Exercises in preparation for transcription.
- Complete Spelling Test 16 with at least 80 percent accuracy.
- Select the appropriate words and the correct spelling according to the context of the dictation when transcribing this section's documents.
- Complete Transcription Test 6.

16.2 SPELLING REVIEW

The dictation for this section contains the words listed here. Study them carefully to help you transcribe more rapidly. If you hear other words in the dictation that you do not know how to spell, make a list of those words and learn their correct spellings. This practice will help you improve your transcription speed.

ambiguous
atrium
comparison
complacent
criticism
curriculum
destination
detrimental
dormitory
forfeiture
fragrance
fulfill
heavily
inferior
landscaping
maintenance
morale
noticeable
nursery
optimistic
particular
prevalent
relied
rescinded
salable
situation
strategy
subtle
suggestion
superior
suspensions
territories
unusually
windows

ASSIGNMENTS

Page 211

Complete the Proofreading Exercises that are located on pages 211–214 at the end of this section. The purpose of these exercises is to assist you with the transcription assignment. Tear the completed exercises out of the textbook, and give them to your instructor before you take Spelling Test 16 and before you transcribe the dictation for this section.

SPELLING TEST 16

Ask your instructor for Spelling Test 16. Complete this test before you transcribe the dictation for Section 16.

SECTION 16 DICTATION

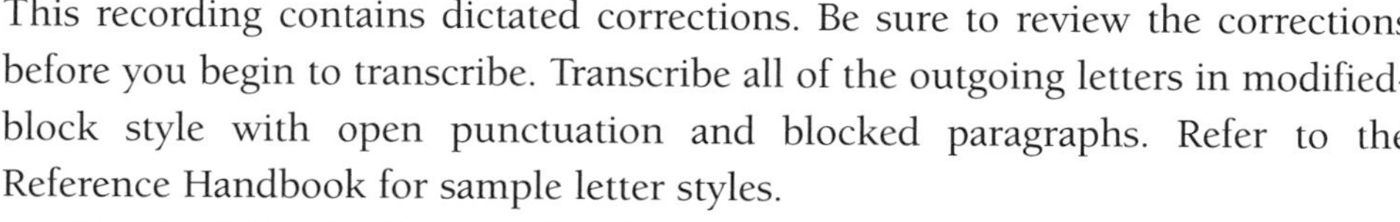

This recording contains dictated corrections. Be sure to review the corrections before you begin to transcribe. Transcribe all of the outgoing letters in modified-block style with open punctuation and blocked paragraphs. Refer to the Reference Handbook for sample letter styles.

Go To... **Recording for Section 16**

Use the following letterheads when you transcribe:

1. Interoffice Memorandum 1
2. No letterhead provided–e-mail message
3. Land Enterprises, Inc.
4. National Automobile Corporation
5. No letterhead provided—e-mail message
6. Jackson College, Admissions Office

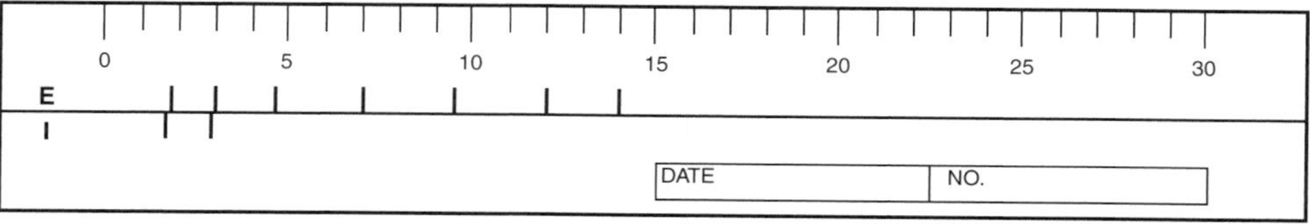

TRANSCRIPTION TEST 6

Ask your instructor for Transcription Test 6. This test contains items you have not transcribed previously. You will transcribe for 30 minutes. Use a spelling checker or a dictionary to look up any words you do not know how to spell.

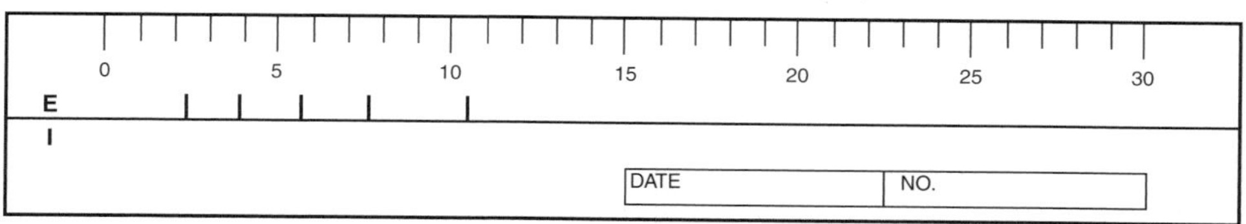

Name/Class ____________________

Section 16 Exercises

When completed, tear these exercises out of the textbook and give them to your instructor.

Proofreading Exercise 16-A

DIRECTIONS: ***Use proofreaders' marks to correct the following calendar. A list of proofreaders' marks is in the Reference Handbook at the back of the textbook.***

CALENDER FOR OCTOBER 30

8:00 a.m.	Board meeting in Conference Room 3
9:45 a.m.	Sales meeting with Jack Kelly, manager of the Mountian District
11:00 a.m.	Betsy Martin - Re: sales contract expirition with Morton
12:00 noon	Lunch with John Miller at Snowmass Country Cub
1:30 p.m.	Reveiw production report with Susan Marks
2:15 p.m.	Interveiw Raymond West
2:45 p.m.	Interveiw Mary Ellen Matual
3:15 p.m.	Interveiw Richard Peters
6 p.m.	Presention to National Committe at Conference Center

Name/Class____

Proofreading Exercise 16-B

DIRECTIONS: ***Use proofreaders' marks to correct the following letter. A list of proofreaders' marks is in the Reference Handbook at the back of the textbook.***

August 9, 20__

St. Charles Hotel
1996 Bayshore Drive
Miami, FL 33139

Ladies and Gentleman

Enclosed is my deposit check for $400.00 for the reservation I made by telephone today. I understand that we well have a two-bedroom suit with a private balcany located at the front of the hotel for seven nights begining on March 20.

Please make a reservation for four for diner at Cafe Chavalle at 8:00 p.m. on March 23.

Sincerly

Thomas Manchester

xxx
Enclosure

Name/Class ____________________

Proofreading Exercise 16-C

DIRECTIONS: ***Use proofreaders' marks to correct the following sentences. A list of proofreaders' marks is in the Reference Handbook at the back of the textbook.***

1. Every person has their own copy of the report.
2. The meetingwill be at 2 o'clock.
3. Please distribute this notice to all personal.
4. We will have time for a vacation in the Spring.
5. Please order 10000 window envelops.
6. The plane leaves at 4:26 p. m.
7. The committee will farther consider the possibility of expanding the present plant.
8. We will of course be glad to help you in any way possible.
9. Please except our apology for the delay.
10. Its time for us to review the equipment needs in the office.
11. Please make a payment on your past due account by March 1.
12. Order 6 dozen no. 24 pens.
13. We must advice you that your account is two months past due.
14. Janes schedule for next semester includes english, keyboarding, computer graphics, and spanish.
15. The add we placed in the June issue of Adventure World magazine was so successful that we are going to repeat the add.
16. Each of the members of the class have at least 3 of their assignments completed.
17. Jason White wrote a book entitled Final Mission.
18. The committee will reveiw the suggestions made by the employees.
19. Please send us you check by May 10.
20. On October 10, we well have been at this location for 15 years.

Name/Class____

21. Each of the three people have appointments.

22. Harry made 5 copies of the report for members of the committee.

23. Mr. Jacobs will meet your plane and Ms. Boner will join you both for lunch at 11:30 a.m. at the Copper Spoon.

24. When you arrive in Chicago, I will meet your plane and we will plan to have dinner at least one evening while you are in the city.

25. We will be happy too assist you in any way that we can.

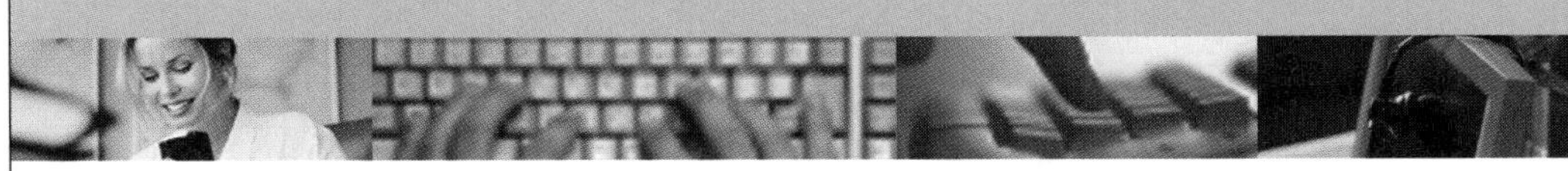

Section 17

17.1 OBJECTIVES

In Section 17, you will work toward the following objectives:

- Correctly complete Proofreading Exercises in preparation for transcription.
- Complete Spelling Test 17 with at least 80 percent accuracy.
- Select the appropriate words and the correct spelling according to the context of the dictation when transcribing this section's documents.
- Complete Transcription Test 7.

17.2 SPELLING REVIEW

The dictation for this section contains the words listed here. Study them carefully to help you transcribe more rapidly. If you hear other words in the dictation that you do not know how to spell, make a list of those words and learn their correct spellings. This practice will help you improve your transcription speed.

NOTE:
You will notice that the text sections are becoming shorter and the recordings longer or more complex. Now that you have the background in language skills and basic transcripton techniques, practice is the key to success.

absence
accident
accrued
acknowledged
allotted
announcements
circulated
collision
comply
construed
duplicating
equitable
erroneously
essential
inducement
injuries
involved
itemized
liability
lien
necessity
occurrence
patient
privilege
recovery
relinquish
substantial
voluntary

ASSIGNMENTS

Go To...
Page 217

Complete the Proofreading Exercises that are located on pages 217–220 at the end of this section. The purpose of these exercises is to assist you with the transcription assignment. Tear the completed exercises out of the textbook, and give them to your instructor before you take Spelling Test 17 and before you transcribe the dictation for this section.

SPELLING TEST 17

Ask your instructor for Spelling Test 17. Complete this test before you transcribe the dictation for Section 17.

SECTION 17 DICTATION

Recording for Section 17

This recording contains dictated corrections. Be sure to review the corrections before you begin to transcribe. Transcribe all of the outgoing letters in modified-block style with mixed punctuation and indented paragraphs. Refer to the Reference Handbook for sample letter styles. Transcribe the manuscripts in unbound manuscript style. (Leave a 2-inch top margin. The title should be in all-capital letters. Double-space after the main heading. Set 1-inch side and bottom margins. Use double spacing. Indent paragraphs ½ inch.)

Use the following letterheads when you transcribe:

1. Sam C. Mitchell
2. Sam C. Mitchell
3. No letterhead provided—manuscript
4. No letterhead provided—manuscript
5. No letterhead provided—e-mail message

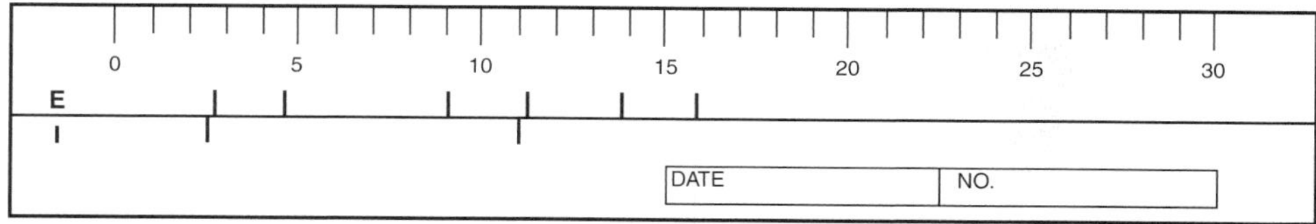

TRANSCRIPTION TEST 7

Ask your instructor for Transcription Test 7. This test contains items you have not previously transcribed. You will transcribe for 30 minutes. Use a spelling checker or a dictionary to look up any words you do not know how to spell.

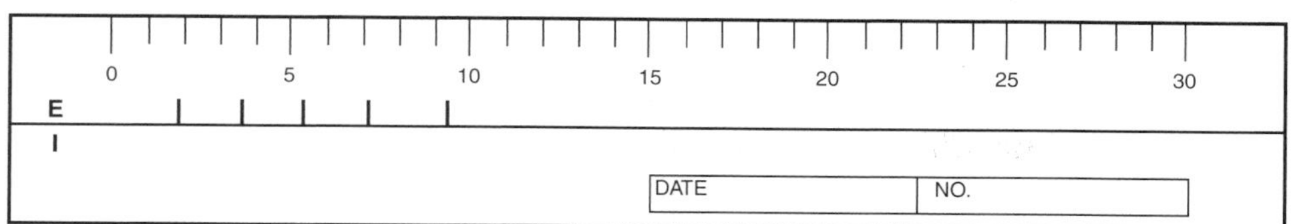

Name/Class ______________________________

Section 17 Exercises

When completed, tear these exercises out of the textbook and give them to your instructor.

Proofreading Exercise 17-A

DIRECTIONS: ***Use proofreaders' marks to correct the following letter. A list of proofreaders' marks is in the Reference Handbook at the back of the textbook.***

May 1, 20__

Mr. Greg Dorris
Happy, the Clown
294 West Melrose Street
Mechanicsville, IA 52306

Dear Mr. Dorris:

Enclosed is the signed copy of the contract for your services as a clown on June 26, 20__, at a birthday party for Angela our daughter. A check for $250.00 is also enclosed.

I understand that you will preform a 45-minute magic show. You will provide party favors, furthermore you will make ballon figures for all 30 children.

I will be sure that the tables you requested are in place before your arrive at 1;30 pm..

Sincerely yours,

Marjorie Land

xxx
Enclosures

EXERCISE Name/Class________________________________

Proofreading Exercise 17-B

DIRECTIONS: ***Use proofreaders' marks to correct the following letter. A list of proofreaders' marks is in the Reference Handbook at the back of the textbook.***

(current date)

Mrs. Martha Hoffman
Apartment 925
Mountainview Apartments
344 Central Avenue
Albuquerque, NM 87106

Dear Mrs. Hoffman:

Thank you for your inquiry concerning Morrow Children's Furniture.

The chest you inquired about is made with dovetail drawer construction. Each drawer has a metal center guide and nylon guides on each side for ease in sliding open on the hardwood drawer guide frame. Each dustproof drawer is custom hand fitted.

All of the exposed surfaces are made from hard maple. This provides a balanced construction that eliminates warpage provides stability during changes of humidity in the home does not chip or crack and provides an extremly hard wood surface to resist scratchs and dents. The H-frames between the drawers are joined to the side panels with dowel joints for added stability. All finishs our durrable and free from toxic substances.

As you can see handcrafted furniture by Morrow is made to be long lasting. If for any reason you should experience a problem you may either contact the retailer where the purchase was made or notify Morrow directly.

The enclosed brochure ilustrates other items in the Morrow line of childrens furniture.

Yours truly,

Harvard Ames

xxx
Enclosure

Name/Class____________________________________

Proofreading Exercise 17-C

DIRECTIONS: ***Use proofreaders' marks to correct the following letter. A list of proofreaders' marks is in the Reference Handbook at the back of the textbook.***

(current date)

M & M Manufacturing Co.
5329 Industrial Parkway
Spring Glen, NY 12483

Ladies and Gentlemen

Please charge our account for the following order:

Style	Description	Quantity	Price	Total
2735	Bocce Ball Set	6	69.95	419.70
6362	Bird Feeder	8	189.95	1515.60
5329	Hot Dog Cooker	10	69.95	699.50
4189	Hose Reel	8	149.95	1189.60
5110	Feather Duster	20	23.95	479.00
			Total	4303.40

Please ship this order by United Parcel Service to our wearhouse address:

109 East Madison
Eagle Harbor, NY 14442

Sincerly

J. L. Cooker
Purchasing Manger

xxx

Name/Class____

Proofreading Exercise 17-D

DIRECTIONS: ***Use proofreaders' marks to correct the following letter. A list of proofreaders' marks is in the Reference Handbook at the back of the textbook.***

June 30, 20__

Mr. Carl Singer
3086 Skyline Drive
Boulder, Colorado 80302

Dear Mr. Singer:

Subject: Subscription to Adventure World

Unless you mailed your renewal to us within the last few days your subscription to Adventure World has expired.

We miss you already and we hop you'll rejoin us as we continue too work to make each issue of Adventure World bigger and better.

Adventure World is written by and for adventure enthusiasts like you and we believe you won't want to be without it in the coming months. Its still available at the same low price of just $6.50 for a year's subscription seven issues. After September 1, a years subscription will cost $7.50.

This is your last chance to renew your subscription and ensure uninterrupted service. Put the enclosed renewal card in the mail to us today and we will bill you latter.

Cordially Yours,

ADVENTURE WORLD

C. A. Robertson
Subscription Supervisor

xxx
Enclosure

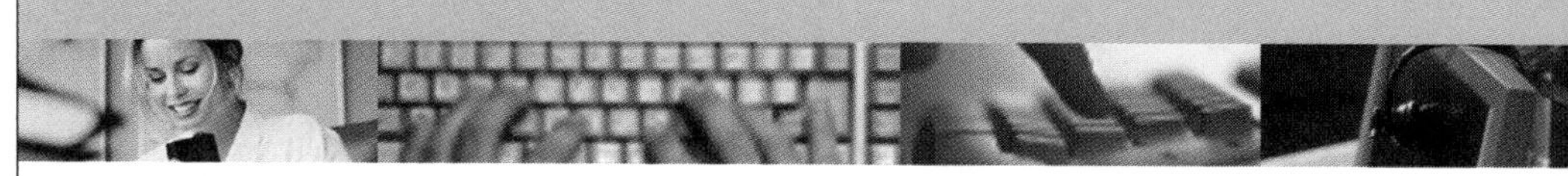

Section 18

18.1 OBJECTIVES

In Section 18, you will work toward the following objectives:

- Correctly complete Proofreading Exercises in preparation for transcription.
- Complete Spelling Test 18 with at least 80 percent accuracy.
- Select the appropriate words and the correct spelling according to the context of the dictation when transcribing this section's documents.

18.2 SPELLING REVIEW

The dictation for this section contains the words listed here. Study them carefully to help you transcribe more rapidly. If you hear other words in the dictation that you do not know how to spell, make a list of those words and learn their correct spellings. This practice will help you improve your transcription speed.

aircraft
allocations
already
aviation
avionics
beginning
bulletin
citizen
competition
coupons
foresee
fuel
improve
literally
maturity
military
parachute
preference
processed
promote
publicity
qualify
satisfaction
soldier
solution
suspect
transaction
virtually
warranty

ASSIGNMENTS

Complete the Proofreading Exercises that are located on pages 223–226 at the end of this section. The purpose of these exercises is to assist you with the transcription assignment. Tear the completed exercises out of the textbook, and give them to your instructor before you take Spelling Test 18 and before you transcribe the dictation for this section.

Page 223

SPELLING TEST 18

Ask your instructor for Spelling Test 18. Complete this test before you transcribe the dictation for Section 18.

SECTION 18 DICTATION

Recording for Section 18

Be sure to review the corrections before you begin to transcribe. Transcribe all of the letters in modified-block style with mixed punctuation and indented paragraphs. Refer to the Reference Handbook for sample letter styles.

Use the following letterheads when you transcribe:

1. Baker Aviation
2. First National Bank
3. Alabama Airways, Inc.
4. Alabama Oil Company
5. American Parachute Association
6. Sam C. Mitchell

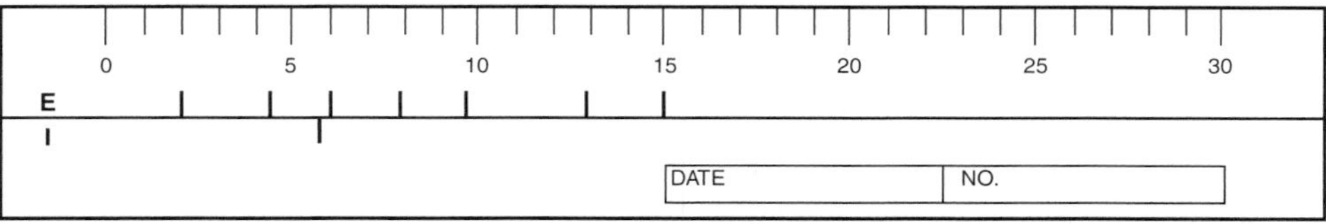

Name/Class ________________________________

Section 18 Exercises

When completed, tear these exercises out of the textbook and give them to your instructor.

Proofreading Exercise 18-A

DIRECTIONS: *Use proofreaders' marks to correct the following table. List the regions in alphabetic order. The figures in the Last Year and Current Year columns are correct. A list of proofreaders' marks is in the Reference Handbook at the back of the textbook.*

MARKETING REPORT

Sales Territory	Last Year	Current Year	Inc/Dec
North Central Region	$2,495,273	$2,503,816	$+8,543
Southern Region	1,792,547	1,850,234	+57,687
Eastern Region	3,052,861	3,278,005	+220,144
Northwestern Regoin	1,951,674	2,321,545	+369.871
Central Region	2,075,913	1,895,767	-180,146
Pacific Region	3,471,258	3,172,987	+298,271
Southwesten Region	2,107,896	2,549,368	+441,472
Mountian Region	2,239,145	2,647,591	+408,556

NOTE:
A table such as this would usually be given to a transcriptionist as a handwritten rough draft rather than as a dictated document.

EXERCISE Name/Class______________________________

Proofreading Exercise 18-B

DIRECTIONS: *Use proofreaders' marks to correct the following letter. A list of proofreaders' marks is in the Reference Handbook at the back of the textbook.*

(current date)

Mrs. Jody Marcus
114 Oak Street
Lakeview, OR 97630

Dear Mr. Marcus:

Congradulations on the upcoming birth of your new baby. Thank you for you interest in the Maxwell portable crib. This crib meets or acceeds all federal safety standards. It is made of sturdy hardwood construction with casters to facilitate maneuverability. The portable crib is equipped with plastic teething rails. One side of the crib can be lowered to allow easier access to your baby. Your baby will sleep in comfort on the thick foam mattress.

The Maxwell portable crib is more than just a crib. The floor of the crib can be adjusted to four different positons. In the upper position, the portable crib becomes a changing table. There are two mattress heights to accomodate the baby as he or she grows. The lowest mattress setting converts the portable crib into a playpin. The crib can be folded into a mere five-inch width for easy storage or travel to grandmothers house.

The enclosed brochure illustrates the portable crib and the accesory items that you will need. The prices in this brochure are effective until July 1 of this year. At that time, we anticepate a price increase.

Order your new Maxwell portable crib today, you will find it to be one of the most usefull purchases you can make for your new baby.

Sincerely,

Karen Miller

xxx
Enclosure

EXERCISE Name/Class

Proofreading Exercise 18-C

DIRECTIONS: ***Use proofreaders' marks to correct the following letter. A list of proofreaders' marks is in the Reference Handbook at the back of the textbook.***

(current date)

Ms. Jane Gilmore
Baker Aviation
1590 Airport Road
Sikeston, MO 63801

Dear Ms. Gilmore;

I would like to sign up for flying lessons. I understand that I must enrol in your ground school class to prepare for the written examination that is required in order to qualefy for a pilot's license.

Please let me know the answers to the following questions;

1. Whin does your next ground school class begen?

2. May I begin taking flying lessons before I complete the ground school?

3. What is the fee for the ground school class?

4. What is the instructor's fee per hour for flying instruction?

5. What is your airplane rental fee per hour if instruction?

6. About how many hours of flight instruction should I expect will be neccessary?

I am eager to begin my flight training and will appreciate your prompt reply.

Sincerely,

Sarah A. Grafton

Name/Class____

Proofreading Exercise 18-D

DIRECTIONS: ***Use proofreaders' marks to correct the following letter. A list of proofreaders' marks is in the Reference Handbook at the back of the textbook.***

(current date)

Mrs. Jane Whitman
5734 Sunset Drive
Glenwood, NM 88039

Dear Mrs. Whitman

Thank you for your order. All items presently in stock are being shiped.

The towel set you choose is temporarilly out of stock but it will be shipped as soon as are new supply arrives next week. Your order from will be returned with the final shipment.

If you find it neccessary to right about your order please enclose the original order form with your letter; and we shall promptly reply. If it is necessary to return any item please use insured parcel post or United Parcel Service however you must return it within 30 days. Include your letter of explanation and the original order form with your return.

We have included a special sale catalog with this letter. This sale catalog is being sent to all our credit card customers a week prior to public anouncement. As you will see their are many choice items at attractively reduced prices. Take advantage of this advance sale notice while supplies last mail your order today.

Cordially yours

WELLER'S DEPARTMENT STORE

James Lee, Manager
Customer Relations

xxx
Enclosure

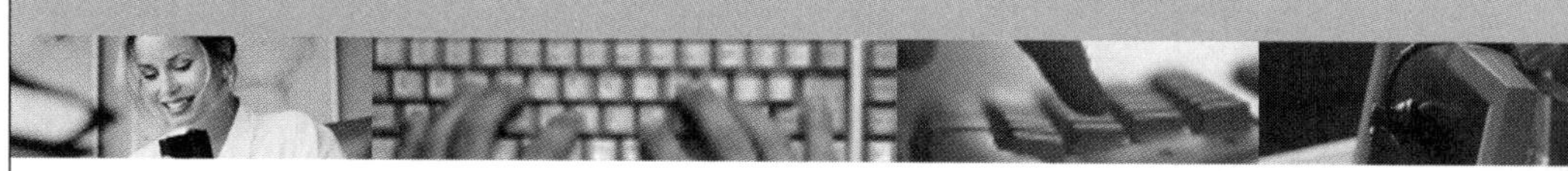

Section 19

19.1 OBJECTIVES

In Section 19, you will work toward the following objectives:

- Correctly format legal documents when transcribing the dictation for this section.
- Correctly complete Proofreading Exercises in preparation for transcription.
- Complete Spelling Test 19 with at least 80 percent accuracy.
- Select the appropriate words and the correct spelling according to the context of the dictation when transcribing this section's documents.
- Complete Transcription Test 8.

19.2 SPELLING REVIEW

The dictation for this section contains the words listed here. Study them carefully to help you transcribe more rapidly. If you hear other words in the dictation that you do not know how to spell, make a list of those words and learn their correct spellings. This practice will help you improve your transcription speed.

aforesaid	intersect	proximately
alleged	litigation	prudent
attorneys	merits	reasonable
consultant	negligent	southerly
contrary	omissions	statutes
endanger	omitting	subsequent
endeavoring	ordinary	vehicle
foregoing	peripheral	violence
hereinafter	propel	witnesses

19.3 TRANSCRIPTION GUIDELINES

Use the following illustrations as format guides when transcribing the first two items.

IN THE CIRCUIT COURT OF FRANKLIN COUNTY, ILLINOIS

JANE DOE,	)	
	)	
Plaintiff,	)	
	)	AT LAW
vs.	)	
	)	No. 2000-L-5000
JOHN SMITH,	)	
	)	
Defendant.	)	

COMPLAINT

Now comes the plaintiff, JANE DOE, by Sam C. Mitchell, her attorney, and for complaint herein against the defendant says:

1.

At all times herein mentioned, Illinois Route 148 was a paved two-lane highway at Zeigler, Franklin County, Illinois, and said Illinois Route 148 was a part and portion of the paved public highway system of the state of Illinois.

2.

On January 19, 2000, at about 11:30 a.m. at a point on the said Route 148 where said highway intersects with Illinois Route 149, the plaintiff herein was operating a Chevrolet automobile in a southerly direction on the said Illinois Route 148.

6.

That the defendant herein did then and there commit one or more of the following careless and negligent acts or omissions to act thereby proximately causing the injuries and damages hereinafter stated:

a. Failed to keep a proper lookout for other vehicles ahead on the said highway when the defendant knew or by the exercise of reasonable care should have known that someone would likely be injured thereby.

b. Failed to apply the brakes on the said Dodge automobile being driven by defendant when it was reasonably necessary to do so in order to avoid the said collision.

WHEREFORE, plaintiff herein prays judgment against the defendant in such amount as may be FAIR and JUST for the treatment expenses and other damages herein sustained together with costs of suit herein.

JANE DOE, Plaintiff,

By: ____________________
SAM C. MITCHELL
Attorney for Plaintiff

ASSIGNMENTS

Complete the Proofreading Exercises that are located on pages 231–234 at the end of this section. The purpose of these exercises is to assist you with the transcription assignment. Tear the completed exercises out of the textbook, and give them to your instructor before you take Spelling Test 19 and before you transcribe the dictation for this section.

Page 231

SPELLING TEST 19

Ask your instructor for Spelling Test 19. Complete this test before you transcribe the dictation for Section 19.

SECTION 19 DICTATION

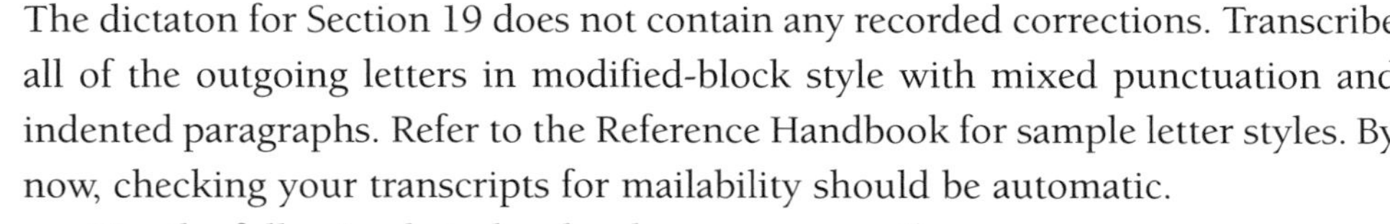

The dictaton for Section 19 does not contain any recorded corrections. Transcribe all of the outgoing letters in modified-block style with mixed punctuation and indented paragraphs. Refer to the Reference Handbook for sample letter styles. By now, checking your transcripts for mailability should be automatic.

Use the following letterheads when you transcribe:

Go To... Recording for Section 19

1 and 2. No letterhead provided—legal documents

3. No letterhead provided—agenda

4. ABC Union Health and Retirement Funds

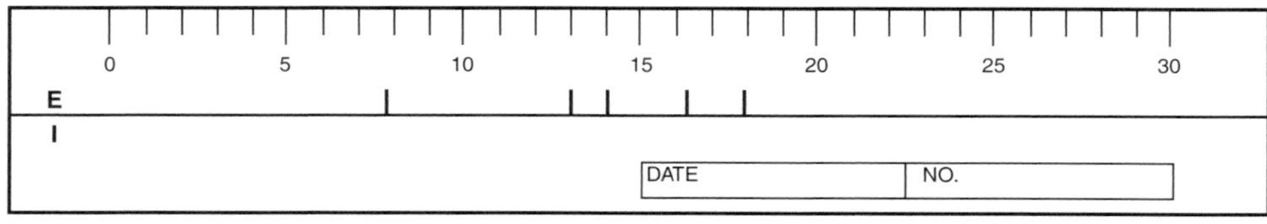

TRANSCRIPTION TEST 8

Ask your instructor for Transcription Test 8, which contains new items. You will transcribe for 30 minutes. Look up any words you do not know how to spell.

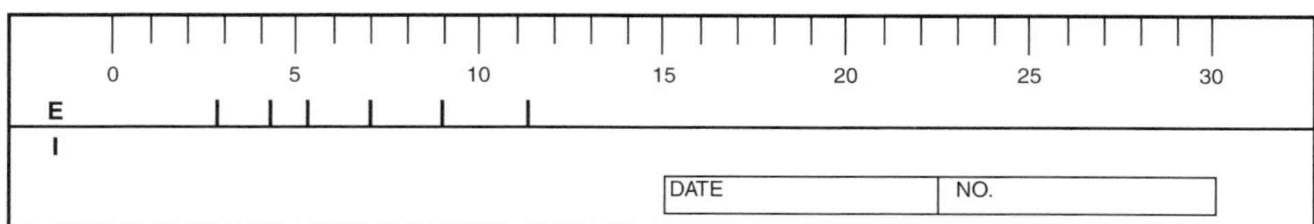

NOTE:
The good news is . . . there are no legal documents on this test. Relax! This is your last transcription test before the final exam. Make this your best test score yet.

Name/Class____

Section 19 Exercises

When completed, tear these exercises out of the textbook and give them to your instructor.

Proofreading Exercise 19-A

DIRECTIONS: ***Use proofreaders' marks to correct the following letter. A list of proofreaders' marks is in the Reference Handbook at the back of the textbook.***

June 26, 20__

Mrs. Margaret Pyszka
1131 North Webster Avenue
Marion, Ill. 62959

Dear Mrs. Pyszka:

We recieved the medical reports from Drs. Raski and Yusko. We will procede to schedule there dispositions in your case.

Please bring any additional medical bills to the office so that they can be included in your file.

We have not yet received a trail date from the court, however, we expect that one will be set when we appear for a pretrial conference that is scheduled in your case next week.

Sincerely yours,

Helen Kunkel

xxx

EXERCISE Name/Class

Proofreading Exercise 19-B

DIRECTIONS: ***Use proofreaders' marks to correct the following letter. A list of proofreaders' marks is in the Reference Handbook at the back of the textbook.***

(current date)

Mr. Steve Randolph
2910 Kentucky Avenue
Lexington, MS 39095

Dear Mr. Randolph:

SUBJECT: Wood Fence Proposal

Today we received your letter that outlined specifications and requirements for a panel wood fence to enclose your yard.

After reading your requirements and specifications we feel certain that we should quote a custom-built fence rather than a panel fence. In a custom-built fence, we build everything on the job cite and all cuts are made to fit the existing grade. This is the only way we can build this fence to meet your requirments.

Please call me at 345-5711 to arange for a convient time for us too meet and discuss your fence. I can explane farther the limititions and advantages of a panel wood fence verses a custom-built fence.

Very truly yours,

David M. Atwood
Sales Represenative

xxx

EXERCISE Name/Class___

Proofreading Exercise 19-C

DIRECTIONS: ***Use proofreaders' marks to correct the following letter. A list of proofreaders' marks is in the Reference Handbook at the back of the textbook.***

(current date)

Mr. Winston Eastwood
627 Washington Avenue
Eldorado, IL 62930

Dear Mr. Eastwood

This will conform your appointment for Thursday October 30 to answer the interogatories that must be sent to the defense attornies in your case.

If you have incured any additional medical bills sense your last contact with us please bring those with you when you come for you appointment.

Sincerely

A. J. Land

xxx

EXERCISE Name/Class________________

Proofreading Exercise 19-D

DIRECTIONS: ***Use proofreaders' marks to correct the following letter. A list of proofreaders' marks is in the Reference Handbook at the back of the textbook.***

(current date)

Mr. Henry A. Casper
Attorney at Law
1305 West Washington Avenue
Miami, FL 33133

Dear Mr. Casper;

Subject: Widgett Estate

If you carefully study the account books and register tapes you will discern the desparity between the income listed in the account books and the amounts shown on the register tapes. This discrepency may collaborate our thoery concerning the origin of the funds we found in the safe.

I think we must hold off dispersing any funds according to the Widgett will until we determine the implecations of these findings. Please let me no your thoughts on this matter.

Yours Truely,

Vincent Ladd

xxx

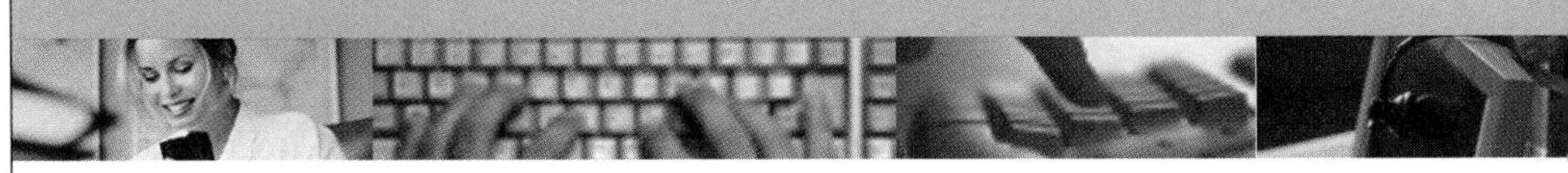

Section 20

20.1 OBJECTIVES

In Section 20, you will work toward the following objectives:

- Correctly format multiple inside addresses when transcribing the dictation for this section.
- Correctly complete Proofreading Exercises in preparation for transcription.
- Complete Spelling Test 20 with at least 80 percent accuracy.
- Select the appropriate words and the correct spelling according to the context of the dictation when transcribing this section's documents.
- Complete the Final Spelling Test.
- Complete the Final Word Study Test on the word study vocabulary in Sections 1 through 14.
- Complete the Final Transcription Test.

20.2 SPELLING REVIEW

The dictation for this section contains the words listed here. Study them carefully to help you transcribe more rapidly. If you hear other words in the dictation that you do not know how to spell, make a list of those words and learn their correct spellings. This practice will help you improve your transcription speed.

accumulated	discretions	per stirpes
affidavit	dissolution	provisions
authorize	estate	residue
bequeath	executor	respect
codicil	instrument	revoking
constraint	memory	surviving
conveyance	nominate	testament

20.3 TRANSCRIPTION GUIDELINES

If a letter is addressed to two or more people at different addresses, the inside addresses may be listed in either of the following two ways:

1. One under the other with 1 blank line separating them.
2. Side by side.

Use the following illustration as a format guide when transcribing the will.

and without giving any additional or special bond for security with respect thereto.

IN WITNESS WHEREOF, I have hereunto set my hand and affixed my seal

this ____________________ day of ________________, 20__.

______________________________(SEAL)
JOHN W. DOE

The foregoing instrument, consisting of three pages of typewritten matter, was on the date hereof signed, sealed, published, and declared as and for his Last Will and Testament by the said Testator, JOHN W. DOE, in the presence of us, who, at his request, in his presence, and in the presence of each other, have subscribed our names hereto as attesting witnesses, fully believing him to be at the time of sound and disposing mind and memory and acting under no undue influence or constraint and at the same time the Testator affixed his initials to each page of this instrument.

___________________________ of ________________________________
___________________________ of ________________________________
___________________________ of ________________________________

STATE OF ILLINOIS)
) SS:
COUNTY OF JEFFERSON)

We, the attesting witnesses to the Will of JOHN W. DOE, on oath state that each of us was present on the _____________ day of _____________, 20___, and saw the Testator sign the Will, of which this affidavit is a part, in our presence; that the Will was attested by each of us in the presence of the Testator; and that each of us believed the Testator to be of sound mind and memory at the time he signed the Will.

____
____
____

Subscribed and sworn to before me this _____ day of _____________, 20 ___.

____
Notary Public

Page Three of My Will____

ASSIGNMENTS

Page 239

Complete the Proofreading Exercises that are located on pages 239–242 at the end of this section. The purpose of these exercises is to assist you with the transcription assignment. Tear the completed exercises out of the textbook, and give them to your instructor before you take Spelling Test 20 and before you transcribe the dictation for this section.

SPELLING TEST 20

Ask your instructor for Spelling Test 20. Complete this test before you transcribe the dictation for Section 20.

SECTION 20 DICTATION

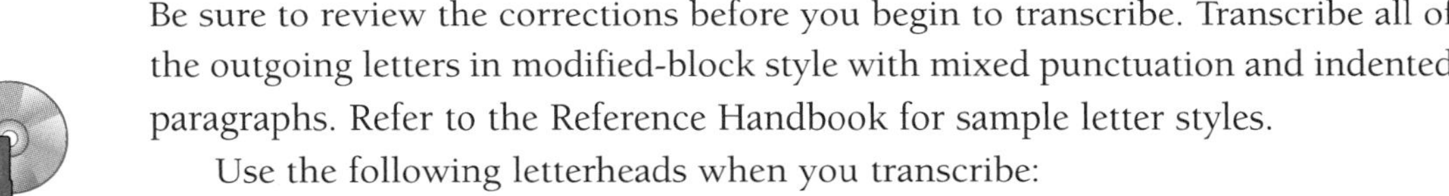

Be sure to review the corrections before you begin to transcribe. Transcribe all of the outgoing letters in modified-block style with mixed punctuation and indented paragraphs. Refer to the Reference Handbook for sample letter styles.

Use the following letterheads when you transcribe:

Recording for Section 20

1. Morton & French, Ltd.
2. No letterhead provided—legal document
3. Morton & French, Ltd.
4. Adventure Tours

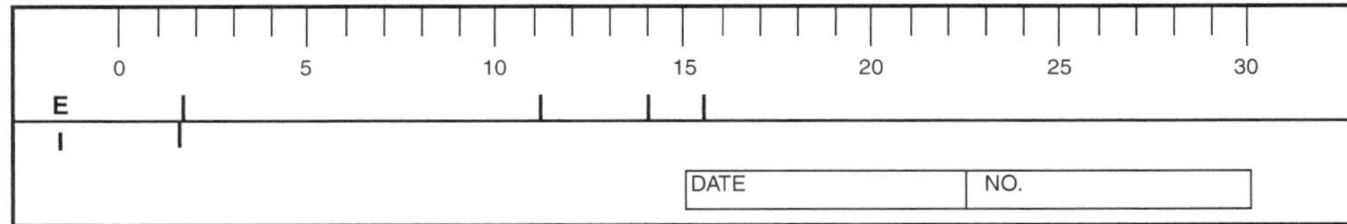

FINAL SPELLING TEST

Ask your instructor for the Final Spelling Test. This spelling test contains 100 words that have been taken from the spelling review words in all 20 sections. The Spelling Word Review Summary in the Appendix is a summary of all the spelling words. Complete this test before you transcribe the Final Transcription Test.

FINAL WORD STUDY TEST

Ask your instructor for the Final Word Study Test. This test covers the information contained in the word studies found in Sections 1 through 14. The Word Study Review Summary, which lists all the Word Study words and their definitions, is in the Appendix. It will help you prepare for this test. Study it before you take the test. Complete this test before you transcribe the Final Transcription Test.

FINAL TRANSCRIPTION TEST

Ask your instructor for the Final Transcription Test. This test contains items you have not previously transcribed. You will transcribe for 30 minutes. Use a spelling checker or a dictionary to look up any words you do not know how to spell.

NOTE:
This test does not contain any dictated corrections or legal documents.

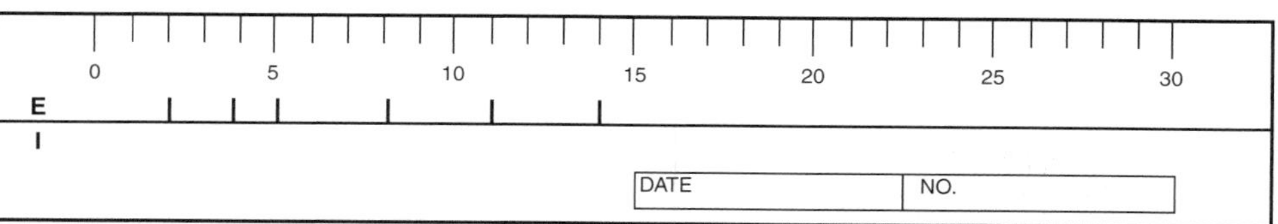

CONGRATULATIONS!!!

Now *you* are a machine transcriptionist.

Name/Class____

Section 20 Exercises

When completed, tear these exercises out of the textbook and give them to your instructor.

Proofreading Exercise 20-A

DIRECTIONS: ***Use proofreaders' marks to correct the following letter. A list of proofreaders' marks is in the Reference Handbook at the back of the textbook.***

October 30, 20__

Mr. Jason Bradshaw
Holly Valley Ranch
2095 Bear Creek Road
Aspen, CO 81611

Dear Mr. Bradshaw:

Please make a reservation for 5 people for a half-day dogsledd ride and lunch at Holly Valley Ranch in December 22. I understand the half-day dogsledd trip begins at 8:30a.m.

Enclosed is my check for the required deposit of $250.00.

Please send a conformation of this reservation.

Sincerely yours,

Loyd Jacobs

xxx
Enclosure: Check

EXERCISE Name/Class____

Proofreading Exercise 20-B

DIRECTIONS: ***Use proofreaders' marks to correct the following letter. A list of proofreaders' marks is in the Reference Handbook at the back of the textbook.***

November 9, 20__

Ms. Alice K. Land
1927 Sand Ridge Road
Lawrenceville, IL 62439

Dear Ms. Land

Congratulations, you have been elected president of the Antique Asociation. Your knowledge of antikues and your experience as a participatant in antique shows thoroughout the years makes you a particularly good choice.

You will be officialy installed as president on December 4 at our annual meeting in Chicago. I would like to meet with you before that date to give you information reguarding our ongoing projects. If their is any assistants I can provide to make the transition a smooth one I will be happy to do so.

I look forward to working with you during the next year; our association is in good hands.

Sincerely

Roy Asbury
President

xxx

Name/Class____

Proofreading Exercise 20-C

DIRECTIONS: ***Use proofreaders' marks to correct the following exercise. A list of proofreaders' marks is in the Reference Handbook at the back of the textbook.***

CALENDER FOR NOVEMBER 9

8:30 a.m.	Adam Jackson - go over proposed new adds
9:30 a.m.	Julie Grayson - interview for sales position
10:30 a.m.	Mark Holder - interveiw for sales position
11:30 a.m.	Jack Isaacs - review monthly sales reports
12:15 p.m.	Meet Carl Fisher for lunch at Anthony's
1:30 p.m.	Finance Commitee Meeting - Conference Room 7
3:30 p.m.	Paul Flowers - interview for sales postion
4:30 p.m.	Cindy Taylor - interview for sales position

EXERCISE Name/Class______________________________

Proofreading Exercise 20-D

DIRECTIONS: ***Use proofreaders' marks to correct the following e-mail message. A list of proofreaders' marks is in the Reference Handbook at the back of the textbook.***

TO: Sam Childers
SUBJECT: New Employees

Dear Sam

Our business is growing so rapidly that we will need to hire at leased ten new employs within the next month. I need your assistants in determining priority postions that must be filled first.

Please right a draft of a notice to be considered for posting to our Web sight concerning these new openings. Can you be available to discuss this farther on Friday at 8 a.m. in my office?

Alice Jacobs

Section 21

21.1 OBJECTIVES

In Section 21, you will work toward the following objectives:

- Prepare for employment opportunities.
- Search for employment opportunities.
- Select the appropriate words and the correct spelling according to the context of the dictation when transcribing this section's documents.

21.2 SECURING EMPLOYMENT

Once you have finished your training, your goal will be to obtain the most rewarding employment available. When you are seeking employment, you are in a sales position. The products you are selling are the education, experience, and skills that you can provide to a prospective employer. Take the time and effort to present yourself in the very best light possible to obtain the position you desire.

There are many sources of information about job openings:

1. College placement office.
2. Internet listings (you will find a partial list at the end of this section).
3. Newspaper ads.
4. Professional journal ads.
5. Previous employers.
6. Relatives.
7. Friends.
8. Private employment agencies.
9. Government employment agencies.

PREPARING YOUR APPLICATION PACKAGE

When you write your letter of application, describe how your education, experience, and skills will benefit the prospective employer. The idea is for your presentation to coincide with the focus of the prospective employer. You need to stress the contribution you can make to the company. Don't merely list courses and previous employment experience; adapt your letter to the reader.

Make sure your letter and resume are absolutely flawless. The employer will see them as samples of your best work, so be sure they are your best work. Keep in mind that your application package (application letter and resume) will be used as part of a deselection process as well as of a selection process. If your materials have errors or are presented in an unattractive manner, you are indicating to the employer that your work on the job may be careless and unprofessional.

Keep your application letter and resume in a smoke-free environment. Knowing that an applicant is a smoker may negatively influence an interviewer, depending on the office's policy and the interviewer's preference. **If the job is important to you, don't restrict your effort to make a good first impression.**

The following is a list of suggestions to help you prepare your application letter and resume:

1. Use 8 1/2 x 11 plain bond paper with a matching envelope. You may want to use an envelope that is large enough to allow your materials to travel flat.
2. Use a laser printer to prepare your materials.
3. For the letter, use the personal business letter style with a return address unless you have your own business letterhead stationery.

"First of all, you spelled 'resume' wrong."

4. Find out who processes applications, and address your letter to that person.
5. Use an appropriate complimentary closing: *Sincerely* or *Sincerely yours.*
6. Don't forget to sign your letter in black or blue ink. Other colors of ink are not appropriate.

Never lie on your resume. Your resume becomes part of your permanent personnel file. If an employer is looking for a reason to terminate an employee, a misstatement on a resume can be used as justification. However, this is not a time for false modesty; honestly state your qualifications for the position.

Your letter and resume must be physically flawless. Don't count on dazzling them in the interview—*first you have to get the interview.* Rarely, if ever, will some-

"You just self-deprecated yourself right out of a job."

one be offered a position based solely on an application package. The objective of your application package is to obtain an interview. The objective of the interview is to secure the position.

If a prospective employer calls you for an interview, your application package has been successful even if you do not get the job.

PREPARING FOR INTERVIEWS

Preparation will help you maintain your poise and confidence during an interview. A good way to practice for an interview is to write possible questions on 3 x 5 cards and ask a friend to practice the interview with you. Shuffle the cards between practice interview sessions to help you learn to think on your feet. (You can find numerous books that list interview questions.) Remember that you are striving to sell your knowledge and skills to a firm that needs them. As you answer questions, point out how your education, experience, and skills will benefit the prospective employer. If you learn all you can about the company before you apply, you will be better equipped to explain how you can be a productive employee.

The following list contains items you may want to take with you to the interview:

- Two copies of your resume and a list of references (if not included in your resume).
- Your social security card.
- Two pens.
- A small notebook for taking notes.
- A personal appointment calendar (the interviewer may ask you to return for a second interview).
- A list of questions to ask the interviewer.
- A portfolio containing samples of your work.
- A small pocket dictionary.
- A school transcript showing dates of attendance.
- Letters of reference (optional).

During the interview, the interviewer will judge the following qualities:

- Appearance.
- Communication skills.
- Ability to solve problems.
- Potential for growth.
- Maturity (more than chronological age).
- Personality (are you friendly, cheerful, and sincere?).
- Manners.
- Ability to think on your feet.
- Ability to fit in with other employees.
- Willingness to work.

The most important thing you can take with you on a job interview is a good work-for-you attitude. The prospective employer is looking for someone who will make the firm run more smoothly and be more profitable and who will be productive without constant supervision. The interviewer is trying to select the applicant who not only is most likely to have the skills necessary to perform productively but who will also be *willing* to work hard and who will be able to perform the necessary tasks without driving everyone else crazy. Judging the applicant's ability to fit in smoothly with the other employees is an important consideration for the interviewer during the interview.

Following are some of the factors that will affect the interviewer's perception of your work-for-you attitude.

- Quality of the application package: application letter, resume, and portfolio (if presented).
- Personal appearance.
- Eye contact.
- Handshake.
- Conduct during the interview.
- Answers to questions during the interview.
- Questions asked by the applicant during the interview.
- Interview follow-up.

Your handshake should give the impression that you are confident. Don't give a limp handshake; don't give a tip-of-the-finger handshake; don't give a bone-crushing handshake; and don't give a two-handed handshake. The web part of your hand should touch the web portion of the other person's hand in a firm handshake.

You want to project a powerful, in-control image during the interview. In the first 5 to 7 seconds, you will have made a first impression that will be hard to overcome later. Make that first impression work for you.

Choose clothing that reflects an understanding of what is appropriate for the position for which you are applying. Choose a color and style that is becoming to you, and do not wear extremes. Ladies, you may have a beautiful pink suit, but don't wear it to the interview. Gentlemen, you may have a great yellow sports jacket, but don't wear it to the interview. Shine your shoes, and be certain your clothes are clean and pressed. Don't wear perfume or cologne. What is quite pleasant to one person may be offensive to another. Perhaps the interviewer is allergic to your cologne. Don't do *anything* that could cause you to be deselected.

You will create a good first impression if you dress appropriately, maintain eye contact, shake hands firmly, hold your head up straight, and keep your hands away from your face or your hair. You want your appearance to convey the image that:

- You are strong.
- You are a business professional.
- You are serious about your career.
- You are confident of your ability.
- The employer can rely on you.

Frank and Ernest

Never be late for an interview. Being late indicates that you are inconsiderate, disorganized, or not serious about the job. Arrive 5 to 10 minutes early. Unless you are quite familiar with the area, drive to the interview site at the interview time a few days ahead of the appointment to determine how long it will take you to get there and find a place to park. (Do not do this on Saturday or Sunday since the traffic patterns will be different.) When you arrive for the interview, park in an area without specific time limits if possible.

Prepare a list of questions before the interview. At some point in the interview, you will probably be asked if you have any questions. Ask the two or three most important questions that have not been covered in the interview.

Thank the interviewer before you leave and also thank the receptionist. Assume that the interviewer will ask the receptionist for an opinion of how you conducted yourself in the waiting room. Never tell the receptionist how nervous you are; act confident even if you are nervous.

The following is a list of things you should *not* do during the interview:

- Don't take anyone with you. It is not professional and might indicate a lack of confidence.
- Don't appear nervous while you are waiting. Don't fidget, tug at your clothes, or tap your pen.
- Don't sit down until invited to do so.
- Don't put personal belongings or your hands on the interviewer's desk.
- Don't argue with the interviewer.

- Don't interrupt. Let the interviewer complete each question or statement before you speak. The interviewer may ask a question to which you have practiced a particularly good answer, but you must not interrupt before the question is completed. If interrupted, the interviewer may be insulted and pay less attention to your answer.
- Don't tell jokes (unless you are applying for a job as a stand-up comedian). What is funny to one person may be offensive to another.
- Don't criticize past employers, former colleagues, your school, or your professors. *Be positive.* Criticisms, even if they are justified, may be perceived as an inability to get along with people.
- Don't smoke. It cannot help you get a job and may prevent you from getting the job. If the interviewer offers you a cigarette, say "No, thank you."
- Don't chew gum.
- Don't look at your watch. The interviewer may think that you are not interested in the position or that you feel you have better things to do.

It is important to get a good night's sleep before the interview. You can't think on your feet if you are dead on your feet.

You can benefit from each interview whether you get the job or not. When the interview is completed, immediately go to a quiet spot and write down as many of the interview questions as you can remember. Later you can transfer these questions to 3 x 5 cards to prepare for the next interview. Objectively evaluate the interview. Were some questions difficult for you to answer? Did you maintain good eye contact throughout the interview? How can you improve your next interview performance? Make notes of information learned about the company, employee names, and procedures. These will be helpful if there is a second interview. If you are offered the position, these notes will help you make a smooth start.

Within 24 hours after the interview, you should write a short letter thanking the interviewer for the opportunity to talk about your qualifications for the position and expressing your continued interest in the position. Briefly mention your most important qualification. You might mention something that was discussed during the interview to help the interviewer remember you. Ask to be notified when a hiring decision is made. The thank-you letter accomplishes at least three things:

1. It reminds the employer of your application and interview and brings your name to mind when the hiring decision is being made. Name recognition is important at this stage.

2. It is the courteous thing to do and will be appreciated by the employer. It shows that you recognize that the interviewer's time is valuable.

3. It underscores your professionalism.

A greeting card or a personal thank-you card is not appropriate in this situation. You must write a short business letter expressing appreciation.

Advances in technology are occurring at an astonishing speed. It will be important for you to keep up with what is new in your field. Refer to Part 1 of this textbook for a review of ways to keep current in your field.

Following is a partial list of employment sites available on the Internet to help you get started on your search for employment:

America's Job Bank	http://www.ajb.dni.us
BridgePath	http://www.bridgepath.com
CareerBuilder Network	http://www.careerbuilder.com
CareerMagazine	http://www.careermag.com
CareerMosaic	http://www.careermosaic.com
CareerPath	http://www.careerpath.com
CareerSite	http://www.careersite.com
Careers/wsj/com	http://www.careers.wsj.com
CareerWeb	http://www.cweb.com
Experience online	http://www.experienceonline.com
Help Wanted USA	http://www.iccweb.com
Job Hunter's Bible	http://www.jobhuntersbible.com
Jobtrak	http://www.jobtrak.com
JobWeb	http://www.jobweb.com
The Monster Board	http://www.monster.com
NationJob Network	http://www.nationjob.com
Online Career Center	http://www.occ.com

ASSIGNMENTS

Transcribe all of the outgoing letters in modified-block style with mixed punctuation and indented paragraphs. Refer to the Reference Handbook for sample letter styles. Refer to the following illustrations to assist you in keying the caption on the legal document.

IN THE CIRCUIT COURT OF WILLIAMSON COUNTY, ILLINOIS

RHONDA GLENN,	)	
	)	
Plaintiff,	)	
	)	AT LAW
vs.	)	
	)	No. 2002-L-278
DAVID HARDCASTLE,	)	
	)	
Defendant.	)	

NOTICE FOR APPEARANCE AT TRIAL

Use the above caption for Section 21 - Item 4

Recording for Section 21

SECTION 21 DICTATION

Use the following letterheads when you transcribe:

1. Interoffice Memorandum 1
2. Dr. James Thornhill
3. Sam C. Mitchell
4. No letterhead provided—legal document

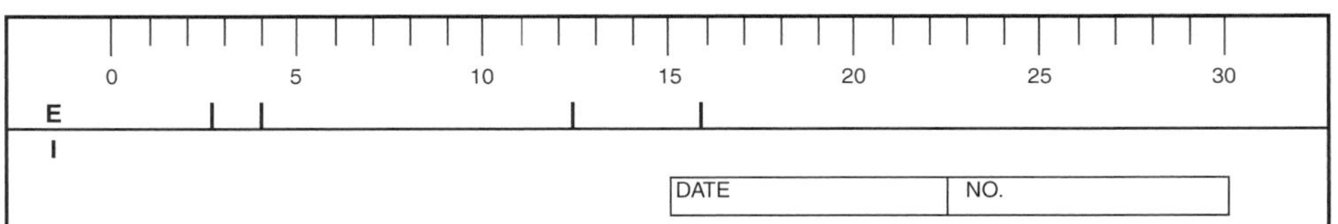

Part 3

Appendix

Spelling Word Review Summary—Keyed to Sections

Word Study Review Summary

Reference Handbook

Spelling Word Review Summary—Keyed to Sections

abandoned—9
absence—17
absenteeism—8
accede—7
accept—3
access—11
accessibility—9
accessories—7
accident—17
accommodations—1
accompanied—4
accomplish—4
accordingly—9
accountants—13
accrued—17
accumulated—20
achievement—12
acknowledged—17
acoustical—9
acquainted—15
acquire—10
acquisition—14
actually—4
adapt—14
addition—3
adept—14
adequate—12
adjacent—2
adjourned—6
adjournment—13
administration—13
adopt—14
advantageous—1
advice—5
advise—5
advisers—6
advocate—12
affidavit—20
aforesaid—19
agenda—1
aircraft—18
align—15
alleged—19
alleviate—10
allocated—12
allocations—18
allotted—17
already—18
altar—6
alter—6
alternate—5
alternative—12
ambiguous—16
amendment—8
among—14
analysis—10
analyze—2
analyzing—10
announcement—17
anticipate—10
apologize—15
apparatus—15
applicable—7
application—1
appointment—4
appraise—4
appreciable—10
appreciate—1
apprise—4
appropriate—4
approximately—11
arrangements—1
arrival—12
ascertain—15
aspects—10
assistance—1
assistants—1
associate—9
assume—7
assuredly—3
atmosphere—2
atrium—16
attached—7
attorneys—19
audience—10
audition—14
authoritative—3

authority—7
authorization—8
authorize—20
automatically—3
auxiliary—15
available—1
aviation—18
avionics—18
bare—11
bear—11
beginning—18
beneficial—4
bequeath—20
between—14
biannual—8
biennial—8
blossoms—8
bookkeeping—13
boutique—12
brake—9
break—9
brilliant—8
brochure—2
buffet—1
bulletin—18
cabana—2
calendar—8
campaign—5
candidate—6
capability—15
capacity—13
capital—9
capitol—9
category—14
cathedral—12
ceremony—6
certificate—2
challenge—12
circulated—17
citizen—18
client—7
codicil—20
cognizant—10
collaborate—12
collateral—15
collision—17
command—10
commend—10
commerce—14
commercial—1
committee—5
community—11
comparison—16
competition—18
competitive—5
complacent—16
complement—5
completion—11
compliance—6
compliment—5
comply—17
concentrated—5
concise—2
conclude—5
conclusion—14
concur—12
condominiums—2
confirm—11
confirmation—2
congratulations—12
conscientious—8
consensus—10
consequently—9
considerably—13
constraint—20
construction—6
construed—17
consul—7
consultant—19
contrary—19
controlling—10
controversial—10
convenience—8
convenient—2
convention—1
conversion—13
conveyance—20
coordinate—9
cordially—2
corroborate—12
costumes—8
council—7
counsel—7
coupons—18
courteous—2
coverage—2
creating—1
credible—14
creditable—14
criticism—16
curriculum—16
custom—3
customers—1
cyberspace—1
decide—6
decline—14
decorations—8
defendant—7
defer—13
definitely—12
delicate—8
delicious—2
demonstrating—5
departure—4
deposition—7
describe—9
descriptions—1
destination—16
deteriorating—6
detrimental—16
device—5
devise—5
differ—13
difference—15
difficult—10
difficulty—4
diligence—10
diminish—10
disappeared—12
disburse—13
disbursement—13
discontinue—7
discouraged—10
discretions—20
discussed—11

injuries—17
innovative—10
inquiries—13
instructions—6
instructor—7
instrument—20
integrity—15
interim—15
interrogatories—9
interruption—4
intersect—19
interstate—14
intrastate—14
introductory—11
investigation—4
invigorating—2
involved—17
irreparable—10
itemized—17
itinerary—7
jeopardize—10
kangaroo—9
koala—9
knowledgeable—3
laboratory—2
landscaping—16
lapse—4
leased—7
least—7
leisure—9
liability—17
lien—17
limousine—1
literally—18
literary—3
litigation—19
Louisiana—7
lounges—7
luge—9
luncheon—13
luxurious—3
magnificent—4
maintenance—16
managerial—10
manifest—12
manuscript—12
maturity—18
memorabilia—11
memorandum—13
memory—20
merchandise—11
merits—19
military—18
miner—4
minimal—3
minor—4
minute—11
miracle—7
modem—5
monetary—14
morale—16
municipal—6
mutually—12
necessary—5
necessity—17
negligent—19
neighbors—11
nominal—5
nominate—20
normally—3
noticeable—16
notifying—15
numerous—13
nursery—16
obedience—10
observed—6
occasionally—8
occurrence—17
occurring—9
officers—14
omissions—19
omitting—19
operation—5
opinion—9
opportunities—1
opposition—14
optimism—10
optimistic—16
ordinance—6
ordinary—19
organization—13
original—11
overdo—4
overdue—4
overlooked—8
paid—7
pamphlet—13
parachute—18
participate—4
particular—16
patience—5
patient—17
per stirpes—20
performance—1
perhaps—4
perimeter—14
periodically—9
peripheral—19
permanent—3
personal—1
personalized—5
personnel—1
pertinent—14
photography—2
physical—10
plaintiff—7
platform—15
podium—1
policies—14
pollution—6
population—11
possibility—7
precede—9
preference—18
preferred—11
premiums—2
prescribed—10
presence—2
presents—2
prevalent—16
principal—7
principle—7
prior—11
privilege—17
probably—11

transferred—12
transition—13
transmission—8
treasure—12
tremendous—1
truly—2
tuition—5
turbine—15
unanimously—6
unconditionally—8
underwriters—8
unforeseen—15
unfortunately—2
unique—3
unparalleled—14
unusually—16
updated—9
upkeep—3
vacancy—13
vacuum—15
valuable—4
variety—1
various—2
vehicle—19
versatile—15
vicinity—15
violence—19
virtually—18
volume—3
voluntary—17
voyage—4
waive—3
waiver—3
warranty—18
waver—3
weak—10
weather—6
week—10
whether—6
widespread—8
windows—16
witnesses—19
wreckage—12
write—12

Word Study Review Summary

Section 1

assistance (noun) help or aid

I need your *assistance* in lifting this box.

assistants (noun) helpers; workers

Mr. White requested three *assistants* to help him in the new division.

desert (verb) to abandon; to leave; to forsake

We will *desert* our plan to build a new factory.

desert (noun) an arid region

Death Valley is a *desert*.

dessert the final course of a meal; such as pie, cake, or pudding

We ate peach pie for *dessert*.

personal (adjective) relating to or affecting a person

Do not make *personal* calls from the office.

personnel (noun) employees

One-half of our *personnel* work on Saturdays.

their (possessive pronoun) belonging to or done by them

This is *their* car. This is *their* work.

there (adverb) at or in that place; used to introduce a clause

I assure you that I will be *there*.

There is plenty of time to finish the report.

they're contraction for *they are*

They're scheduled to arrive at 7 p.m.

to (preposition) in the direction of; toward; used to introduce a verb in the infinitive; regarding or concerning

John was on his way *to* work.

She did not want *to* be late for the meeting.

He was attentive *to* the telephone while everyone was at lunch.

too (adverb) more than enough; also

Jane ate *too* much for lunch.

He wanted to help *too*.

two (adjective) one plus one

Mr. Davis dictated *two* letters before the meeting.

Section 2

allowed (verb) permitted

Three representatives of our division were *allowed* to attend the conference.

aloud (adverb) in an audible voice

Please state your objections *aloud.*

cite (verb) to quote

Please *cite* your favorite poem.

sight (noun) something seen; the act of seeing

The sunset was a beautiful *sight.*

The *sight* of the tornado terrified them.

sight (verb) to observe

The soldier used binoculars to *sight* enemy planes.

site (noun) location

This is the *site* for the new building.

envelop (verb) to surround

The convention hotel is designed to *envelop* a center courtyard.

envelope (noun) a folded paper container for a letter

The assistant addressed the *envelope* before inserting the letter.

farther (adverb) to a greater distance

Mr. Whitmer has come *farther* than anyone else.

further (adverb) to a greater degree or to a greater extent

We will discuss the plans *further* at the next meeting.

it's contraction for *it is*

It's time for the meeting to begin.

its (possessive pronoun) belonging to or done by it

The budget committee made *its* position clear in the report.

presence (noun) the fact or condition of being present

His *presence* could be felt in the room.

presents (noun) gifts

She received three *presents* on her birthday.

presents (verb) gives

Listen carefully as he *presents* his report.

NOTE:
Be careful not to confuse the possessive pronoun ***its*** with the contraction ***it's***. Try to substitute the words ***it is*** in the sentence. If the substitution makes sense, use the apostrophe and key ***it's***. If the substitution does not make sense, key the possessive ***its***. You can make similar substitutions for other possessive pronouns and contractions to determine whether you need an apostrophe.

Section 3

accept (verb) to receive; to give approval to

We will accept applications for this position tomorrow.

The representatives for the other company will accept the proposed changes.

except (preposition) with the exclusion or the exception of

Everyone in the department attended the conference except John.

addition (noun) something added

The addition of the Iowa plant brings our total to 50.

edition (noun) one version of a publication

This is the latest edition of the book.

currant (noun) a kind of berry

He ate *currant* jam on his toast.

current (adjective) occurring at the present time; now in progress

Mr. Jamison obtained the loan at the *current* interest rate.

waive (verb) to give up something, such as a right, a claim, or a privilege

The corporation decided to *waive* the right to renew the option on the property.

waiver (noun) the act of giving up right, claim, or privilege; a document containing declaration of such an act

We received the *waiver* in the mail yesterday.

wave or waver (verb) to sway; to fluctuate in opinion

The only juror voting against the defendant was beginning to *waver*.

wave (noun) a sweeping movement of the hand used as a signal or a greeting

She motioned to the door with a *wave* of her hand.

your (possessive pronoun) belonging to you

This is *your* book.

you're contraction for *you are*

We hope *you're* planning to go to the lecture.

Section 4

appraise (verb) to decide the value of

The real estate agent will *appraise* our house on Thursday.

apprise (verb) to inform; to notify

I will *apprise* you of any change in the meeting time.

miner (noun) a person who works in a mine

The coal *miner* was tired after working all day in the mine.

minor (adjective) lesser in size, amount, extent, or importance

The *minor* problem did not cause a delay in the completion of the building.

minor (noun) a person who is under legal age

A *minor* is not admitted unless accompanied by an adult.

overdo (verb) to do too much

Don't *overdo* on your first day of jogging.

overdue (adjective) past the time for payment

Your account is *overdue*.

Section 5

ad (noun) an advertisement

The new *ad* will appear in the November issue of the magazine.

add (verb) to join or unite; to combine in one sum

Please *add* this letter to the Williams file.

She had to *add* many columns of numbers to finish the chart.

advice (noun) a recommendation; an opinion given about what to do

Paul did not heed his brother's *advice*.

advise (verb) to inform; to recommend

My attorney will *advise* me on the matter.

complement (verb) to complete or make complete; to fill out

A husband and wife *complement* one another in a marriage.

complement (noun) something that completes or fills up

The team does not have its full *complement* of players.

compliment (noun) an expression of courtesy or respect; a flattering remark

He received a *compliment* on his fine job.

device (noun) a thing created for some purpose; a plan

This *device* is used to open envelopes automatically.

devise (verb) to plan; to work out

Please *devise* a slogan for marketing the new product.

passed (verb) moved on; transferred

She *passed* the report around the conference table.

past (noun) a former time

I have attended the meetings in the *past*.

past (adjective) at a former time; gone by

I have been out of town on business for the *past* two weeks.

stationary (adjective) fixed; not movable

The flagpole is *stationary*.

stationery (noun) paper

He ordered new engraved *stationery* for the office.

Section 6

air (noun) the atmosphere

The *air* is polluted around some industrial complexes.

heir (noun) a person who inherits property or a hereditary title

He is the sole *heir* to the Hamilton estate.

altar (noun) a raised structure that serves as a center for worship

They exchanged wedding vows at the *altar*.

alter (verb) to change; to modify

We must *alter* the plans.

weather (noun) the general condition of the atmosphere

The raincoat provided protection against the foul *weather*.

weather (verb) to endure exposure to the atmosphere

The siding will *weather* well.

whether (conjunction) used to introduce an indirect question with alternatives

Whether he arrives or not, I will be there.

NOTE:
Use *whether*, not *if*, to indicate which one of two.

Did she indicate *whether* we made a profit or lost money?

Section 7

accede (verb) to agree to; to give in

I will *accede* to your request.

exceed (verb) to go beyond; to be greater than

The cost will not *exceed* $100.

affect (verb) to influence

The information did not *affect* her decision.

effect (noun) a result; an outcome

What effect did the medicine have on your cold?

effect (verb) to bring about; to cause to happen; to accomplish

Prompt payment will *effect* a change in the status of your account.

consul (noun) an official in a foreign country appointed to look after his or her country's citizens and businesses

Send my mail in care of the American *consul* in Paris.

council (noun) an advisory group

The town *council* will meet to vote on the mayor's proposal.

counsel (noun) advice; a lawyer who gives advice

I will seek *counsel* from my attorney concerning this matter.

He sought advice from *counsel* before talking with the police.

counsel (verb) to give advice to; to advise

The attorney will *counsel* you regarding your rights.

deposition (noun) a written statement made under oath by a witness

The *deposition* of the defendant will be taken at 1:30 p.m. on Friday.

disposition (noun) a proper arrangement; the power or authority to arrange, settle, or manage; temperament, natural attitude toward things

They agreed on the final *disposition* of the matter.

She has a pleasant *disposition*.

leased (verb) rented

The apartment was *leased* for three years.

least (adjective) smallest in size, degree, or importance

That was the *least* amount of work he could do under the circumstances.

principal (noun) an amount of money borrowed or invested in stocks or bonds on which interest is paid; the head of a school

John earned 12 percent on the *principal*.

The *principal* at Sally's school also taught an English class.

principal (adjective) main; first in importance

His *principal* income came from his job as a letter carrier.

principle (noun) a rule of action; a law of conduct; a fundamental truth

They studied the *principle* of democracy in their government class.

verses (noun) lines of a poem or song; short divisions of a chapter in the Bible

They sang all three *verses* of the song.

The sermon was based on the first four *verses* of Psalm 99.

versus (preposition) against; in contrast with

Battling the flood made the rescuers feel it was the town *versus* nature.

Section 8

biannual (adjective) twice a year

He makes *biannual* insurance premium payments.

biennial (adjective) every two years

Our *biennial* celebration will be held on August 8.

calendar (noun) a table that shows the months and days of the year

I will check my *calendar* to see whether I am free on that date.

calender (noun) a machine with rollers used to process paper or cloth

The paper finishing stopped when the *calender* broke down.

cent (noun) a penny; a unit of money equaling 1/100 of a dollar

The candy costs 1 *cent* at the school fair.

scent (noun) a smell; an odor

The perfume's *scent* was pleasant.

sent (verb) caused to go (past tense of *send*)

She *sent* the letter yesterday.

sense (noun) normal intelligence and judgment; an agreement with such intelligence and judgment; meaning

He is a person of good *sense*.

This solution makes *sense*.

Can you make any *sense* of the situation?

sense (verb) to become aware of

The dog could *sense* his fear.

employ (verb) to provide work for; to make use of

The new plant will *employ* 300 people.

employee (noun) a person hired by another

She has been an *employee* of the company for ten years.

Section 9

brake (noun) a device used to slow or stop the motion of a vehicle or machine

The accident was caused by a defective *brake* on the machine.

brake (verb) to slow down or to stop

He knew not to *brake* too hard on an icy road.

break (verb) to cause to come apart

The Board of Directors voted to *break* off the merger negotiations.

break (noun) a broken place; a separation; a crack

The Water Department repaired the *break* in the water line.

capital (adjective) chief; principal; main

Our *capital* concern was the completion of the project before the deadline.

capital (noun) money; a city or town that is the official seat of government of a state

Jennifer provided 51 percent of the *capital* to start the business.

Denver is the *capital* of Colorado.

capitol (noun) a statehouse; the building in which the state legislature meets

We will meet with State Representative Green at 8 a.m. at the *Capitol*.

precede (verb) to be, come, or go before

A coffee break will *precede* the final afternoon session.

proceed (verb) to advance or go on

We will *proceed* with negotiations as soon as Howard arrives.

Section 10

command (verb) to give an order to

In an hour the general will *command* his troops to break camp.

command (noun) an order

She issued the *command* to march.

commend (verb) to praise; to entrust

We *commend* your act of bravery.

Julie's grandfather will *commend* his rare-book collection to her when she turns 21 years old.

fiscal (adjective) having to do with financial matters

The *fiscal* year is the 12-month period between settlements of financial accounts.

physical (adjective) of the body as opposed to the mind

He has a *physical* examination every year.

quiet (adjective) calm; motionless; not noisy

It was a *quiet* library.

quit (verb) to stop

He *quit* his job.

quite (adverb) completely; entirely

He was *quite* surprised.

weak (adjective) not strong

He was still *weak* from his long illness.

week (noun) seven days

This was her first *week* of work.

Section 11

access (noun) approach; admittance, entrance

He gained *access* through the west door.

excess (adjective) more than needed; extra

The *excess* merchandise will go on sale Saturday.

excess (noun) an amount that is more than enough; a surplus

An *excess* of water in the stream caused a flood.

bare (adjective) exposed; revealed; uncovered

The walls were *bare* in the new office.

bear (verb) to carry; to transport; to withstand; to endure

The porters will *bear* the supplies to base camp.

Let him *bear* the expense of the trip.

choose (verb) to select; to make a choice

She decided to *choose* the first applicant for the job.

chose selected (past tense of *choose*)

He *chose* to postpone the meeting.

eminent (adjective) outstanding; remarkable; distinguished

She is an *eminent* scientist.

imminent (adjective) near at hand; likely to happen without delay

The completion of the new building is *imminent*.

Section 12

collaborate (verb) to work together, especially in reference to literary, artistic, or scientific work

They will *collaborate* on the book.

corroborate (verb) to strengthen; to make more certain; to confirm; to support

The witness will *corroborate* his story.

right (adjective) correct

Her answer was *right*.

right (noun) privilege under the law

He has a *right* to an attorney.

rite (noun) a ceremonial or solemn act

The old book contained the *rite* that we had been discussing.

write (verb) to form or inscribe words on a surface

She will *write* a letter.

suit (noun) a set of clothes; a legal procedure

He wore a blue *suit*.

He will bring *suit* against the company.

suit (verb) to please; to adapt

We will change the paint color to *suit* you.

The orchestra will *suit* its music to the occasion.

suite (noun) a series or group of rooms occupied as a unit

We reserved a *suite* in the hotel.

sweet (adjective) having a taste like sugar or honey; having any agreeable taste, smell, sound, appearance; pleasant

The dessert was *sweet*.

She is a *sweet* girl.

Section 13

NOTE:
You differ ***with*** someone.

One thing differs ***from*** another thing.

defer (verb) to postpone; to submit in opinion or judgment

The school will *defer* its fees until he receives his check.

He will *defer* to his father on this matter.

differ (verb) to disagree; to be unlike

They *differ* on the resolution of the matter.

They *differ* with your decision.

This book cover *differs* from the other book cover.

disburse (verb) to pay out; to expend

It is Jane's responsibility to *disburse* the profits.

disperse (verb) to break up and scatter in all directions

The policemen were there to *disperse* the crowd.

NOTE:
If you are referring to a series of more than two, use ***first*** rather than ***former***.

formally (adverb) in a customary form; with regard to form, fixed customs, and rules

The new constitution was *formally* adopted by the organization.

formerly (adverb) previously; in the past

Formerly the company name was Quinn, Mason & Peabody, but it was changed to Mason & Peabody.

former (adjective) previous; occurring in the past; the first in a series of two

She was a *former* employee.

Of the two spellings, the *former* is preferred.

The chairs are available in brown, blue, and green; but I prefer the *first*.

latter (adjective) the second in a series of two

The chairs are available in blue and in green, but I prefer the *latter*.

imply (verb) to suggest; to hint; to intimate

She went on to *imply* that she did not approve.

infer (verb) draw a conclusion

I *infer* from your statements that you do not approve.

Section 14

adapt (verb) to make suitable; to conform

She will *adapt* to her new position and her new employer.

adept (adjective) highly skilled; expert

They are *adept* downhill skiers.

adopt (verb) to take and use as one's own

We have voted to *adopt* the new designs.

among (preposition) in company or association with; Use *among* when you are referring to one of three or more persons or things

Mr. Kennedy was *among* the three applicants called for a second interview.

between (preposition) in relation to; one or the other; use *between* when you are referring to two persons or things.

Mr. Kelly was seated *between* the president and the treasurer.

can (auxiliary verb) implies ability or power

Can you finish the report by Tuesday?

The police *can* arrest that man for stealing.

may (auxiliary verb) implies permission or possibility

You *may* present your report at the meeting.

It *may* rain this afternoon.

credible (adjective) believable

His version of the story was *credible*.

creditable (adjective) praiseworthy

The plans for marketing the new product are *creditable*.

hear (verb) to become aware of something through your sense of hearing

Do you *hear* his voice?

here (adverb) in this place

The meeting will be *here* at 9 a.m.

interstate (adjective) between or among states

The firm is involved in *interstate* commerce within a three- state area.

intrastate (adjective) within a state

The firm confines its activities solely to *intrastate* commerce. (one state only)

Reference Handbook

Reference Handbook Contents

Dictation Equipment Manufacturers

Dictaphone Corporation
3191 Broadbridge Avenue
Stratford, CT 06497-2559
203-381-7000
www.dictaphone.com

Grundig-Stenorette
NTI Business Corporation
8150 Devonshire
Montreal, PQ H4P 2K3
CANADA
514-736-1616
www.grundig.com

Lanier Worldwide, Inc.
2300 Parklake Drive, N.E.
Atlanta, GA 30345
770-496-9500
www.lanier.com

Olympus America, Inc.
Two Corporate Center Drive
Melville, NY 11747-3157
631-844-5000
www.olympusamerica.com

Philips Speech Processing (USA)
14140 Midway Road
Dallas, TX 75244
972-726-1200
www.philips.com
www.speech.philips.com

Sanyo Fisher (USA) Corporation
21605 Plummer Street
Chatsworth, CA 91311
818-998-7322
www.sanyousa.com

Sony Corporation of America
One Sony Drive
Park Ridge, NY 07656
201-930-1000
www.sony.com

Letter Placement Chart—Word Processors

Length of Letter	Number of Minutes	Margin Settings Courier New 10-point	Margin Settings Courier New 12-point	Top Margin Inches	Top Margin Line
Short	1 or less	2"	2"	3.32	20
Medium	1½	1.75"	1.7"	2.96	18
	2	1.75"	1.5"	2.61	16
	2½	1.5"	1.2"	2.25	14
Long	2½–3	1.25"	1.2"	2.07	13
Two-page	3 or more	1"	1"	2.07	13

The letter must begin at least a double space below the letterhead. If the letter contains extra lines such as attention line, subject line, company name in the closing lines, and mailing notations, adjust the position of the date line upward. Return four times after keying the date. If you choose a different font, the placement may need to be adjusted.

Proofreaders' Marks

After reading the keyboarded copy, the dictator may occasionally make revisions or corrections. You should be familiar with proofreaders' marks so you will know what changes to make. Below are the most commonly used proofreaders' marks.

PROOFREADERS' MARK	MEANING	EXAMPLE
	Transpose	hte is it
	Delete	and thee
	Move to the right	The meeting will
	Move to the left	The meeting will
	Move down	heading
	Move up	heading
	Close up space	YM CA
#	Insert space	Themeeting
^	Insert a word	Send your check.
⊙	Insert a period	in the library
	Insert comma	If you come we
∨	Insert apostrophe or quotation marks	"I cant go.
SS	Use single spacing	SS It is our We will send
DS	Use double spacing	DS It is our We will send
TS	Use triple spacing	TS It is our We will send
//	Align vertically	// January February
○	Spell out	2 people will
	Move as indicated	from our office
¶	Start a new paragraph	¶ The report
≡	Capitalize	i will go.
....	Ignore change indicated (Stet)	The final report
___	Italicize	The book, Gentle Winds,
___ US	Underscore	Gentle Winds US
/ or l.c.	Use lowercase	In the Spring
~~word~~ /	Change word or letter	We wall remain
=/	Insert hyphen	selfmade

Punctuation Guide

Colons

Enumerations and Lists

Use a colon before an enumeration or when the items in a series are listed on separate lines. Indent the numbered items that are written on separate lines if the paragraphs are indented; block them if the paragraphs are blocked. Double-space between numbered items.

> **NOTE:**
> For more in-depth information about punctuation, consult an office reference manual such as ***The Gregg Reference Manual*** by William A. Sabin.

Examples: At lunch, we ate the following: shrimp cocktails, club sandwiches, cheesecake, and iced tea.

The meetings will be held in the following cities:

1. Chicago

2. New York

3. Seattle

4. St. Louis

Do not use a colon if the series is immediately preceded by a verb or a preposition, unless the items are listed on separate lines.

Examples: He took courses in math, word processing, and English.

The last ones to arrive were John, Betty, and Karl.

Quotations (See Also *Commas*)

Use a colon to introduce a long one-sentence quotation or a quotation of more than one sentence. If a quotation takes up four or more printed lines, key it single-spaced and indented ½ inch from each margin. Double-space above and below the quoted material. Quotation marks are unnecessary; the indention takes the place of the quotation marks.

Examples: In the conclusion of the report, he wrote:

> The proposed new plant location at Centerville appears to be ideal for our purposes. The power supply is sufficient. After talking with city officials and various other members of the community, I believe the local work force can meet our demand for employees. The proposed site includes adequate space for future expansion.

Commas

And Omitted

When two or more consecutive adjectives modify the same noun, they should be separated by commas. To help you decide whether a comma is necessary, try inserting *and* between the adjectives or try reversing the adjectives. If the meaning is not changed, you need to insert a comma between the two adjectives.

However, do not use a comma between the adjectives if the first adjective modifies the combined idea of the second adjective plus the noun. Do not use a comma between adjectives connected by *and*, *or*, or *nor*.

Examples: She was an intelligent, conscientious student.

The accounting department prepared the annual financial statement.

In the first example, *and* could be inserted between the two adjectives without changing the meaning, and the adjectives could be reversed. Therefore, a comma is necessary. In the second example, *annual* modifies the combined idea of the adjective *financial* and the noun *statement*. Therefore, no comma is needed.

Appositives

Use commas to set off an appositive. An appositive explains or identifies the noun or pronoun that precedes it.

Example: Mr. Loyd Jacobs, chairman of the board, will deliver the dinner address.

Compound Sentences

A compound sentence contains two or more independent clauses connected by a coordinating conjunction (*and*, *but*, *for*, *nor*, or *or*). Use a comma before the coordinating conjunction in a compound sentence.

Example: The personnel manager interviewed four applicants for the job, but she hired only one.

Be sure not to confuse compound sentences with sentences that have only compound predicates. Do not use a comma before the conjunction if the sentence contains only a compound predicate.

Example: The personnel manager interviewed four applicants for the job but hired only one.

If you are unsure, look for the subject and verb in each clause before inserting the comma. If there is only one subject for both verbs, do not use a comma. If each verb has its own subject, use a comma before the conjunction.

If both independent clauses are imperative, insert a comma before the conjunction.

Example: Give the report to me on Friday, and give copies of the report to Mr. Martin and Mrs. Fuji.

Dates

Insert a comma between the day and the year. If the sentence continues after the date, insert a comma after the year. If the date consists of only the month and year, do not use a comma to separate them.

Examples: Angela was born on June 26, 1980.

November 2002 is the projected completion date of the new facility.

Independent Words or Expressions

Independent words or expressions are not necessary to the meaning of the sentence; therefore, they are set off by commas. The following are some examples: *besides, consequently, furthermore, however, I hope, I think, in addition, in my opinion, indeed, nevertheless, of course, on the contrary, therefore, unfortunately*.

Examples: We all knew, however, that he would succeed.
In my opinion, we should reject the proposal.

If you are unsure of whether the words are independent, read the sentence without them. If the meaning is unchanged, the words are independent.

Use commas to set off names and titles used in direct address.

Example: Chris, please sharpen these pencils.

Introductory Dependent Clauses

Use a comma after an introductory dependent clause. Dependent clauses begin with subordinating conjunctions such as *although, as, because, before, even though, if, since, unless, when*, and *whether*. A sentence containing an independent clause and one or more dependent clauses is called a complex sentence.

Example: When Mr. Carson calls, be sure to tell him about the change in the program for the sales conference.

No comma is needed when the independent clause is stated before an essential dependent clause. However, if the dependent clause is nonessential, it should be set off by commas.

Examples: Be sure to tell Mr. Carson about the change in the program for the sales conference when he calls.

The sales conference will take place in New York, which is an exciting city.

Introductory Prepositional Phrases

It is recommended that you use a comma after all introductory prepositional phrases. You should use a comma after an introductory prepositional phrase that contains a verb form or is five or more words long. If the introductory prepositional phrase is less than five words long and does not contain a verb form, you may omit the comma. However, use a comma if one is needed for clarity.

Introductory Prepositional Phrase Containing a Verb Form:
After hearing the news, we planned our sales strategy for the new marketing territory.

Introductory Prepositional Phrase Containing Five or More Words:
Between Angie's desk and the elevator, there is a spot marked for the new copy machine.

Introductory Prepositional Phrase Containing Fewer than Five Words and No Verb Form:
By five o'clock he had completed all the dictation.

or

By five o'clock, he had completed all the dictation.

Introductory Prepositional Phrase Needing a Comma for Clarity:

For our committee, meetings will be scheduled every Wednesday at 9 a.m.

Quotations (See Also *Colons*)

Use a comma before a *short* quotation.

Example: He said, "Be at work on time every day."

Remember: Periods and commas always go inside quotation marks. Semicolons and colons always go outside quotation marks.

Series (See Also *Semicolons*)

Use a comma to separate three or more items in a series. Place a comma before the conjunction. Do not use a comma to separate a series of only two items.

Examples: Bob ordered ballpoint pens, paper clips, computer disks, and file folders from Fisher Office Supply Company.

Chicago and Atlanta are on the itinerary for Mrs. Jacobs.

Hyphens

Compound Expressions

Compound expressions such as *past due* and *follow up* sometimes require hyphens. If a noun follows the expression, use a hyphen.

Examples: The results of the follow-up survey surprised the research team.

Please make a payment on your past-due account.

If the compound expression is not followed by a noun, do not use a hyphen.

Examples: To check on the efficiency of the new procedure, we must follow up with employees in June.

Your account is seriously past due.

Do not use a hyphen if the first word of the compound expression is an adverb ending in *ly*.

Examples: He was a poorly trained employee.

Semicolons

Conjunctive Adverbs

The independent clauses in a compound sentence may be connected by a conjunctive adverb rather than by a coordinating conjunction. Use a semicolon before and a comma after the conjunctive adverb. The following are examples of conjunctive adverbs: *accordingly*, *consequently*, *furthermore*, *hence*, *however*, *moreover*, *nevertheless*, *otherwise*, and *therefore*.

NOTE: No comma is needed after ***hence, so, then, thus,*** and ***yet*** unless you want the reader to pause at that point.

Examples: My car is in the garage; consequently, we will have to take your car to Chicago.

Coordinating Conjunction Omitted

Use a semicolon to separate two independent clauses when the coordinating conjunction has been omitted.

Examples: It's the only answer; sell the business.

Other Commas

Use a semicolon instead of a comma to separate independent clauses when other commas appear in either independent clause and misreading might occur.

Examples: Andrew Jacobs, chairman of the board, will preside over the meeting; and the seminar, which follows immediately, will be introduced by Francesca Jamison, president.

Series (See Also *Commas*)

Use a semicolon to separate items in a series when the individual items contain commas or when the individual items are complete sentences.

Examples: The sites of the division headquarters are located in Chicago, Illinois; Baltimore, Maryland; Phoenix, Arizona; Portland, Oregon; and Sarasota, Florida.

Before you leave today, please do the following: arrange for the conference room for our meeting on Wednesday; schedule an appointment with Mr. Benton for Thursday; call the printer to approve the proof copy; and cancel the meeting with Mrs. Monroe.

Transitional Words

When transitional words or phrases such as *for example, namely,* or *that is* link two independent clauses or introduce an explanation or an enumeration, use a semicolon before the word or phrase and a comma after it.

Examples: Tell me what you can about the new employee; that is, her training, her previous experience, her personality, and her appearance.

We have many tasks to complete before we can turn the project over to the Production Department; for example, we must perform stress tests on the frame.

Transcription Guidelines

AGES

See *Numbers*

ATTENTION LINE

The attention line is keyed as the first line of the inside address. The word *attention* should be followed by a colon. When an attention line is used, the appropriate salutation is *Ladies and Gentlemen*. The trend is to omit attention lines.

Examples: Attention: Mr. John Williams (Most efficient)

ATTENTION: MS. JOAN WILSON

An alternate location is a double space below the inside address at the left margin. Double-space between the attention line and the salutation. However, if you are using a word processing program to create the envelope, this location will not work.

June 26, 20__

Attention: Human Resource Manager
M & M Industries
115 East Main Street
West Frankfort, IL 62896 ↓**2**

Ladies and Gentlemen

See also *Envelopes* for an illustration of attention line placement.

BLIND COPY NOTATION

A blind copy (*bc*) notation is used when you do not want the person to whom the letter is addressed to know that someone else received a copy of the letter. The *bc* notation should be one of the last items on the letter and should begin a double space below the last item at the left margin. An alternate location for the *bc* notation is at the left margin in the upper left corner on line 7. Be sure the *bc* notation appears on your file copy (hard copy, electronic copy, or both). The format is the same as for a regular copy (*c*) notation.

If you are using a typewriter, you may prevent the notation from appearing on the original by placing a small card over the original before typing the *bc* notation. Alternatively, you may wish to remove the original and any copies on which the *bc* notation is not to appear before typing the *bc* notation.

Examples: bc Peter T. McClaron
bc: Peter T. McClaron

BOOK AND MAGAZINE TITLES

You may enter the titles of books and magazines in one of the following three ways:

1. Enter the titles in italics, and capitalize the first letter of each important word (preferred).
2. Underline titles, and capitalize the first letter of each important word.
3. Key the titles in all-capital letters.

Examples: *Angie's Secret* Angie's Secret ANGIE'S SECRET

COMPANY NAMES

If the company name appears in the closing lines of a letter, double-space after the complimentary closing, and key the company name in all-capital letters. Use a comma to separate *Inc.* or *Ltd.* from the rest of the company name if the company uses a comma. Then return four times before keying the signature line.

NOTE:
When you are using company stationery, the company name is not necessary; however, some firms prefer to use the company name in the signature block. When you start working in a new position, check the preference of your employer.

Example: Sincerely yours,

↓**2**

M & M PRINTING COMPANY, LTD.

↓**4**

E. G. Mitchell

COPY NOTATION

A copy (*c*) notation is used when you want to send a copy of the letter to someone in addition to the addressee. The order of the notations at the end of a letter is as follows:

1. Reference initials
2. Enclosure notation
3. Delivery notation
4. Copy notation
5. Postscript
6. Blind copy notation
7. Blind postscript

Examples: c Mr. L. V. Jacobs
c: Ms. Angela Mitchell

DELIVERY NOTATION

The delivery notation is keyed at the left margin on the line after the enclosure notation (after the reference initials if there is no enclosure). See also *Copy Notation* and *Envelopes*.

Examples: By certified mail, By registered mail, By Express Mail, By Federal Express, By fax, By special delivery, By messenger

An alternate location for the delivery notation is a double space above the inside address. The notation placed in this position should be keyed in all capitals.

DEPARTMENT AND DIVISION NAMES

Capitalize the official name of a division or a department within your own firm.

Examples: Send this invoice to the Accounting Department.

Notify Human Resources that we will need a part-time employee during November 1–20.

The Board of Directors must approve the budget for this year before we can approve this purchase order for the new word processing equipment.

Capitalize the names of divisions and departments in other firms only if you definitely know that they are the official names.

Examples: Your marketing department would benefit from our Star Sales Training Program.

The Department of Research and Development at Madison Manufacturing Company requested a copy of our report on chemical tolerances.

E-MAIL

Keep in mind that e-mail messages are not private. Do not send an e-mail message that you would not want everyone in your firm to read. Always use a subject line. When composing the subject line, think of what you would write on a file folder label to help you keep it brief. Restrict each e-mail message to one subject. If you have more than one subject to write about, send more than one e-mail message.

In the e-mail dialog box, type the recipient's name and e-mail address after *To or Mail To,* and type the subject after *Subject or Re.* The date, your name, and your e-mail address will be inserted automatically.

You may omit the salutation or insert the recipient's name at the beginning of the message. The complimentary closing is generally omitted. You may close simply with your name. These items are a matter of personal preference.

E-Mail Addresses

When you type an e-mail address, never change the capitalization, punctuation, or symbols contained in the address. Also, note that e-mail addresses do not have spaces. The first part of the address is the name the person has chosen for his or her *mailbox.* This is followed immediately by the @ symbol. The @ symbol is followed by the *domain* name (the system used to deliver the e-mail message). If an e-mail address falls at the end of a line, you may divide the address before the @ symbol or before a dot in the address. Do not insert a hyphen. However, it is best to avoid dividing e-mail addresses.

ENCLOSURE NOTATION

The enclosure notation is keyed at the left margin on the line below the reference initials. If you have more than one enclosure, you may want to list enclosures.

Examples: Enclosure
Enclosures 3
Enclosures:
1. Contract
2. Check
3. Credit application

The notation *Attachment* is more appropriate on a memorandum if you are not using an envelope.

If you are sending additional material under separate cover (that is, separately), you should key a separate cover notation in the same location as you would enter the enclosure notation. If you are sending enclosures with the letter and items under separate cover, list the separate cover notation under the enclosure notation.

Examples:	Separate cover 2	Enclosures 2
		Separate cover 2
	Under separate cover:	1. Contract
		2. Book

NOTE:
It is common practice to accept the positioning of word processing programs when formatting envelopes.

ENVELOPES

On the envelope, place the attention line as the first line of the address.

The delivery notation should be placed on line 9. It should end about 1/2 inch from the right edge of the envelope. Delivery notations should be in all capitals.

Be sure to use the ZIP Code + 4 if possible.

Position the address as shown in the following illustrations:

No. 10 Envelope
9 1/2 by 4 1/8 inches

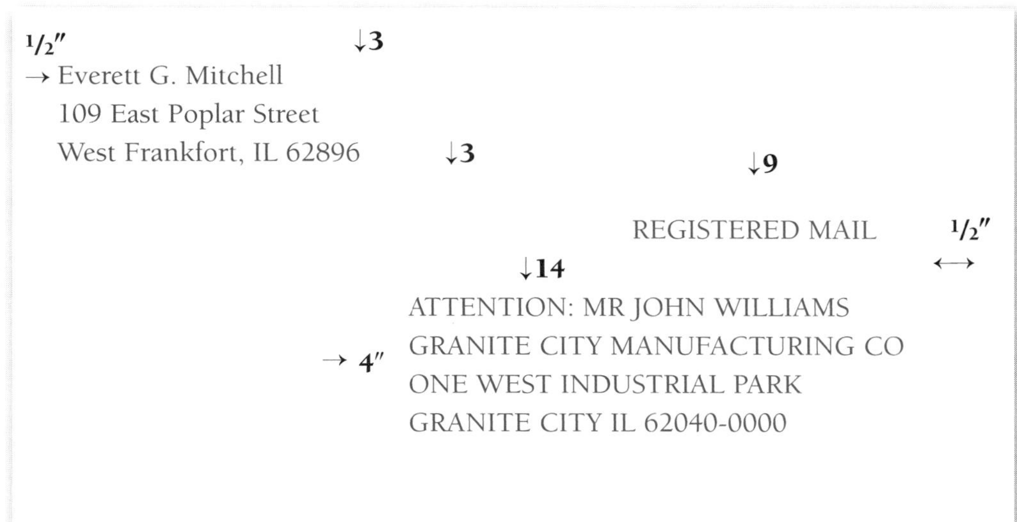

1/2″
↓3
→ Everett G. Mitchell
109 East Poplar Street
West Frankfort, IL 62896
↓3
↓9
REGISTERED MAIL
1/2″
↓14
ATTENTION: MR JOHN WILLIAMS
GRANITE CITY MANUFACTURING CO
ONE WEST INDUSTRIAL PARK
GRANITE CITY IL 62040-0000
→ 4″

No. 6 3/4 Envelope
6 1/2 by 3 5/8 inches

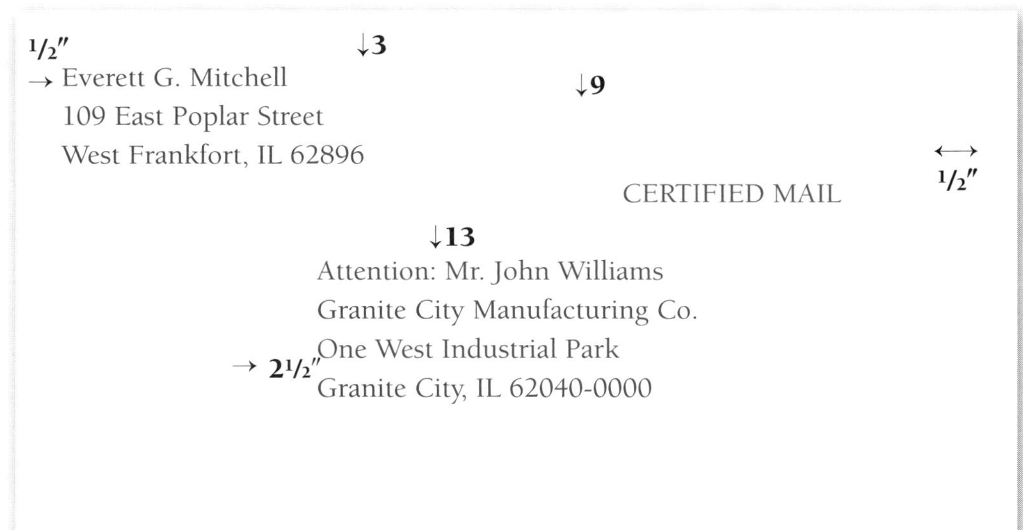

1/2″
↓3
→ Everett G. Mitchell
109 East Poplar Street
West Frankfort, IL 62896
↓9
1/2″
CERTIFIED MAIL
↓13
Attention: Mr. John Williams
Granite City Manufacturing Co.
One West Industrial Park
Granite City, IL 62040-0000
→ 2 1/2″

FAX COVER SHEET

Your word processing software may have a template you can use to create a fax cover sheet. If you are creating a template for your use only, fill in any information that will remain constant. However, if you are creating a template that many different people will use, create a form with blank lines that can be filled in with the appropriate information. Try to create entry lines that have a common left margin to make the form easier to use. You may want to add graphics that include the firm name and address to the top of the form. The following is a sample form:

FAX COVER SHEET

Date: ______________________________

To: ______________________________

Fax Number: ______________________________

From: ______________________________

____

Fax Number: ______________________________

Number of pages (including this cover sheet): ______________

Message: ______________________________

____

____

____

____

____

____

____

____

____

If any part of this fax transmission is missing or not clearly received, please call:

Name: ______________________________

Phone Number: ______________________________

FOREIGN ADDRESSES

When you are addressing a letter to a foreign country, the name of that foreign country should be keyed in all-capital letters as the last line of the address on the envelope and as the last line of the inside address on the letter. The following example illustrates the address for a letter being sent to England:

Example: Mr. Jerome Swanson
Lancaster Apartments
36 Queen's Gate
London SW7 5JA
ENGLAND

HOUSE NUMBERS

See *Numbers*

ITINERARY

After the heading, ITINERARY, a secondary heading should list the name of the person for whom the itinerary was prepared and dates covered by the itinerary. Use side headings that are in bold to clearly indicate the day of the week and the date. List the times in a column at the left margin. Set a tab for all the descriptive information to the right of the times.

JR., SR., II, AND SO FORTH

Use a comma between a person's name and *Jr.*, *Sr.*, or *II* if the person uses a comma in his signature. Use a comma after *Jr.*, *Sr.*, or *II* if a comma precedes the designation in the sentence.

LETTER AND MEMORANDUM STYLES

The following pages contain sample letter and memorandum styles. These are not the only acceptable formats available to you. You should follow the style manual for your firm if one is available. You should also obtain a good reference manual. *The Gregg Reference Manual* by William A. Sabin is a well-recognized resource.

Block Style, Open Punctuation. All lines begin at the left in block style. When you use open punctuation, do not put any punctuation after the salutation or the complimentary closing.

December 30, 20__

Mrs. Jane Michaels
Office Decor, Inc.
2975 Elm Street
Chicago, IL 60010

Dear Mrs. Michaels

Subject: Office Furniture

Enclosed is our check for $5247.19 to cover your Invoice 468-310 for the office furniture we ordered from you. All the furniture arrived in fine condition.

We are planning to redecorate our reception area and would like to make an appointment to discuss the plans with you. If you are free next Thursday at 10 a.m., we can get started. If this time is not convenient for you, please contact my assistant, Alice Jacobs, to set up another appointment.

Sincerely yours

M & M ADVERTISING AGENCY

Angela C. Mitchell
Office Manager

xxx
Enclosure
c Mrs. A. K. Land

Modified-Block Style, Standard Format (Blocked Paragraphs), Open Punctuation. In modified-block style with a standard format, the date and closing lines begin at the center. All paragraphs begin at the left margin. When you use open punctuation, do not put any punctuation after the salutation or the complimentary closing.

December 30, 20__

Mrs. Jane Michaels
Office Decor, Inc.
2975 Elm Street
Chicago, IL 60010

Dear Mrs. Michaels

Subject: Office Furniture

Enclosed is our check for $5247.19 to cover your Invoice 468-310 for the office furniture we ordered from you. All the furniture arrived in fine condition.

We are planning to redecorate our reception area and would like to make an appointment to discuss the plans with you. If you are free next Thursday at 10 a.m., we can get started. If this time is not convenient for you, please contact my assistant, Alice Jacobs, to set up another appointment.

Sincerely yours

M & M ADVERTISING AGENCY

Angela C. Mitchell
Office Manager

xxx
Enclosure
c Mrs. A. K. Land

Modified-block Style, Indented Paragraphs, Standard (or Mixed) Punctuation. In modified-block style with indented paragraphs, the date and closing lines begin at the center. The first line of each paragraph is indented 5 spaces. When you use standard, or mixed, punctuation, put a colon after the salutation and a comma after the complimentary closing.

December 30, 20__

Mrs. Jane Michaels
Office Decor, Inc.
2975 Elm Street
Chicago, IL 60010

Dear Mrs. Michaels:

Subject: Office Furniture

Enclosed is our check for $5247.19 to cover your Invoice 468-310 for the office furniture we ordered from you. All the furniture arrived in fine condition.

We are planning to redecorate our reception area and would like to make an appointment to discuss the plans with you. If you are free next Thursday at 10 a.m., we can get started. If this time is not convenient for you, please contact my assistant, Alice Jacobs, to set up another appointment.

Sincerely yours,

M & M ADVERTISING AGENCY

Angela C. Mitchell
Office Manager

xxx
Enclosure
c: Mrs. A. K. Land

Interoffice Memorandum. The following is an acceptable format for an interoffice memorandum. There are many different acceptable formats.

MEMO TO: All Department Managers

FROM: Angela Mitchell, Office Manager

DATE: December 30, 20__

SUBJECT: Time-Management Seminar

Please inform this office of the names of those from your department who will be attending the Time-Management Seminar at the Palmer Plaza on January 19.

If you need to hire temporary employees for your department to allow more of your full-time employees to attend, I will be glad to assist you.

xxx

MONEY

See *Numbers*

MULTIPLE INSIDE ADDRESSES

If a letter is addressed to two or more people at different addresses, the inside addresses may be listed in either of the following two ways:

1. One under the other with one blank line separating them.

2. Side by side.

NEWS RELEASE

The author suggests using the following format from *The Gregg Reference Manual,* Ninth Edition by William A. Sabin (Glencoe/McGraw-Hill, New York, 2001, pp. 512–513).

Heading. The heading should indicate the name and address of the organization sponsoring the news release. It should also show the name and phone number of the person to contact in case more information is needed.

The heading should also indicate when the information contained in the news release may be distributed to the public. In many cases the phrase *For immediate release* is sufficient. If the information is to be kept confidential until a specific time and date, the heading should carry a notation like this:

For release 9 a.m. EST, May 7, 2001

Headline. The text of the news release should begin with a descriptive title and, if desired, a subtitle.

Content Considerations. The first paragraph should begin with a bold run-in head that indicates the city and state of origin and the date on which this material is to be released. This run-in head is usually followed by a colon or a dash (typical newspaper practice) rather than by a period.

At the end of the text, leave 1 blank line and type one of the following notations, centered: three spaced pound signs (# # #) or the phrase -30-. These notations, derived from long-standing newspaper practice, signify "the end."

Illustration of Press Release

News Release Griffin Hospital

233 Lakeland Ave.
Coventry, CT 08765

Contact: Ahmed Aradian
Phone: 203-555-1294
Fax: 203-555-1295

FOR IMMEDIATE RELEASE

GRIFFIN HOSPITAL OFFERS NEW PROCEDURE

Noninvasive Procedure Relieves Angina Symptoms and Pain

Coventry, Connecticut, December 5, 2002: Griffin Hospital today announced a new, noninvasive procedure to relieve angina symptoms and pain. Enhanced External Counterpulsation, or EECP, is a nonsurgical procedure that can reduce or eliminate symptoms of angina, according to hospital officials. Angina is characterized by agonizing chest pain brought on by exercise or emotional stress. Many candidates for EECP have had angioplasty and/or open heart surgery, and there are no other medical options available to them.

The Centers for Medicare and Medicaid Services (CMS) announced that EECP will be covered for Medicare patients effective October 1. Many other insurers cover the procedures based on the individual member's insurance plan.

# # #

> **NOTE:**
> For a more in-depth list of number rules, consult an office reference manual such as ***The Gregg Reference Manual*** by William A. Sabin.

NUMBERS

As a general rule, the numbers *one* through *ten* are written as words, and numbers *11* and above are written as digits. There are some exceptions to this general rule.

If a number appears as the first word in a sentence, it must be written in word form.

Example: Fifty-three members were present for the meeting.

Line, page, paragraph, size, and verse numbers are always typed in digits. The words *line, page, paragraph, size,* and *verse* are not capitalized unless they appear as the first word in the sentence. Other words appearing with numbers are capitalized.

Examples: Our new copier is Model 4956X.
We will be on Flight 482.
This refers to Invoice 2371.
We received Model 684.
I will need the dress in a size 4.
We will meet in Room 2.
They broke Rule 896.
Please read paragraph 2, line 29 on page 3.
Page 2 shows the music for the next song.
We will sing verse 4.

Ages. Ages are generally expressed as words. Use digits for expressing age when the age immediately follows the person's name or when the age is used in a technical sense. Use digits when expressing age in years, months, and days.

Examples: Karen, 60, has chosen early retirement.
Your insurance policy will be paid up at the age of 65.
When we bought the house, William was 5 years 11 months and 3 days old. (Do not separate the years and months with commas.)
Angela is nineteen years old.
The applicant is in her twenties.

House Numbers. Always use digits to express house numbers. *One* is always spelled out, however. Do not use commas in house numbers.

Examples: 2475 East Main Street One West Hickory Avenue

Millions or Higher. For easier comprehension, use the words *million or billion* instead of writing out the zeros in even amounts.

Examples: 1 million 3 billion 55 million 2.5 million

Money. Do not use a decimal point and zeros when you type an even amount of money. Use a comma to separate dollar amounts of five figures or more. (The trend is to omit the comma in amounts of four digits unless they appear with larger amounts.) Amounts that are less than $1 are written in digits and words. Even amounts in millions or more may be expressed in digits and words for clarity.

Examples:	$12,500	$35.90	$534,827.65
	50 cents	$1400 or $1,400	
	$1 million	$3 billion	

Room Numbers. All room numbers are expressed in digits. Do not use a comma in a room number.

Examples: The meeting will be held in Room 5.
The office is in Room 2003.

Street Numbers. Spell out *one* through *ten* in street names. Use digits for higher numbers. Do not abbreviate direction designations such as *East* or *West* before the street name. Abbreviate compound direction designations when they appear after street names, and insert commas before them. Spell out *North, South, East*, and *West* following a street name, and omit the comma.

Examples: One East Fifth Street
2 West 78th Street
293 Oak Street, NW
161 Maple Avenue South

Symbols. Use symbols (#, ¢, %, @) in technical writing, in tables, and on business forms only. Spell out or abbreviate these designations in business letters. All percentages are expressed in digits.

Examples: Please send 25 No. 39 shirts.
Please send 50 cents for handling.
We expect to increase profits 2 percent over last year.

Time. Use digits to express time with *a.m.* or *p.m.* Omit the colon and the zeros when keying even times. However, in lists containing several hour and minute expressions, add two zeros to exact times to maintain a uniform appearance. Use either words (for formality) or digits (for emphasis) to express time with *o'clock*.

Examples:	6:35 p.m.	8 a.m.	ten o'clock
Wrong:	five p.m.	9:00 a.m.	11:00 o'clock

POSTAL ABBREVIATIONS

United States Postal Abbreviations. The following is a list of United States postal abbreviations for states, districts, and territories:

AL	Alabama	MT	Montana
AK	Alaska	NE	Nebraska
AZ	Arizona	NV	Nevada
AR	Arkansas	NH	New Hampshire
CA	California	NJ	New Jersey
CZ	Canal Zone	NM	New Mexico
CO	Colorado	NY	New York
CT	Connecticut	NC	North Carolina
DE	Delaware	ND	North Dakota
DC	District of Columbia	OH	Ohio
FL	Florida	OK	Oklahoma
GA	Georgia	OR	Oregon
GU	Guam	PA	Pennsylvania
HI	Hawaii	PR	Puerto Rico
ID	Idaho	RI	Rhode Island
IL	Illinois	SC	South Carolina
IN	Indiana	SD	South Dakota
IA	Iowa	TN	Tennessee
KS	Kansas	TX	Texas
KY	Kentucky	UT	Utah
LA	Louisiana	VT	Vermont
ME	Maine	VI	Virgin Islands
MD	Maryland	VA	Virginia
MA	Massachusetts	WA	Washington
MI	Michigan	WV	West Virginia
MN	Minnesota	WI	Wisconsin
MS	Mississippi	WY	Wyoming
MO	Missouri		

Use these two-letter abbreviations in business addresses when you know the appropriate ZIP Codes. Use a ZIP Code directory to determine the appropriate ZIP Code if you do not have that information available on previous correspondence. Use a ZIP Code + 4 whenever possible.

Canadian Postal Abbreviations. Use the following two-letter abbreviations in Canadian addresses:

AB	Alberta	NU	Nunavut
BC	British Columbia	ON	Ontario
MB	Manitoba	PE	Prince Edward Island
NB	New Brunswick	QC	Quebec
NF	Newfoundland	SK	Saskatchewan
NT	Northwest Territories	YT	Yukon Territory
NS	Nova Scotia		

You may use the two-letter Canadian abbreviations for the provinces and territories, or you may spell out their names. The following are examples of Canadian addresses if you are mailing a letter from the United States. Key the name of any foreign country on the last line in all-capital letters.

Preferred Forms:

Ms. R. G. Quinn
1473 Carling Avenue
Vancouver, BC V6C 1P8
CANADA

or

Mr. Robert Caswell
230 Slater Street
Ottawa, Ontario
CANADA K1P 5H6

If you were mailing a letter in Canada to a Canadian address, you would not key the word *CANADA* in the address, just as you would not key the words *UNITED STATES* on a letter to be mailed from Chicago to New York. The following are examples for keying Canadian addresses on Canadian letterheads:

Preferred Forms:

Ms. R. G. Quinn
1473 Carling Avenue
Vancouver, BC V6C 1P8

or

Mr. Robert Caswell
230 Slater Street
Ottawa, ON K1P 5H6

or

Ottawa, Ontario K1P 5H6

POSTSCRIPT

A postscript is keyed a double space below the copy notation or previous notation. See also *Copy Notation* for the order of closing notations. If the paragraphs in the letter are indented, you should also indent the first line of the postscript. If the paragraphs are in block style, begin the postscript at the left margin. You may omit the *PS* abbreviation.

ROOM NUMBERS

See *Numbers*

SPACING GUIDE

1. Space once after a comma or a semicolon in a sentence.
2. Do not space after a comma in a number.
3. Do not space after a period within an abbreviation.
   Example: p.m.
4. Space once after a period used at the end of an abbreviation.
   Example: Mr. Banks
5. Space once after a period used with an initial.
   Example: R. G. Quinn
6. Space twice after terminal punctuation: period, question mark, exclamation point.
7. Space once after a question mark in the middle of a sentence.
8. Do not space before or after a dash.
9. Do not space before or after a hyphen used to connect two parts of a compound word.
   Example: self-made
10. Space twice after a colon used to introduce a series.
11. Do not space before or after a colon used to separate hours and minutes in stating time.
12. Space once between a whole number and a fraction made with a diagonal.
    Example: 2 1/8
13. Do not space between a figure and the diagonal when you make a fraction.
14. Do not space between a whole number and ½ or ¼.
15. Space once before and once after & (ampersand) and @ (meaning "at a cost of"). Do not space before or after @ in an e-mail address.
16. Do not space between a figure and ¢ (cents sign) or *(asterisk).
17. Do not space before or after ' (apostrophe) in a contraction.
18. Do not space between the parentheses and the words that are enclosed.

19. Space once before the left parenthesis and once after the right parenthesis.

20. Do not space between $ (dollar sign) and the following figure. An exception occurs in a column of figures where the $ is positioned to accommodate the longest amount.

    Example: $ 5.00
    175.37
    53.25

21. Do not space between # (number sign) and the figure with which it is keyed.

22. Do not space between % (percent sign) and the preceding figure.

23. Do not space between the quotation mark and the word it encloses.

24. Use the spacing that normally follows the punctuation mark when a quotation mark occurs with that mark of punctuation.

    Examples: "What?" "We lost the game!"
    "Very good," he said.

STREET NUMBERS

See *Numbers*

SUBJECT LINE

A subject line of a letter is keyed a double space below the salutation. The subject line is centered or indented the same amount as the paragraphs are indented. If you are using block style for the letter, you must key the subject line at the left margin. Double-space after the subject line before you start the first paragraph.

October 30, 20__

Mrs. Shirley Bronson
XYZ Corporation
6401 West Main Street
Belleville, IL 62223

Dear Mrs. Bronson: ↓2

Subject: National Management Conference ↓2

Would you serve as the master of ceremonies for the National Management Conference that will be held in Chicago on March 25–27?

SYMBOLS

See *Numbers*

TIME

See *Numbers*

TWO-PAGE LETTERS

The heading on the second page of a two-page letter may be keyed in block style or in horizontal style. The margins should be the same on all pages of the letter. The first line of the heading is keyed on line 7 from the top of the page. Double-space or triple-space before you key the rest of the letter. Do not leave fewer than two lines of a paragraph at the bottom of the first page. Do not carry fewer than two lines of a paragraph to the second page.

The second page should be typed or printed on plain paper that matches the letterhead stationery.

Block Style

↓7

Mr. George Russell
Page 2
June 5, 20__

↓2 or 3

available to take these depositions. It is their opinion that they need this information before they can proceed to make an evaluation of this case. The

Horizontal Style

↓7

Mr. George Russell 2 June 5, 20__

↓2 or 3

available to take these depositions. It is their opinion that they need this information before they can proceed to make an evaluation of this case. The

Word Division Guide

A divided word is harder to read than a word written as a single unit. However, it is sometimes necessary to divide words in order to keep the right margin attractive.

1. Always carry at least three key strokes over to the next line.
2. Avoid dividing words of five letters or fewer. (You must have at least three key strokes on each line. Some references allow one of these to be a punctuation mark.)
3. Divide only between syllables. If you are unsure of the syllabication, use a dictionary.
4. Avoid dividing a word at the end of the first line or last full line of a paragraph.
5. Do not divide a word at the end of the last line of a page.
6. Avoid dividing words at the end of more than two consecutive lines.
7. Do not divide one-syllable words.
8. Do not divide abbreviations.

   Examples: f.o.b. UMWA UNICEF
9. Do not divide contractions.

   Examples: doesn't o'clock wouldn't
10. Do not divide a one-letter syllable at the beginning or end of a word.

    Wrong: . . . . a-
mount . . . . bacteri-
a
11. Do not divide a two-letter syllable at the end of a word. Since a hyphen is required, only one space would be saved. At least three key strokes should be carried over to the next line. (Some references allow you to count a punctuation mark as one of the three strokes.)

    Wrong: . . . . apparent-
ly . . . . accura-
cy
12. If possible, avoid dividing a two-letter syllable at the beginning of a word. (See also Rule 18.)

    Wrong: . . . . be-
ginning . . . . in-
troduce
13. Divide hyphenated words at the hyphen only.

    Examples: . . . . self-
control . . . . sister-
in-law
14. Divide a solid compound word between the elements of the compound.

    Examples: . . . . business-
person . . . . home-
owner
15. Divide after single-letter syllables.

    Examples: . . . . para-
keet . . . . para-
lyze

    . . . . regu-
late . . . . sepa-
rate

16. Divide between two single-letter syllables.

Examples: . . . . concili-
ation . . . . evalu-
ation

17. If possible, divide after the prefix.

Examples: . . . . circum-
navigate . . . . super-
structure

18. Avoid word divisions that will be confusing to the reader.

Wrong: . . . . inter-
pret **Better:** . . . . in-
terpret

. . . . read-
just . . . . re-
adjust

19. Divide between the suffix and the root word. If the final consonant is doubled before adding a suffix, divide between the double letters. If the root word ends in a double letter, divide after the double letters.

Examples: . . . . begin-
ning . . . . occur-
ring

. . . . progress-
ing . . . .recall-
ing

20. Avoid dividing in the middle of word endings such as *able*, *ible*, and *ical*.

Correct: . . . . reach-
able . . . . vis-
ible

Wrong: . . . . logi-
cal

21. Avoid dividing proper names. If necessary, divide the name before the surname.

Examples: . . . . Angela C.
Mitchell . . . . Mr. Loyd V.
Jacobs

22. Avoid dividing dates. If necessary, divide between the day and the year.

Example: . . . . June 26,
2002

23. Avoid dividing numbers. When absolutely necessary, divide a long number after a comma. (Divided numbers are very difficult to read.)

Example: 395,890,-
123,746

24. Avoid dividing street addresses. If necessary, divide a street address between the street name and the word *Street*, *Avenue*, or similar designation.

Example: . . . . 414 Walnut
Street

25. Avoid dividing names of places. If necessary, divide between the city and the state or between the state and the ZIP Code. (Dividing at the comma is preferred.)

Examples: . . . . Chicago,
Illinois 60606 . . . . Chicago, Illinois
60606

26. Divide an itemized list before any number or letter.

Examples: . . . . these items: (1) . . . ., (2) . . . .

Wrong: . . . . these items: (1) . . . ., (2) . . . .

Communicating Without Gender Bias

NOTE: Adapted from William C. Himstreet, Gerald W. Maxwell, and Mary Jean Onorato, ***Business Communications***, 2d ed., Glencoe Publishing Co., Encino, CA, 1987, p. 298.

Roles played by men and women continue to change. Women have entered such traditionally male-dominated fields as skilled labor, engineering, and business management. With less stereotyping in the workplace, larger numbers of men are working in fields once dominated by women, such as nursing and secretarial work.

The following are examples of discriminatory terms that were coined when most workers were men:

common man	fellow man	salesman
countryman	man-hour	sportsmanship
craftsman	mankind	statesman
draftsman	manpower	workmanship

Because thoughtless use of language can offend customers and colleagues, modern business communicators avoid gender bias in their choice of words. Gender bias, or stereotyping, occurs when the words chosen suggest that everyone involved in an activity is or ought to be male, as in the previous examples, or female.

Good transcriptionists help dictators eliminate gender bias in their communications. A dictator concentrates on the overall structure of the message and may let biased wording slip into the dictation. For example, in a letter to Adrian Walker, the dictator may routinely say "Dear Mr. Walker." When the sex of the recipient is not known, "Dear Adrian Walker" or "Dear Customer" is appropriate. The dictator may say "Gentlemen" to a company in general when "Ladies and Gentlemen" or possibly "Friends" would be better. The transcriptionist can help with these changes.

Eliminating such gender bias from communication is not difficult. An awareness of terms that might convey bias to a reader is all that is required. The following guidelines will help you avoid stereotyping in business language.

AVOID JOB-TITLE STEREOTYPES

In general references, do not use job titles that could single out a person as male or female. Instead, use an alternate term.

AVOID	USE
chairman	coordinator, chairperson, moderator, presiding officer
businessman	businessperson, business executive
newsman	reporter
councilman	council member

policeman, policewoman	police officer
fireman	firefighter
six-man commission	six-member commission
cleaning lady	house (or office) cleaner
maid	housekeeper
housewife	homemaker
steward, stewardess	flight attendant
spokesman	spokesperson

AVOID JOB–TITLE QUALIFIERS

Do not use gender words to describe job titles.

AVOID	USE
woman lawyer	lawyer
male nurse	nurse
female truck driver	truck driver
male model	model
woman doctor	doctor

AVOID CONDESCENDING TERMS

Select words and terms that are not disrespectful to either of the sexes. Adults should be referred to as *women* or *men*, never as *girls* or *boys*. Children may be referred to as *girls* or *boys*, but whenever there is doubt, *young woman* or *young man* is the better choice.

AVOID	USE
girl Friday	assistant
career girl	professional (or name the profession)
man and wife	husband and wife
ladies	women (Exception: *Ladies* may be used with *gentlemen*.)

AVOID THE GENERIC USE OF MASCULINE AND FEMININE PRONOUNS.

Do not use the pronouns *he* and *him* or *she* and *her* when you are referring to people in general. Use the plural forms of pronouns when appropriate. If a sentence must remain in the singular form, rewrite it to replace the masculine or feminine pronoun with *one*, *you*, or (sparingly) *he or she*. In some cases, you may alternate the use of *he* and *she* in a passage, but not too frequently or the wording will become awkward.

Avoid: Have each *employee* return *his* forms as soon as *he* is finished.

Use: *Employees* should return *their* forms as soon as *they* are finished.

Avoid: *He* who applies *himself* to the task will be successful.

Use: *Those* who apply *themselves* to the task will be successful.

Avoid: Any *nurse* who wants to go to the convention should bring *her* registration fee tomorrow.

Use: *Nurses* who want to go to the convention should bring *their* registration fees tomorrow.

Avoid: If the applicant is not satisfied with *his* performance on the first test, *he* may retake it.

Use: *You* may retake the test if *you* are not satisfied with *your* performance.

or

Applicants who are not satisfied with *their* performance on the first test may retake it.

Avoid: Allow each *council member* to participate in a discussion. Has *he* had the opportunity to speak? Could *he* possibly feel left out?

Use: Allow each *council member* to participate in a discussion. Has *she* had the opportunity to speak? Could *he* possibly feel left out?

or

Allow each *council member* to participate in a discussion. Have *all members* had the opportunity to speak? Could *any* possibly feel left out?

REWORD TO ELIMINATE UNNECESSARY GENDER REFERENCES.

Neutral words or terms can be substituted for those that refer to gender.

Avoid: As a *coed* at Yale University, *she* received many academic awards.

Use: As an *undergraduate* at Yale University, *she* received many academic awards.

Avoid: The *common man* is not aware of the extent of the crisis.

Use: The *average person* is not aware of the extent of the crisis.

Avoid: This *man-made* fiber will outlast every natural fiber on the market.

Use: This *synthetic* (or *manufactured* or *artificial*) fiber will outlast every natural fiber on the market.

Avoid: How much *manpower* will you need to complete the job?

Use: How many *people* will you need to complete the job?

Avoid: This is a *man-sized* job.

Use: This is an *enormous* job.

Index

PHOTO CREDITS

Bill Aron/Photo Edit 109; Scott Barrow/International Stock; Tim Brown/Stone 43; Steve Chenn/Corbis 45; Dictaphone Corporation 8, 13; Rachel Epstein/Photo Edit 17b; Tony Freeman/Photo Edit 139; Spencer Grant/Photo Edit 2; Howard Grey/Stone 41; Grundig AG 9; Kevin Horan/Stone 47; Lanier Voice Products 10; Michael Newman/Photo Edit 31; Olympus America Inc. 11; Jose Palaez/The Stock Market 24; Steven Peters/Stone; Philips Dictation Systems 1, 6, 17t, 53, 112, 147, 195; Patrick Ramsey/International Stock 30; Steven Rubin/The Image Works 156; Sanyo Inc. 23; Rhoda Sidney/Photo Edit 48; Sony Corp. 176(3); Superstock 4, 21; Sam C. Mitchell/Wilkey's Café, Belle Rive, Illinois 167

© Cartoons by Johns 28, 85, 146, 185.
PEANUTS reprinted by permission of United Feature Syndicate, Inc. 243.
© 2001; Reprinted courtesy of Bunny Hoest and Parade Magazine 244.
© The New Yorker Collection 2000 Frank Cotham from cartoonbank.com. All rights reserved 245b.
FRANK & ERNEST reprinted by permission of Newspaper Enterprise Assn., Inc. 245t, 247, 248.